The
EVERYTHING®
Sewing Book

Dear Reader:

I began sewing when I was only six or seven. I started with doll clothes, of course, learning through trial and error that I should put seam allowances on the inside and that stitches ½" long don't hold too well. Cutting the fabric so it would sew into three-dimensional garments wasn't instinctive. It was a good thing my fashion doll couldn't sit down, because the pants I made her wouldn't have let her, anyway. However, all this messing around and mistake-making gave me confidence to try some real sewing some five or six years later.

It may be easier when you are young to begin something you don't know how to finish. As adults we worry about failure: the expense or the time we've wasted, the project that doesn't look the way we wanted it to. Forget all that. You won't *fail*. You'll probably make some mistakes, but you'll find a way around them. What you learn will be worth the expense and the time, even if what you make might not seem like it. Besides, who needs to know what you *wanted* it to look like? Dig deep inside. Find a bit of that childish sense of adventure, and plunge in.

Sandra Detrixhe

The EVERYTHING® Series

Editorial

Publishing Director	Gary M. Krebs
Managing Editor	Kate McBride
Copy Chief	Laura MacLaughlin
Acquisitions Editor	Eric M. Hall
Development Editor	Karen Johnson Jacot
Production Editor	Jamie Wielgus

Production

Production Director	Susan Beale
Production Manager	Michelle Roy Kelly
Series Designers	Daria Perreault
	Colleen Cunningham
Cover Design	Paul Beatrice
	Frank Rivera
Layout and Graphics	Colleen Cunningham
	Rachael Eiben
	Michelle Roy Kelly
	John Paulhus
	Daria Perreault
	Erin Ring
Cover Artist	Eulala Conner
Interior Illustrator	Eric Andrews

Visit the entire Everything® Series at www.everything.com

THE
EVERYTHING®
SEWING
BOOK

From threading the needle to
basting the hem, all you need to
alter and create beautiful clothes,
gifts, and decorations

Sandra Detrixhe

Adams Media
Avon, Massachusetts

To my first reader and darling daughter Eden

An Everything® Series Book.
Everything® and everything.com® are registered trademarks of F+W Publications, Inc.

Published by Adams Media, an F+W Publications Company
57 Littlefield Street, Avon, MA 02322 U.S.A.
www.adamsmedia.com

ISBN: 1-59337-052-0
Printed in the United States of America.

J I H G F E D C B A

Library of Congress Cataloging-in-Publication Data
Detrixhe, Sandra.
The everything sewing book / Sandra Detrixhe.
p.   cm.
(An everything series book)
ISBN 1-59337-052-0
1. Sewing. 2. Dressmaking. I. Title. II. Everything series.
TT705.D48   2004
646.2–dc22   2003026251

This book is available at quantity discounts for bulk purchases.
For information, call 1-800-872-5627.

Contents

Acknowledgments

Special thanks to Michael Wentz for letting me watch him clean my sewing machine and Pat Gerhardt, County Extension Agent, for information on crib safety, vest patterns, and other things.

Top Ten Reasons
to Learn to Sew

1. Learning to sew will teach you about fabric and construction, making you a better consumer when you buy ready-made items.

2. You can save money by mending clothes you would otherwise have to throw away.

3. Store-bought clothes can be altered to fit you better.

4. You can construct clothing that exactly suits your style.

5. Your home can be decorated with your own personal touch.

6. Sewing allows you to express yourself creatively.

7. Whether you're mending or constructing new items, sewing promotes self-esteem and a sense of independence.

8. Sewing can relieve stress by being a rewarding and absorbing hobby.

9. You can sew unique gifts tailor-made for the recipient.

10. You can sew practical items that simplify or organize your life.

Introduction

▶SEWING USED TO BE CONSIDERED A SURVIVAL SKILL.
Girls were taught to sew at an early age, along with their lessons in
cooking and housecleaning. All but the wealthiest would be
expected to make all their families' clothes once they were married.
Those wealthy few who could hire tailors and seamstresses were
still expected to do some fancy needlework in their leisure time.

Even after ready-made clothing became widely available late in
the nineteenth century, a lot of women continued to sew some or
all of their families' clothes in order to save money. This was
especially true during the 1930s, when so many people were out of
work. Clothing was often made out of feed sacks, and the unfrayed
parts of worn-out clothes were remade to fit a smaller member of
the family.

In the mid-1940s, as more women entered the work force, they
began to think of their time as having value. The cost of a pattern
and fabric might be less than the cost of a similar garment ready-
made, but what about the time it would take to construct it? When
this cost was figured in, many women gave up sewing. The next
generation, having not learned to sew from their mothers, rejected
all but the most basic mending as not worth their time.

As fewer women were sewing, the cost of fabric and patterns
went up. When clothing is mass-produced, often in offshore factories
where labor is cheaper, the cost of the finished product is often
less than the retail cost of the materials to make it. Occasionally,
there are fabric or pattern sales, but it's generally questionable

whether home sewing saves any money, even if you *don't* count your labor.

So why would anyone want to learn to sew at all? One answer is to get exactly the clothes you want, not what the manufacturers think we all should be wearing. Another is to get clothing that really fits, though that might take some practice. An important side benefit to learning to sew is an increased knowledge of fabric and garment construction, of grain lines and shrinkage, of finished seam allowances and well-made facing. All of these things will make you a better consumer when you shop for ready-made clothes.

However, those aren't the primary reasons people sew. They sew because they enjoy it. Hobbies like sewing give you a creative outlet and a sense of accomplishment. Sewing is an enjoyable way to spend some leisure time, and the crafts or clothing you create for yourself or as gifts are the by-products of the hobby, not the reason.

People who love to sew love the look and feel of fabric, the clever way odd-shaped pieces stitch together to form sleeves or plackets or baby toys. They love being able to say, "I made this myself," or they love keeping quiet and letting people think they bought it at an expensive boutique. How can you know if you'll love to sew unless you give it a try?

Something has brought you to this book. Perhaps you've tried sewing just enough to know you enjoy it, but you need a little more instruction. This book begins with the very basics of sewing. The instructions are designed to alert you to possible pitfalls, and they offer lots of choices, so the projects are truly your own. This book will take you through progressively more advanced projects until you have enough knowledge and, more importantly, confidence, to tackle anything you want to sew. Ⓔ

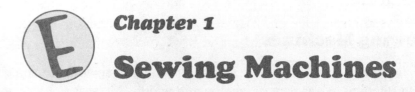

Chapter 1

Sewing Machines

While anything can theoretically be sewn by hand, the sewing machine makes sewing much easier. Seams sewn on a machine are stronger and neater. Most people wouldn't consider doing construction sewing without a machine. The savings they can give you in time alone makes them worth the investment.

Choosing a Machine

There are a wide variety of machines available, in an even wider range of prices. In general, the more your machine does, the more it will cost. But how much do you really need your machine to do? Having your sewing plans well in mind before you shop can save you from paying for features you never use.

Basic Sewing Machines

The bare essentials you'll need for construction sewing are straight and zigzag stitching in a variety of lengths and widths. Most, if not all, modern machines will also do a hemstitch and make buttonholes, possibly with an attachment. Most machines will offer a few other stitches as well that are more or less combinations of straight, reverse, and zigzag stitches.

If you're planning on doing a small or moderate amount of sewing, this may be as much as you'll ever need. This type of machine starts around $100 at a discount store and can go up to the neighborhood of $1,000, depending on the brand of the machine. The more expensive machines may be less prone to failures and last longer than the cheaper models. Consider, too, whether you are buying from a dealer who offers service as well as sales.

Computerized Machines

The next step up from the basic machine is the computerized machine. These offer a lot more versatility—from fancy edging and appliqué stitches to computerized embroidery patterns. Most computerized machines make any kind of stitch adjustment as easy as touching a button. They offer features that can be real time-savers if you are doing a great deal of sewing, like the option to set the needle to stop in the up position when you are doing regular stitching or to stop in the down position if you are pivoting around an odd-shaped piece.

Manufacturers have been putting computers in sewing machines for around thirty years. These have gotten better and, relative to other machines, less expensive. The discount-store price for a computerized machine is around $250. For machines from higher-end makers, you can expect the price to take a $400 or $500 leap above their noncomputer-ized models. You can easily spend well over $1,000 for one of these sewing machines. When shopping, consider whether the machine is limited to the patterns in its memory or if you can buy discs of additional stitching and embroidery designs to add to its versatility.

FACT

Isaac Singer invented the foot-operated treadle sewing machine. Before this invention, people operated their machines by hand-turning the balance wheel. Singer's promotional skills and use of mass production made his the bestselling sewing machine by 1860 and allowed him to retire at age fifty-two just three years later.

Specialty Machines

There are some sewing machines with very specialized uses. Rather than replacing them, these are meant to complement regular sewing machines in one particular area. The most common of these is the serger. A serger will clean-finish the seam allowance edge as it sews a seam. Some specialty machines have attachments to allow them to do additional things like gathering or rolled hems. Extremely stretchy fabrics can be sewn on a serger without stretching them out of shape. The serger is also faster than a regular machine and saves the additional step of finishing the seam allowance. If you will be doing a great deal of construction sewing, you may find a serger to be worth the extra expense. They tend to cost more than regular machines, starting at $200 in discount stores to upwards of $2,200 for the top of the line.

Another specialty machine is the embroidery machine. This is similar to the computerized sewing machine that includes embroidery, except it is used for embroidery exclusively. Because that is all it does, it can do it in a big way. If you are interested in a great deal of embroidery and already have a regular sewing machine, they might be worth looking into. They start in the $600 range.

A less common specialty machine is the jeans machine. This machine is specifically designed to handle heavier fabrics. Most regular machines can sew through denim adequately if you use a heavy-duty needle.

However, if you are interested in the many crafts that feature old jeans or new denim and canvas-type fabrics, you might consider getting one of these to save wear on your regular machine. They cost around $300.

Another specialty machine is the quilting machine, also called a long-arm machine. These machines follow a quilting pattern down the length of a quilt. The sewing machine moves instead of the fabric. Very few people own one unless they are doing quilting commercially, but for these quilters, they are a huge investment in both money and space.

Regular sewing machines that include a few features intended to make specialty sewing easier are available and cost only slightly more than standard machines. Machines called mid-arm machines are made to work like the long-arm machines on a smaller scale and at a price more for home use, starting at around $600.

Used Machines

Parts are still available for some surprisingly old machines. In fact, some older machines—from the 1960s or earlier—may have fewer plastic parts in them, and it's the plastic parts that need replacing the most. Because of these facts, it's not as big a risk as it might seem to buy a used machine.

Old machines sometimes go at garage sales for under $30. Add to that a $30 to $50 fee to have the machine cleaned and serviced, and your investment isn't very great. Chances are the machine can give you years of service.

Be a little cautious of buying a used machine that contains computer chips unless you're buying from a dealer who resells trade-ins and who will stand behind the machine if there is any problem with it. Computerized machines can be expensive to fix, so you want to be sure it works before you buy it.

Knowing Your Machine

Your sewing machine will come with an owner's manual. This is your best source for information about your particular machine. Yet there are some things that will be the same on all sewing machines.

FIGURE 1-1

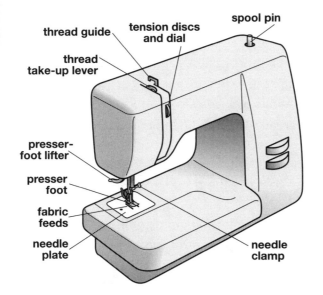

thread guide
tension discs and dial
spool pin
thread take-up lever
presser-foot lifter
presser foot
fabric feeds
needle plate
needle clamp

◀ **Sewing machine:** Learn the name and use of these parts of your machine.

FIGURE 1-2

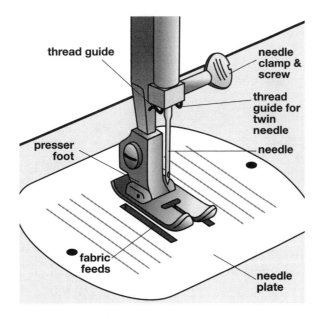

thread guide
needle clamp & screw
thread guide for twin needle
presser foot
needle
fabric feeds
needle plate

◀ **Needle area:** More parts to learn.

Identifying Basic Parts

Use the diagrams of the sewing machine (**FIGURE 1-1**) and the needle area (**FIGURE 1-2**) to locate the following parts on your machine:

- **Thread take-up lever:** Controls the thread as it is fed to the needle.
- **Tension discs:** Keep the thread at just the right tautness for perfect stitches.
- **Presser foot:** Holds the fabric against the fabric feeds.
- **Fabric feeds:** Move the fabric.
- **Presser-foot lifter:** Allows you to raise and lower the presser foot.
- **Needle clamp and screw:** Hold the needle in place. Loosen the screw to change needles.
- **Needle plate:** Surrounds the fabric feeds and has a hole, which the needle goes through to carry the thread to the bobbin thread.

Somewhere on the top of your machine you'll find the spool pin. There may be a bobbin pin or spindle on top or at the base of the trunk for winding thread onto your bobbin. The balance wheel, which is used to raise or lower the needle, will be on the right side of the machine.

Your machine should also have a light under the body of the machine. Generally this light comes on automatically when the machine is switched on. Like all light bulbs, this one can burn out. Check your manual for replacement instructions.

You will also have a foot pedal, which plugs into the machine and operates much like a gas pedal on a car. A few machines have knee press levers instead.

Making Adjustments

Every machine has a few things that can be controlled or adjusted. Exactly where these controls are and what they look like will vary with each machine. They may be touch pads, buttons, dials, or knobs. They will probably be labeled on your machine.

The tension adjustment control is often found near the tension discs. To see if you need to adjust the tension, sew a straight stitch with contrasting thread in the bobbin. If the stitches on the top and bottom of the cloth look alike except for the color, the tension is balanced. If the bobbin thread is visible on top, the thread tension is too tight and should be loosened. If the top thread shows on the bottom stitches, the tension is too loose. Make tiny adjustments and test again.

The reverse stitching control allows you to backstitch. This control is often found near the base of the trunk of the machine.

Stitch length and width controls regulate the size of the stitches. Width refers to the width of zigzag and other stitches for which the needle moves from side to side.

Understanding Attachments

Most machines come with a few attachments that expand what you can do with your machine. Each has a specific purpose. Other attachments may be available at additional cost to fit your machine, adding to its versatility.

Machine Presser Feet

The most common attachments available are alternate presser feet. There are dozens available. Some will make a task easier, while others will make it possible to do things with your machine you couldn't do otherwise. The one most likely to be included with your machine is the zipper foot. A zipper foot is narrow with a groove on either side for the needle, instead of a hole or slot in the middle. This allows you to stitch close to a zipper without having the zipper's teeth under the presser foot.

Another common foot is the straight stitch foot. The all-purpose foot, which is generally on the machine when you buy it, is used for either straight or zigzag stitching. The straight stitch foot is only necessary when close control is needed, such as topstitching or stitching delicate fabrics.

A buttonhole foot is included with most machines. This might be a special clear plastic foot with markings that help you stitch on either side of a buttonhole line you've marked on your fabric, or it might be a one-step buttonhole foot that sews the buttonhole almost automatically. A button fits in a sliding slot; the machine uses that to determine the size of the buttonhole that's needed for it.

Your machine attachments may also include a satin stitch foot. This foot has a groove on the bottom, behind the needle hole, to keep it from getting hung up on the bulky zigzag stitches.

A walking foot or even-feed foot may be worth buying separately if one doesn't come with your machine. This presser foot has feeds on it to feed the top layer of fabric along with the bottom layer. This is very helpful for matching strips or plaids where a slight slip of the fabrics will be visible. It is also helpful with stretchy fabric and with machine quilting.

Needle Plates

Most of the time the needle plate on a machine is actually a zigzag plate. Leaving it on allows you to switch from straight stitching to zigzag without switching plates. However, occasionally it is preferable to use the straight-stitch plate. The only difference is a round or narrow needle hole instead of an oblong one designed to accommodate the needle during zigzag stitching. Use the straight-stitch plate along with the straight-stitch foot when special control is needed. For instance, if you are sewing with delicate fabrics that tend to follow the needle down the hole, using a smaller hole decreases the problem.

ALERT!

If your fabric is following the needle down the hole at the beginning of your seams, make a thread bunny. Fold a small scrap of fabric to a couple of inches square and put it toward the back of the presser foot as you start the seam.

Another plate you may have with your machine is a cover plate. This plate is thicker and prevents the feed from moving the fabric. This is used with free motion sewing such as self-guided embroidery, which requires a special hoop to hold your fabric as well. The cover plate is also used for button sewing, which requires a special button foot.

Another less common cover plate is the chain stitch plate. This is used in conjunction with a special bobbin case insert that replaces the bobbin. The machine catches the loop from the last stitch with the next one to make a chain stitch instead of the usual interlocking stitch.

Other Attachments

Other attachments might include a seam guide. This is often an adjustable slide that screws into your machine near the needle plate. There are also circular sewing guides to make sewing curves more accurate. Stick-on magnetic pin catchers are another common addition to sewing machines.

The Necessary Needle

Sewing machine needles have an interesting shape. Look closely at one, and you will see it has a groove down the back. This is where the thread is tucked as the needle takes its stitch. One side of the top is flat. This is to make sure you don't put your needle in backward. It also assures your needle is held tightly by the needle clamp.

Needles come in a variety of sizes and styles. The most common is the size 14 sharp-pointed needle. This is used for nearly all woven fabrics. The size 16 sharp-point is thicker and better for use on denim and other heavy fabrics. Size 11 needles are extra fine and will leave smaller holes in some delicate fabrics. In knit fabrics, a ballpoint needle works better than a sharp-pointed needle. That's because the rounded needle point will slide past the individual threads instead of catching them and dragging them through the hole in the needle plate.

There are also special twin needles designed for topstitching or for double stitching on stretch fabrics. Be sure your machine is designed to accommodate twin needles before you try these.

The needle is the first thing you should check when your machine doesn't seem to be working properly. If your needle is dull, it can poke your fabric through the hole instead of penetrating the fabric. This will cause your machine to skip stitches because the bobbin hook is prevented from catching the thread. If your needle is bent, it may be missing the exact spot where it needs to pass the bobbin hook. Needles can become dull after use on heavy fabric, especially when thick seams cross one another, from hitting pins, or because the needle clamp is loose.

Threading Your Machine

Your machine needs to be threaded properly to work. Threading is the second thing you should check if you are experiencing any problems. Your owner's manual will describe how to wind your bobbin and thread your machine. The routes may even be marked with arrows on your machine's surface. Nevertheless, a description of the purpose of each step might be helpful. You can identify most of the contact points on the sewing machine diagrams.

Needles are cheap, so lay in a good supply. Don't wait until your machine's skipping stitches to change them. Some experts recommend you change your needle every time you start a new project.

Threading the Bobbin

The bobbin will need to be wound with your sewing thread before you can sew. A few machines with drop-in bobbins are designed to wind the bobbin directly in the bobbin case after the machine is threaded. Most, however, require winding at some other point on the machine before the machine is threaded. The most common place for this is on the top, where the spool of thread can be in its usual place on the spool pin. Another common location is on the right side of the machine, where the spool sits in a secondary spool pin at the base and the bobbin is wound somewhere up the side. The thread is then brought around a thread guide that serves as a tension for the thread.

The end of the thread is poked through a hole in the bobbin from the inside out, and the bobbin is mounted on a bobbin pin or spindle. Often, the spindle either slides toward a stop or a stop slides toward the spindle, engaging the spindle so it will turn. The stop prevents the bobbin from being overwound by popping back to the former position when the thread in the bobbin applies pressure, thus disengaging the spindle.

Cut the thread near the bobbin and drop the bobbin into the bobbin case. Threading the bobbin into the case is usually little more than pulling the thread into a slot and under the tension spring.

The bobbin case itself is removed and inserted into place by holding a latch open with the tip of your finger while you move it in or out.

Threading the Machine

Begin by raising the presser foot. This releases the tension discs. Slide your spool onto the spool pin. If your machine has a horizontal pin, slide the spool holder on after it. Lead the thread around the upper thread guide. This puts the thread in line with the tension discs. Lead the thread firmly between the discs. You will need to hold the thread above the discs as you bring it through to be sure the thread is all the way between them.

From the discs, the thread needs to be led straight down, held by either a thread guide or a check spring, and led straight up again. The purpose of this is to give the take-up lever something to pull against. Slide the thread through the slot in the take-up lever and all the way to the eye at the end.

Next, the thread goes down to the lower thread guide, which is just above the needle bar. After one last thread guide, which is on the needle clamp itself, you can thread the needle. Most modern machines are designed with slotted guides so the only place you actually have to poke the thread through a hole is at the needle. Some machines even make that easier with built-in needle threaders. When you pull the threader down to engage it, a tiny hook goes through the eye of the needle from the back. Thread guides on the threader will help you get the thread under the hook. Release the threader slowly, and it pulls a loop of thread through the eye. Disconnect the thread from the threader and pull the loose end through.

Cleaning and Maintenance

Your sewing machine is going to give you more years of service if you get into a habit of regular cleaning and maintenance. Lint that gathers between the tension discs or clogs the needle's entry area in the bobbin case is often a reason for the machine not working properly. Be sure to unplug your machine from the power source before doing any maintenance.

Routine Cleaning

A nylon brush is sometimes included with the accessories for a machine. It is ideal for cleaning lint out of all the little crevices where it collects. Clean any visible lint out of any thread guides whenever you notice them. Keep the surface of your machine free of dust, either with frequent dusting or by covering your machine. Your thread will carry these tiny dust particles into the machine.

FACT

One of the biggest sources of lint in your machine is the thread itself. In fact, some manufacturers recommend you use high-quality polyester thread and avoid the cheap all-purpose thread, which is cotton-wrapped polyester and can leave behind tiny cotton fibers.

Raise the presser foot, and clean between the tension discs with a long-bristled nylon brush or with a very narrow pick. Lint here can affect the tension. If you are having repeated trouble with the tension in spite of adjustments, lint might be the culprit. Clean it each time before you thread the machine.

Remove the needle plate to clean around the feeds. The plate may slide out, or you may need to remove a screw. Clean inside as far as you can reach with your brush. Hard-to-reach places can be cleaned with the narrow-edge attachment on a hose-type vacuum cleaner. Canned air used to clean computers can be helpful for blowing the lint away from tiny crevices too small to be picked up by the vacuum.

Get into a habit of brushing away any visible lint in and around the bobbin case every time you change the bobbin. Occasionally, clean under the tension spring on the bobbin case. This may require loosening a screw. Be careful not to bend the spring, and be sure it is seated properly when you tighten the screw again.

Oiling Your Machine

Some machines have parts that have been "permanently" lubricated. This means that, under normal conditions, you should never need to oil your machine. Your service technician will examine these parts and decide if they need to be oiled.

If your machine is one that requires oiling, you will probably receive a small bottle of sewing machine oil along with your accessories. The owner's manual will also tell you what parts need to be oiled and how to get to them. Annual oiling is usually recommended.

Be sure to use only sewing machine oil, which is a light, pure oil. A single drop is all you will need at any of the lubrication points. Excess oil will only attract dirt and stain your thread or fabric.

Periodic Service

If you are the mechanically minded type, you might try removing the covers of your machine and doing a more thorough cleaning once a year or so. Be sure to make note of which screws came from where because they are often all different. When replacing a screw that threads into plastic, screw it backward until it clicks into place or the screw will ruin the threads in the plastic.

Add a scant drop of oil where shafts run through bushings. Be careful not to oil plastic parts because the plastic will absorb the oil and become soft. Clean dirt out of gears, taking care not to break any teeth.

ALERT!

Be wary of turning screws found inside the machine. These may be set screws that determine tensions, clearance or timing. If your machine has a drop-in bobbin, do not attempt to remove the bobbin case.

Using the Machine

You shouldn't expect to sew perfectly the first time you use a sewing machine. If the process is new to you, you will need some practice. Use some scraps of fabric, and get to know your machine.

Getting Started

You should be seated directly in front of the needle. Position your chair at a comfortable distance so you lean forward only slightly to operate your machine. The foot pedal should be slightly forward of your right foot when it is flat on the floor in front of you.

If you are using a seam guide, set it at $5/8$" from the needle. This is the standard seam allowance used in construction sewing. If you don't have a seam guide, identify the line on the needle plate that represents $5/8$".

With right sides together, pin two pieces of fabric together. The pins should be a couple of inches apart and run perpendicular to your planned stitching line. Normally the heads of the pins should extend beyond the edge of the fabric and point inward. However, if you are using a seam guide, they will need to come from the other direction. They should not extend beyond the fabric edge, or they will catch on the seam guide.

Raise the presser foot, and slide the fabric under it. With the edge of the fabric aligned at $5/8$", use the balance wheel to lower the needle into the fabric about $1/2$" down from the top edge of your fabric. Lower the presser foot, and you're ready to sew.

Sewing a Seam

Engage the reverse-stitch control, and backstitch to the edge of the fabric. Release the reverse stitch control, and allow the machine to stitch forward.

With your hands resting lightly on the fabric, guide it under the presser foot. Do not pull the fabric. Watch that the edge continues to line up with the $5/8$" mark or the seam guide. Work at creating an even pressure on the foot pedal. If your pins are in straight, your machine should stitch right over them with no problem.

When your stitching reaches the end of the fabric, backstitch for four or five stitches. Stop and raise the needle. Raise the presser foot, gently pull the fabric out from under it, and cut the threads.

Check Your Work

How did you do? Does your seam look straight, and is it a consistent distance from the raw edge? If the stitches are not consistent in length, you may have been dragging on the fabric occasionally, preventing the feeds from pulling it along. If the fabric is puckered, you may have been urging it forward under the presser foot. Next time relax, and let the presser foot move the fabric.

Check to see if the stitches look identical on the top and bottom of the fabric. Adjust the tension if necessary.

Remove the pins, and open out the fabric. Your finished seam will always look better from the right side.

More Practice

Practice making zigzag stitches next. Try to guide the fabric so the zigzags are an even distance apart.

Curves can be a bit of a challenge at first. The temptation is to watch the seam gauge lines in front of the presser foot instead of those that are even with the needle. Practice inward curves and outward curves, and measure to see how you did. If you need to make a sharp turn with your stitching, stop with the needle down, raise the presser foot, and pivot the fabric under it. Have fun trying a little of that.

When you feel you and your sewing machine are working together, you've had enough practice. Let's get the rest of the supplies together and get ready to sew. Ⓔ

Chapter 2

Sewing Tools and Notions

A certain number of tools are necessary for even the simplest sewing project. Others are more specialized and can be purchased when they become necessary. There are others that are never necessary but can make certain tasks easier. Consider them as your budget allows.

Choosing Shears and Scissors

Scissors come in a wide variety of sizes and shapes. Shears are scissors with blades more than 6" long. Whichever you choose, be sure they are good quality, and keep them sharp to avoid damaging your fabric. With proper care, a good pair can last your whole sewing career.

Cutting Fabric

Dressmakers' shears have long blades and angled handles. The handle allows the fabric to remain flat on the cutting table while you are cutting. These are a necessity and should be used only for cutting fabric—and nothing else—to keep them from becoming dulled.

Sewing scissors are similar to the shears except they are a little shorter and the blades themselves are a little thinner. This makes them ideal for trimming seams and interfacing and other close work. The shears and the sewing scissors can double for each other if your budget won't allow for both.

Rotary cutters can be very helpful when you are cutting out geometric shapes by measure rather than with a pattern. They are always used with a special cutting mat and often with acrylic rulers.

Good quality scissors and shears can be sharpened. Don't discard an old pair simply because they are dull. Inquire at your favorite fabric store for recommendations on a good place to have them sharpened.

Pinking shears have serrated blades that allow them to cut a zigzag pattern. They are used to trim seam allowances to stop, or at least slow, fraying. They are not a necessity but are helpful. If you intend to do a lot of construction sewing with woven fabrics, they may be worth the investment.

Clipping Threads

Embroidery scissors are handy to have next to the sewing machine for cutting threads. They are small, sharp-pointed scissors with blades that may be only 1" or so long. Since they are small, they fit easily into the sewing bag if you take hand sewing with you.

There are also special thread clippers with spring-action blades. Consider these as an alternative to the embroidery scissors, and get at least one pair of one or the other.

Ripping Out Seams

Even if you never make a mistake, you will at some point need to take out stitches—basting stitches, if nothing else. You can take out a seam with embroidery scissors, but you risk cutting your fabric along with the stitches. Seams can be taken out with a pin, but it's a slow process. A seam ripper is specifically designed for the purpose. They are considered such a necessity that they come among the attachments with some sewing machines.

A seam ripper is easy to work. The narrow point slips under stitches. The cutting surface is in the crook of the hook. A ball on the upper tip acts as a guide through the fabric. Seam rippers can also be used to open buttonholes. With them there is less chance of your cutting the reinforcing stitches than if you used scissors.

Knowing Your Needles and Pins

It's probably pretty obvious that you'll need needles and pins if you are going to sew. It may not be quite so obvious that you have a wide range of sizes and styles to choose from. A little information about the advantages and uses of each will make shopping easier.

Needles

Sewing machine needles were discussed in Chapter 1, but you will need a few needles for hand sewing as well. The most basic needles are the sharps. These are used for nearly all hand sewing. Buy a variety pack of sharps that includes sizes 7, 8, and 9, and wait for specific projects to start your collection of other types of needles.

Embroidery needles will be required for some decorative stitches. They are longer than sharps and have an elongated eye to accommodate the strands of embroidery floss.

Tapestry needles are a longer version of the embroidery needles and are used for embroidery with yarn. Chenille needles are bigger yet and used with heavier yarns. Chenille needles come with either sharp points for sewing into fabric or with rounded points for sewing knitted garments.

Darning needles are only slightly thicker than the sharps needles, but they are much longer. The length makes it possible to work a weaving pattern with your thread over a hole being darned. Beading needles look very similar to darning needles except they are finer. As their name suggests, they are used for attaching beads and sequins.

If you are doing finishing stitches by hand, between needles will make it possible to keep your stitches very fine. They are used primarily for quilting or topstitching.

FACT

Darning gourds, shaped like a child's rattle, and darning mushrooms, which are similar but with a broader top, might seem terribly old fashioned, but they are useful for more than just darning socks. Nearly any hand mending will be neater if you use one. You can find them in well-stocked fabric stores, but the ones you find in antique stores will have more character.

Pins

Standard dressmaker's pins are the cheapest and will serve nearly all the needs of a beginner. Buy a box and some kind of cushion or magnet-topped container to make them easily accessible. Discard any pins that become bent, or they will catch on the presser foot of your machine.

Some people prefer glass-headed pins, sometimes called silk pins, because they are a little longer than standard pins. They are also finer, so they leave smaller holes in your fabric, making them a necessity for silks and other delicate fabrics. The colored heads make them easier to find if they get dropped in the carpet.

However, if you are working with looser weave fabrics, the thinner pins aren't going to hold. You'll need T-pins. They are heavier, and, instead of the usual head, the top of the pin is bent to form a T, which prevents it from slipping between the threads of the loose weaves.

The other type of pin you will use occasionally is the safety pin. They are especially useful for holding fabric pieces in place that you will be hand-stitching. They won't fall out with all the handling you'll have to do and won't scratch you like straight pins.

Learning about Thread

We're all familiar with the spools of thread available almost everywhere. Those common spools contain cotton-wrapped polyester thread and are often labeled as all-purpose. This kind of thread can be used for almost all sewing. But like needles and pins, there may be more to choose from than you realize. A slightly more expensive alternative to all-purpose thread for machine sewing is polyester thread. Its advantage, as mentioned in Chapter 1, is that it won't leave fibers behind in your machine.

An alternative for hand sewing is mercerized cotton thread. It won't tangle and knot as much as all-purpose thread, but it is sometimes difficult to find. Other threads available from some specialty stores that are used less often are silk thread for sewing silk and wool, buttonhole twist for hand-stitched buttonholes, metallic thread for decoration, darning thread, and upholstery thread.

Embroidery thread, often called floss, is used for decorative stitching. It comes in 6-ply skeins. The thread is separated into two or three strands after each length is cut. Tapestry wool, a 2-ply yarn, is also used for decorative stitching.

ALERT!

Thread that is twenty years old or more may have become brittle. This will make it prone to breaking during sewing or afterward. You can use it up as basting thread, but don't use it for regular sewing.

Choosing Measuring Tapes and Gauges

Accurate measurements are important to assure a good fit in garment construction and a successful completion of craft sewing projects. Discard wooden or plastic rulers with nicks or faded markings, metal gauges that are bent, and cloth tape measurers that have frayed or stretched. (In fact, it's a good idea to avoid cloth tapes entirely because if and when they do stretch, you might not even realize it.)

A plastic tape measurer is a necessity. You will use it to take body measurements as well as during several other steps in the sewing process.

A rigid ruler or yardstick will be useful for altering patterns and for drawing straight lines. An 18" by 6" acrylic ruler is highly recommended. It will serve all the functions of a conventional ruler, but, because of its width and because you can see through it, it will help you measure more quickly and accurately. It also serves as a straight edge if you are cutting with a rotary cutter.

A measuring gauge is so useful that if you've ever used one, you probably consider it a necessity. They are 6" metal measurers with a sliding tab. They are particularly helpful when you are pressing under seam allowances or hems. A new version of this gauge has a short sliding ruler in place of the tab. They are intended for spacing and marking buttonholes.

FACT

There are other tools you'll find that have more specialized purposes, such as standard and complex French curves, flexible curves, and set squares. Their primary use is for drawing patterns, though they might also be useful for altering them. You likely won't need these unless you are interested in creating your own patterns.

Choosing Marking Tools

Certain details on a pattern, such as the placement of darts or slits, will need to be marked onto your fabric. This can be done by taking loops of thread loosely through the pattern and the fabric pieces, then snipping them between the layers of fabric, leaving thread tails to mark the location. Often there are faster ways to do it.

One of the most accurate methods of making these marks is with dressmaker's carbon and a tracing wheel. You use the spur-like wheel to trace the pattern (with the carbon between the pattern and fabric), and it leaves a dotted line on the "wrong" side of the fabric. The wheel does less damage to the fragile pattern paper than tracing with a pencil does.

At some point you might need to mark alterations or other information on your fabric. You have your choice of tailors' chalk, chalk pencils, and fabric marking pencils and pens. Some will work better on certain fabrics. Read the packages for recommendations.

Considering Pressing Tools

An iron, preferably with steam, and an ironing board are absolute necessities. Your ironing board doesn't have to be a full-sized one; a small version that sits on a table will do fine. Beyond that, there are a few other tools you might need depending on the type of sewing you plan to do.

A sleeve board that looks a little like a miniature ironing board is used for narrow items such as cuffs and sleeves. A point presser is a wooden stand that looks like an anvil. It is used to press points into collars and other turned points.

ALERT!

Check the cords on older irons to be sure they haven't started to wear, and think safety whenever the iron is plugged in. Use only distilled water in steam irons because minerals in water will coat the elements and shorten the life of your iron.

A tailor's ham is a hard-packed cushion about the size of a large ham. It's used to press curved seams and darts that might pucker if they were pressed on a flat ironing board. A seam roll is an oblong cushion made the same way. It's used to press seams on certain fabrics that would form ridges along the edge of the seam allowance if they were ironed flat. The roll allows you to iron directly on the seam and not on either side of it.

A needle board is used with velvet and other nap or pile fabrics that would be permanently crushed if they were ironed normally. Some other delicate fabrics need only a press cloth to protect them from the iron.

Learning about Interfacing

Interfacing is used between layers of fabric to add a small amount of stiffness. Nearly every collar and cuff pattern is going to call for interfacing.

Interfacing comes in a few different weights. It is generally white, off-white, black, or gray. Occasionally you can find it in other colors. It doesn't need to color coordinate with your fabric—it just needs to be invisible on the finished product, and so you don't want it to show through the fabric.

Interfacing is generally sold by the yard, but occasionally you can find it packaged. Since you will be using only small amounts of it for most projects, keeping some medium-weight white interfacing on hand will probably take care of most of your needs.

Fusible interfacing, which adheres to fabric when it is ironed, can save some time and is indispensable for some projects. It is usually more expensive than the nonfusible, sew-in kind.

Understanding Trims and Bindings

There are so many types of bindings, ribbons, and tapes available that it can seem confusing. You'll get to know them gradually, but understanding the purposes of the most common kinds will help you find exactly what you need to get started.

Bias Binding

Bias binding, sometimes called bias tape, is a narrow strip of fabric cut on the bias. Bias binding is used to finish edges as an alternative to hemming on anything from pot holders to quilts to skirts. It can be used for decorative finishes and can cover cord for piping. Because it's cut on the bias, it stretches slightly. This makes it possible to stitch it around curves either flat on a surface or as edging.

With bias binding, the edges of the fabric have been pressed under. While both edges have been pressed under, it is still called single fold. "Double fold" means it has been folded again down the center and pressed. Bias binding is sold in packages usually containing three yards. It comes in a wide range of colors.

It also comes in several widths, and this is where it becomes confusing. Narrow or ¼" double-fold bias binding is the same actual width of regular of ½" single fold, except it has been folded in half, making it look half as wide. The measurements on the package indicate the folded width. Extra-wide double fold looks like it's the same width as single fold, except the package is fatter. Both packages will say ½", but the double fold is really twice as wide and folded in half.

Quilt binding is usually displayed at the same place with bias binding. It is ⅞" wide and double folded. You may also find blanket binding, which is usually satin and not cut on the bias at all. Be sure to read the package to see that you are getting the type and width you need.

There are a variety of bonding and tacking tapes used to hold fabrics together permanently or temporarily to make stitching easier. Some are paper backed, and others iron on. These are especially useful for projects with tiny pieces.

Seam Binding

Seam binding, sometimes called hem tape, is a tightly woven, narrow ribbon ½" wide. It comes in a wide variety of colors and is packaged like bias binding. It is used to add support to certain seams. For example, if you are sewing with a stretchy fabric, seam binding sewn along the seam will keep the garment from losing its shape. It can be used to clean-finish hems when you want to avoid having an extra layer of folded fabric. One edge is sewn along the raw hem edge, and the other is hemmed to the garment.

Lace seam binding, sometimes called flexi-lace, is a lighter weight version of the same thing and is used the same way.

Twill Tape

Twill tape is a sturdy cotton tape. It is generally available only in black or white in widths from ¼" to ¾". It is indispensable behind snaps or other fasteners that might pull and tear away from the fabric.

Decorative Trims

Decorative lace, ruffles, and fringes come in a wide array of styles and colors. They are generally sold by the inch off oblong spools. Some of these, especially the cotton fringes, will shrink. Buy a few inches extra and wash it by hand before you sew it to anything you intend to machine wash and dry.

Decorative lace comes either flat or ruffled. Notice the bound edge of the ruffled lace. Sometimes it is finished appropriately to sew externally on a garment. Other times it's designed to be hidden inside a seam. Consider your purpose when making your choice.

Rickrack is a zigzag-shaped trim usually used for decoration. Because it is so tightly woven and stiff, a straight row of stitches down the center will generally hold even the widest rickrack without the tips folding with wear or washing.

Understanding Elastic and Fasteners

Extra notions like elastic and snaps that you will need for a particular pattern will be noted on the pattern envelope. The pattern will specify the size required, but within those requirements you may have some choices to make.

Elastic

The most common type of elastic is called corded elastic. It is a long-wearing, firm elastic that comes in a variety of widths up to about ¾".

Nonroll elastic is wider and designed not to fold in half in waistbands or other places that call for wide elastic. Both of these types of elastic are intended to be encased in fabric.

Elastic made for specific purposes include sports elastic, made to tolerate chlorine; lingerie elastic and trunk-top elastic, with one soft side to be worn against the skin; drawstring elastic with a built-in casing along the center; and extra-soft elastic for baby clothes.

Zippers

Zippers come in several weights as well as lengths. Some have metal teeth, while others are made of polyester. Among the polyester zippers are regular and invisible zippers. In the latter style, the teeth are curved inward so after the zipper is sewn into the garment, it looks like a seam except for the tiny teardrop pull hanging at the top.

Separating zippers open at the bottom end. The heavier weight ones are usually called heavy jacket. Again, the weight of the fabric and the ultimate use of the article will determine which one is appropriate.

QUESTION?

When was the zipper invented?
It's hard to imagine living without zippers, but they are relatively new. The first slide fastener was patented in 1893. The first zipper with teeth—similar to what we know now—was patented in 1913.

Snaps

There are two basic types of snaps—those that are riveted on, and those that are sewn on. Both come in a variety of sizes and weights.

The rivet type requires a hammer and a kit that includes a punch and a tool to keep the parts in place without damage while they are hammered together. There is also a snap tape available which is a twill tape with snaps attached at regular intervals. This can be a time-saver on projects that need a whole row of snaps, such as the inside legs of toddler clothes.

Hooks and Eyes

These standard little fasteners are sometimes preferable to snaps. If pressure on the fastening might cause a snap to open, use the hook and straight eye. If you want the two pieces of fabric to be flush against each other instead of overlapping, use a hook and the horseshoe-shaped hoop eye and sew both on the inside of the garment. Usually they are sold in packages that contain several hooks and an equal number of both types of eyes.

There are also heavyweight hooks and bars for use in skirt and pants waistbands, and decorative hook and hoop eyes for coats and jackets.

Buttons

We all know about buttons—plastic buttons, glass buttons, metal buttons. There are flat buttons with two or four holes, ball buttons, and shank buttons. Ball and shank buttons have protruding stitching holes or metal loops on the bottom. They are better than flat buttons for thicker fabrics.

If the perfect button is flat, and the thickness of the cloth indicates a need for a shank button, you can make the shank from thread. Simply place a toothpick on top of the button and stitch over it when you attach the button. Remove the toothpick, and the button is sewn on loose enough to fit the thicker fabric.

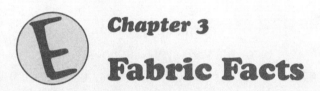

Chapter 3

Fabric Facts

The fabric will be a major factor in the success of your sewing projects. The more you know about the qualities and difficulties of different fabrics, the better a decision you'll be able to make. There are many different types of fabrics to fit every style and taste. Some, of course, are better suited to certain projects than others, so it's important to learn as much as you can.

Comments on Cotton

Cotton is the most versatile fabric there is. It's been used for textiles for centuries. The primary thing to look for in cotton and cotton-blend fabrics is the weight and texture to be sure your choice will give you the finished product you're hoping for.

Cotton's Strengths and Weaknesses

Either as pure cotton or mixed with synthetic fibers, cotton is often the best choice because it is soft, washable, generally colorfast, and easy to work with. Most cotton is plain weave, which means the fabric has a flat even texture. Cotton can range in weight from sheer gauze to heavy canvas. It comes in a seemingly limitless array of solids and prints.

Cotton will fade eventually with repeated washing but is actually more vulnerable to the sun. In spite of this, it is a very popular cloth for outdoor wear because it breathes; that is, it allows air to pass through it. It is also absorbent and wicks sweat away from your body.

ALERT!

Most pattern envelopes will include fabric suggestions. Pay particular attention to any fabric the pattern specifies as unsuitable. There will be reasons these particular fabrics will not work with this pattern, though they may not be apparent simply by looking at the picture.

Types of Cotton

Most cotton fabric is dyed after it has been woven, but some are woven of dyed threads. Gingham has a checked pattern created by weaving colored and white yarns together. Chambray and denim are woven of colored warp threads and white weft threads. Chambray is a light- to medium-weight plain-weave fabric used often for shirts, while the heavier denim is a twill-weave fabric used for jeans and jackets. Seersucker alternates tightly woven stripes with more loosely woven ones. This makes the fabric crinkly. It is often a lightweight fabric ideal for summer wear.

Cotton flannel has one fuzzy side, which makes it a napped fabric. Velvet is another napped cotton fabric, but its nap brushes smooth in one direction and stands up or feels rough in the other, making it a directional nap. The nap on corduroy is directional, too, but it is in rows called wales.

Fabrics that are made primarily or solely out of cotton include:

Calico
Cambric
Chintz
Damask
Jersey
Lawn
Muslin
Poplin
Terry cloth
Voile

A Look at Linen

Linen is similar to cotton and is made from the fibers in the stems of the flax plant. It has been around for more than 7,000 years. Ancient Egyptians grew flax along the Nile River and wrapped their mummies in it before placing them in their tombs. Through Roman times, the Middle Ages, and colonization of the Americas, it remained the most popular fabric. It wasn't until the invention of the cotton gin in 1793, which made cotton cheaper to produce, that linen slipped in popularity. Flax isn't grown commercially in the United States, and all linen is imported.

Linen fabric is tougher than cotton and wears longer. It is even more absorbent than cotton, making it particularly popular in hot climates. It tends to wrinkle worse than cotton and is often mixed with other fibers to make it more crease-resistant. Linsey-woolsey is a mixture of linen and wool and has been around since the fifteenth century. A silk-and-linen mix is shiny and softer than pure linen.

FACT

While flax doesn't grow well in the United States, hemp would. While hemp fiber is generally used for making rope, it can also be woven into a heavy linen-like cloth. It is occasionally discussed as an alternative crop to tobacco, but it is illegal to grow in this country. Although hemp is not a drug-producing plant, it belongs to the same family as the notorious *cannabis sativa*—the source of marijuana.

A Word about Wool

Wool is sometimes avoided because it needs some special care. It will shrink with a combination of heat and water. Wool garments can be dry-cleaned or hand-washed and laid flat to dry. Hanging will cause them to stretch. Don't use steam when pressing wool, and use a press cloth or press only on the underside of the fabric to prevent a shine.

Wool comes in two distinct types. Worsted, made from longer fibers, has a smooth finish. Woolen, made from the shorter fibers, is rough and hairy.

Most people don't like the feel of wool against their skin. Usually it is the prickly fibers of woolen fabric that are to blame, although occasionally it is a true allergy to the lanolin in the wool. Wool garments are almost always lined to make them more comfortable.

Specialty fabrics, similar to wool, include angora, cashmere, and mohair, which come from the hair of particular breeds of goats; and alpaca, made from the fleece of alpacas. These fibers are often blended with wool, cotton, or synthetics.

Studying Silks

Silk is woven from the threads spun by the silkworm. What most people think of when they think of silk is silk satin, which has a shiny finish that is susceptible to water spots. The synthetic imitations or blends, often called washable silks, are less expensive and easier to work with.

Silk is often mixed with other fibers, giving it very different qualities. Silk and wool is soft and lustrous. Silk and cotton has the drape of silk with much easier care. Silk and linen is a shiny dense fabric. Depending on the weight, these fabrics are used in suits, jackets, pants, dresses, and blouses.

ALERT!

Fabrics with satin finishes may show pinholes. Extra care will be needed to keep all pins within seam allowances, both when laying out a pattern and when pinning seams to sew. Incorrectly placed seams that are ripped out and sewn again may leave a visible line of holes.

Selecting Synthetics

Technically speaking, synthetics such as polyester and nylon are produced chemically, while rayon is made from plant material regenerated into fibers. They are often grouped together because they are all man-made fibers and because they share many of the same characteristics.

Rayon has been available since 1910. It has improved a great deal since then and is nearly as comfortable as cotton, only more flowing. It can be hand washed and ironed with a warm iron. Never use a hot iron on it or it will burn.

Though they are usually easy to care for, washable, and permanent press, pure synthetics do not breathe. Because of this, they are not as comfortable to wear as natural fabrics. They also fray more than natural fabrics, making them unsuitable for some projects.

When they are mixed with linen, cotton, or wool, however, synthetics add many of their desirable qualities to the natural fibers. These blends, especially cotton/polyester, are often the best choices for garment construction, being both easy to sew and easy to care for afterward. They keep their crisp, like-new appearance longer than the natural fabrics do.

Knowing Your Knits

Nearly any of the fibers already mentioned can be knitted instead of woven. The most common knit fabrics, however, are cotton jersey and polyester knits.

Jersey is lightweight, stretchy, and a bit tricky to work with. Special care needs to be taken to ensure the pieces keep their shape while you are stitching. If the fabric stretches and the seam does not, the thread in the seam is going to break. To avoid this, you must stitch with a narrow zigzag stitch or a special stretch stitch, which is usually two stitches forward and one back.

The heavier polyester knits, especially double knits, were very popular in the 1970s. They are less stretchy than jersey, so they are easier to work with and make extremely easy-care garments.

They are mostly out of style now, but a few polyester knits might be found. They are great for some craft projects because they do not ravel, and the interlocking double-knit process keeps them from being prone to runs like regular knits.

FACT

Items made from mohair, angora, and wool, or acrylic yarns are usually knitted into the pattern shape and sewn together rather than cut from a flat piece of knitted fabric. Therefore, they are primarily available as yarn for home knitting rather than fabric for home sewing.

Choosing Wisely

Besides a little background into the types of fabric available, there are a few general things to consider as you shop for fabric. To make this easier, let's begin with some fabric and fabric store terms.

Fabric is generally sold by the yard or fraction of a yard and is sometimes referred to as yard goods. It is usually displayed at the store in large rolls called bolts. The tightly woven edges of the fabric are called selvages. The threads that run parallel to them are called lengthwise or warp threads. The cut edge is called the raw edge, and the threads running along that direction are called crosswise or weft threads.

The bias is an imaginary line running diagonally across these two threads at a 45-degree angle. This line has the most stretch.

What Does It Look Like?

Once you've found the type of fabric you need for your project, you will probably be attracted to certain colors or prints. If you are buying fabric to coordinate with something else, be sure to bring it (or a swatch of the material you're trying to match, if it's difficult to carry around) with you so you can see them together. Take the bolt of fabric near a window if you can, so you can see how the fabric looks in natural light. It may look very different than it does under artificial lights in the store.

Often fabric is folded right sides together when it is wound on the bolt. Be sure you unroll it enough that you can see both sides. In fact, you ought to unroll enough of the fabric that you can play with it a little. Let some fall over your hand. Does it drape the way you want it to? Will it be too limp or too crisp for your purposes?

To determine if you have chosen a one-way fabric, arrange the cloth so it is turned back on itself, allowing you to see the right side of the fabric as it runs in two directions. If it is one-way, it will not look the same in both directions. If there are prints that must be right side up, it will be more noticeable now. If there seems to be a difference in the color of the fabric, it has a one-way shine or one-way nap.

Don't eliminate the fabric because of this. Simply buy a little extra or follow the "with nap" instructions for yardage on your pattern envelope. All your pattern pieces will need to run in the same direction on the fabric.

Because nearly all fabrics are slightly off grain, stripes, plaids, and checks that are printed on the fabric are not likely to be straight. Choose instead fabrics in which these patterns have been woven in. The back of the fabric will look like the front if the colors are woven.

What Care Will It Need?

Along with the price per yard, the end of the cardboard center of the bolt will tell you the fabric content. This will offer a clue to the care of the fabric. The end might also include specific laundering instructions. To find out how much ironing the fabric will need, squeeze a small handful and see how badly it wrinkles.

Is It Going to Fray?

One special problem some fabrics have that isn't always obvious until you try to work with them is excessive fraying. To determine how much the fabric frays, check the cut edge. If the thread ends are clinging close to the fabric, it is not likely to fray much.

If the ends are sticking out, perform another test. Scratch outward from the edge with the fabric between your forefinger and thumbnail. No more than a thread or two should come loose, and a second scratch should not bring more threads off the fabric. If it frays more than that, consider that it may be more difficult to stitch and you will have to do something to finish the seam allowances. This, again, isn't reason to reject the fabric if you are willing to do a little extra work. There are even nonfray liquids available, which are essentially light glues, that you can apply to raw edges to stop fraying. If your fabric seems especially likely to fray, treat the edges of all your fabric before you wash it and the pieces before you begin to sew them.

Is It Off-Grain?

One last thing to check, and perhaps the most serious, is the grain of the fabric. Severely off-grain fabric will be difficult to cut and will never hang properly.

To determine if the fabric is off-grain, look first at the way the fabric is folded and rolled around the bolt. If the selvage edges cannot meet without creating crosswise wrinkles in the fabric, reject it. If the fabric seems to fold all right, but the raw edge shows an abundance of cut threads as if it were cut on the bias, it may be off-grain. Look closely to see if the problem might simply be the result of a poor job of cutting. See if you are able to follow a thread from one corner of the fabric. Does it seem to run at an angle instead of straight across? If so, it is off grain.

Almost all fabric will be slightly off grain. You can correct this when you are preparing your fabric. But severely off-grain fabric is difficult, if not impossible, to straighten. It's hard to give up on an otherwise perfect fabric, but be glad you discovered it before you wasted any more time and money. With practice, you will recognize this problem quickly before considering a fabric further.

Preparing Your Fabric

That lovely fabric you've just brought home from the store isn't quite ready to cut yet. There are a few things you need to do first before you begin your sewing project.

Preshrink Your Fabric

Any machine-washable fabric with natural fibers ought to be washed. Cotton and linen both might shrink slightly the first time they are washed. Wash the fabric in the way you plan to wash the project when it is finished. Clipping the corners of the fabric through the selvage seems to keep new fabric from fraying quite as much. After it's washed, cut away the worst of the tangled threads and shake the fabric out before putting it in the dryer, so it won't wrinkle as badly. To prevent fraying entirely, zig-zag-stitch along the cut ends of your fabric.

Hand wash-only and dry clean-only fabrics don't need to be laundered before sewing. You will be taking special care throughout the life of the finished product to see that they don't shrink.

Synthetic fabric will not shrink anyway, so washing is optional. Some have a crisp finish when they are new, which makes them slightly easier to work with if you don't wash it out. However, if the fabric is slightly off-grain, that finish is going to make it impossible to straighten. In this case, you'll have to go ahead and wash it before working with it.

FACT

Though it isn't necessary, some people like to wash synthetic fabrics before they work with them. Their choice isn't because of any worry about shrinkage but because of the chemical smell that is often evident on new fabrics. This generally washes out easily.

Straighten Woven Fabrics

Straightening fabric simply means putting the lengthwise and crosswise threads into as nearly a perpendicular position as possible. Before you can check to see if your fabric needs to be straightened, you must trim one raw edge of your fabric along a thread line.

If your fabric has woven stripes, checks, or plaids, you can simply follow one of the stripes. For other fabrics, clip through the selvage near the edge and pull a thread until it breaks. Cut along the line you've created. Pull a thread again and trim and so on across to the other selvage. One edge of your fabric is now cut along the crosswise threads. Fold this line in half to determine if the selvages are perpendicular. If they hang together when you hold up the folded end, your fabric is straight with the grain.

If they do not, pull on the appropriate diagonal all along the length of your fabric. Remember the true bias isn't going to be corner to corner unless your fabric is exactly as long as it is wide. To determine which direction to pull, notice which edge of your fabric is hanging closer to the center fold. That is the edge that needs to be pulled outward from the opposite corner above.

Straighten Knit Fabrics

Knits don't have weft and warp threads; instead, they have lengthwise and crosswise stitches. Pulling a thread is not going to be possible. Cut the end following a row of stitches as closely as possible. It may be easier to follow a row from the back of the fabric. Test the same way you would woven fabric. Pull very gently on the bias to straighten.

Iron Your Fabric

If your fabric is heat tolerant, you may need to iron it before you lay out your pattern or measure to cut patternless crafts. Wrinkles will make your cutting inaccurate. Choose the iron setting appropriate for your particular fabric. Some extremely wrinkled fabrics may be difficult to even test for straightness until they've been ironed. In that case, iron it again after you've straightened it to help set the new position.

Some permanent press fabrics and knits will not need to be ironed. As soon as they are straightened, they are ready to go. And now you are ready to sew!

Chapter 4

Basic Mending and Altering

Before you tackle a new sewing project, practice some machine and hand-sewing techniques by doing a little mending or altering. Don't expect an old garment to look like new when you're done, although the goal is to make your efforts as invisible as possible. Knowing how to fix tears, repair ripped seams, or raise a hemline will always be useful.

Why Bother?

Ready-made clothes can be bought for relatively little nowadays, leading many people to dismiss the notion of mending or altering in favor of buying something new. Your time, after all, is worth more than a lot of these clothes. However, the very policies that make clothes cheap also increase the chances that a brand-new piece will have some little thing wrong with it. Knowing how to quickly fix whatever is wrong will mean your money wasn't wasted.

There are some other reasons to give mending and altering a try. You will get some sewing practice and a more intimate knowledge of clothing construction as you notice how store-bought items are put together. It will also make you a better shopper as you become more adept at recognizing flaws and potential problems.

If you've had some practice stitching missed seams on T-shirts and mending a few tears, you'll be ready when the opportunity arises to save a favorite dress or an expensive new jacket from the rag sack.

Mending Hems and Seams

Two of the most common problems that arise are hems and seams that are starting to come loose. This is where the old saying "A stitch in time saves nine" has the most application. A tiny hole in a seam or a short loosening of a hem can be ignored. However, every time the garment is washed, these problems get just a little bigger. Fix them as soon as you notice them.

ALERT!

Don't assume that technique alone will make your stitches invisible. In order to hide your mending, you will need to make your stitches disappear on the fabric. When mending or altering, the trick is to mimic the stitches that are already there. Match the color, the size, and the style as nearly as possible.

Invisibly Stitched Hem

The hem you need to fix may have been stitched with a hemstitch, that is, every inch or so on the outside of the garment, you can see a tiny loop of thread. The best way to mend this kind of hem is by hand.

FIGURE 4-1

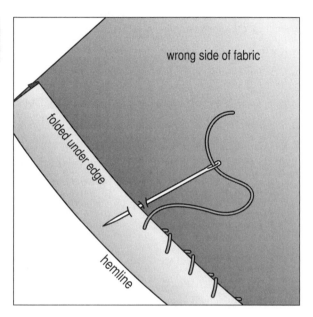

wrong side of fabric

folded under edge

hemline

◀ **Hand hemstitch:** Take tiny stiches in the garment and larger ones in the allowance.

The hand hemstitch consists of taking a tiny stitch—consisting of only a couple of threads—in the underneath fabric right above the hem edge, as illustrated in **FIGURE 4-1**. This is followed by a larger stitch through the hem edge, from the back of the hem allowance through to the top. This leaves visible vertical stitches over the hem edge that help to hold it in place.

Knot the end of the thread that is working loose, if possible, to prevent the hem from coming further undone. Trim off any hanging threads. Pin the hem into the position where it needs to be.

Use a single strand of matching thread with one end threaded through the eye of a sharp needle and the other tied in a small knot. Anchor your thread in the hem allowance a couple of inches before the open portion of the hem.

Bring the needle out at one of the remaining catch stitches. Make a tiny stitch through to the front of the garment along with theirs. Catch your thread in the allowance again. Be careful you don't pull your stitches too tight. When you run out of stitches to match, make your own. Try for the same size and spacing as the originals. When you've come to the end of the opening, copy a couple more of their catch stitches. Take several tiny stitches on top of each other in the hem allowance to keep your stitches from coming loose, and cut your thread.

FACT

Any time you are hand sewing, the beginning and end of your thread will need to be anchored to the fabric. Knotting the end of your thread before you start is the easiest way. At the end of your stitching, it's difficult to tie a knot flush with your fabric. It's easier to take several stitches on top of each other to secure the end.

Visible Hems

The hem may have been stitched with a row of stitches that are visible on the outside. This is easy to fix. Cut away loose threads, pin the hem into position and stitch it with your sewing machine as nearly like it was as possible.

However, if the article is a knit and you can see two rows of stitches on the outside, you may have a little more trouble. The hem was stitched with twin needles in a special stretch-stitch your machine may not be able to do. Check your manual. If your machine has this option, and a pair of twin needles came with it, here's your chance to try it out.

If not, the next best thing is two rows of straight stretch-stitch. If your machine won't do a stretch stitch either, use a straight stitch and stretch the fabric slightly while you stitch. This will make the stitches loose enough that they won't pop the first time the fabric stretches. Don't overdo it, or you'll end up with a ruffle where your hem should be.

Popped Seams

A seam that's opened up with no damage to the cloth itself can simply be stitched up the way it was. The only time this is tricky is when another seam or facing or pocket keeps you from being able to get to the opened seam. In these cases, you have two choices—either remove some more stitches, fix the seam and put things back together, or blind-stitch the seam from the outside.

FIGURE 4-2

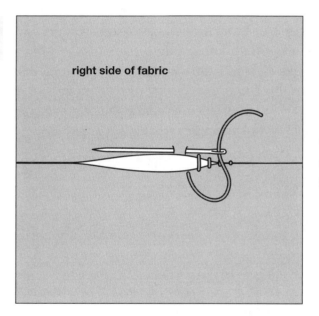

right side of fabric

◀ **The blind stitch:** Try to make your stiches look like machine stiches.

The blind stitch might not be the best choice every time, but it is very useful in a lot of applications. If it's done properly, it's almost invisible. Refer to **FIGURE 4-2**, and follow the steps below.

1. Begin along the remaining seam about ½" before the opening.
2. Hide your knot on the inside seam allowance.
3. Bring the needle out along the stitching line.
4. With the right side of the garment facing you, insert the needle into the opposite fabric and directly across from where it exited.
5. Bring it out again along the seam, trying to match the size of the existing stitches.

6. Take another tiny stitch along the seam line on the opposite fabric, being sure to enter directly across from the end of the previous stitch.
7. Repeat all along the open seam and at least ½" into the stitched seam beyond.
8. Insert the needle through to the back and take three or four tiny stitches on top of each other through the seam allowance and cut the thread.

The blind stitch can be made even stronger by using a sort of half backstitch. When the needle is under one side of the seam, it progresses the length of two stitches. On the other side it moves backward the length of one. See **FIGURE 4-3** and **FIGURE 4-4**. The result is a seam with a little more give and two threads in every stitch. Be sure you still do all your movement along the seam on the underside and your stitches bridge the gap between the fabric directly rather than at an angle.

FIGURE 4-3

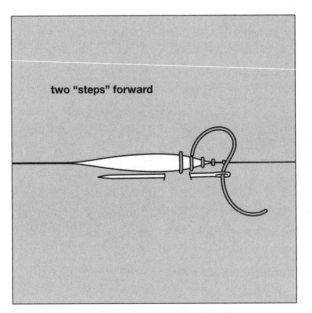

two "steps" forward

◀ **Half backstitch:** Two steps forward . . .

FIGURE 4-4

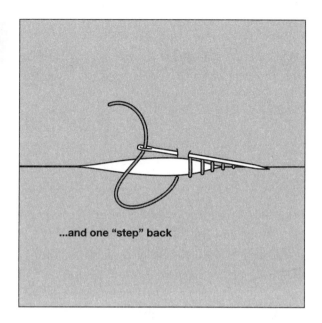

...and one "step" back

◀ . . . and one step back.

Missed Seams

It's not uncommon to get a new article of clothing home and discover that one layer of fabric was missed in a seam. Or, after only a few washings, fabric that was only caught by a thread may have pulled away from the stitching.

If this is a simple straight seam, begin the repair by removing the stitches on either end of the opening where the loose fabric angled away from the seam line. Realign the two layers and stitch them together, matching the thread and stitches as closely as possible. Use a similar method if the problem is a hem.

If the loose fabric is part of a cuff or collar, it may be a little more difficult. In order to save money, some clothing manufacturers allow very little fabric for seams, which was the cause of the problem to begin with. This leaves you very little to work with.

Turn the raw edge under the best you can and blind-stitch it down, even if part of the seam underneath shows. If you leave it as it is, it will fray and look progressively worse, if it doesn't actually catch on something and tear. Fixing this flaw is usually a matter of making the problem as inconspicuous as possible without expecting invisibility.

What if the fabric has torn at the seam?
In that case, remove the seam stitches from about 1" on either side of the tear. Patch the tear with an iron-on patch. Restitch the seam.

Changing Hemlines

One of the most common tasks in altering is changing the length of a hemline. The first step is to take out the old hem and press the allowances flat. Next, determine exactly where you want the hem to be. Then press the hem allowance under along this new hemline.

Before you can decide how best to hem the garment, you need to determine how much flaring or tapering is going on at the bottom couple of inches of the garment. Check for this by laying your garment flat and folding the edge up a couple of inches. If the width at the bottom edge is equal to the width of the garment where it's lying, your hem allowance will lie flat. If the bottom edge is wider, your garment flares. If it's narrower, your garment tapers.

Straight Hem Allowances

Exactly how you proceed will depend on the weight of the fabric. Heavyweight fabrics, such as jeans or denim skirts, should be hemmed to minimize bulk. Hems on jeans are usually turned twice. Press the raw edge up to the desired length. Trim the allowance to 1" of your fold line. Fold the raw edge almost to the fold line. Machine-stitch the hem in place with a straight stitch, using a heavy-duty needle.

An alternative is to trim the hem allowance to ½" and finish the raw edge with a zigzag or other finishing stitch. Fold the hem up and machine-stitch. You will still need a heavy-duty needle but will be sewing through two layers instead of three. A neater version of finishing the raw edge of heavy to medium weight fabrics is to overlap the very edge with seam tape. Machine-stitch the tape to the edge and stitch the actual hem along the other edge of the tape. This will hide the raw edge on the inside while allowing you to stitch through fewer layers of the dense fabric.

Lightweight fabrics are nearly always turned twice. Trim the hem allowance to anywhere from 1 to 2. Turn the raw edge under ¼" or ½". Pin the hem in place and hem with a machine hemstitch or by hand.

FIGURE 4-5

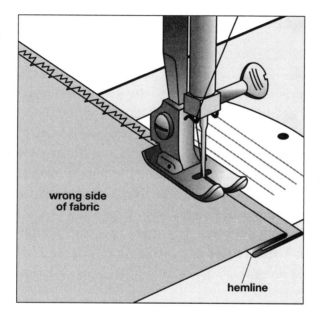

wrong side
of fabric

hemline

◄ **Machine hemstitch:**
Fold the fabric carefully so
your stitches are even.

If you have a hemstitch on your machine, this would be a perfect time to try it out. Adjust the pins so they run parallel to the edge instead of perpendicular. With the wrong side toward you, fold the hem back under the main fabric, exposing about ⅛" of the hem edge. Stitch along this edge as shown in **FIGURE 4-5**. The hemstitch consists of three or four straight stitches that go through the hem edge, followed by one zigzag stitch that extends over onto the main fabric. On the outside, it will look much like a hand-stitched hem. Care must be taken to keep the fabric folded so that the zigzag stitches extend into the main fabric at approximately the same distance.

If you prefer to hand-stitch your hem, refer to the hand hemstitch illustration and description earlier in this chapter.

When raising a hem, the temptation is to fold over an existing hem in case you want to lengthen the garment later. Do this only for a fast-growing child and only if you are confident the article won't wear out before it's outgrown.

Flared Hem Allowances

If your hem allowance is flared, you will need to gather the edge of the fabric slightly to make it fit. The best way to minimize this is to make the hem as narrow as possible. Also, because the gathers will add bulk, finishing the edge with zigzag stitches or seam tape is preferable to folding the edge under on any but the lightest weight fabrics. Lace seam binding can be helpful here. Stretch it slightly as you stitch it to the raw edge.

You will have to be especially careful pinning the hem in place so your gathers along the hem edge will be at the appropriate places to make the finished hem lie flat. Extremely flared hems will be difficult to ease in with the machine and should be hand sewn. If you are using seam tape or lace, take a running stitch, that is, tiny in-and-out stitches in the tape edge between the stitches that go through the fabric underneath. See **FIGURE 4-6**.

FIGURE 4-6

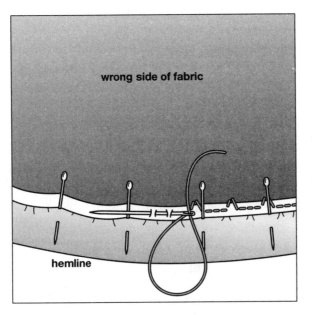

wrong side of fabric

hemline

◄ **Stitching flared hems with binding:** Gather the excess allowance until it fits between the pins.

If you are folding the raw edge of your hem allowance under, use the longest stitch setting on your machine and stitch along this single fold. Pin your hem in place. With a pin, pull a few of the stitches between the anchor pins to gather the edge. See **FIGURE 4-7**. Hem with the regular hemstitch by machine or by hand.

FIGURE 4-7

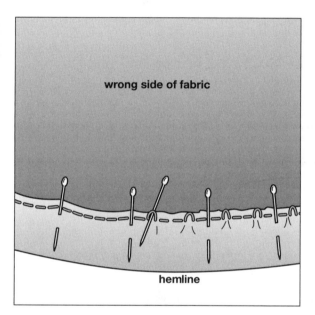

wrong side of fabric

hemline

◀ Stitching flared hems with turned edge.

Tapered Hem Allowances

Tapered hems are the most difficult. Essentially, you need to gather the garment to fit the hem, but you don't want it to show that you've done that. If you were constructing a new garment that tapered, at the point where you wanted the hem to fold, you would flare out your garment pieces to make up for the taper. With a ready-made garment you are altering, it's too late to do that. Instead, make the hem as narrow as possible and place your stitches a little farther apart to minimize the pinched look on the outside.

Lowering a Hemline

If you want to shorten a ready-made garment, you will have plenty of hem allowance to work with. Lengthening a garment is a different matter.

First of all, there has to be enough fabric in the hem allowance to work with. Unless it is a garment that lends itself to some creative inserts, trims, or ruffles, you'll want the lower hem to be part of the garment fabric itself. After ripping out the original hemstitches, use seam binding to minimize the amount of fabric you will need. Sew the seam binding to the raw edge so it just barely overlaps onto the fabric. Fold the seam binding under enough that it doesn't show and hem. This will use only about ¼" of fabric.

The other problem with lowering hems is the crease from the old hem. The crease can be difficult to press out even in new garments, and garments that have had some wear will almost certainly have a permanent crease line. If these are everyday clothes for a growing child, ignore the crease. If you are altering dress pants to fit a taller person or a skirt to reflect a new, longer style, consider whether the finished product is going to be satisfactory enough to make it worth the effort.

To tell if a crease is going to show before you take out the old hem, separate the two layers of fabric at the hem. If the fold line appears lighter than the fabric around it, it's going to show.

Taking In or Letting Out a Seam

Like lowering a hem, the amount of seam allowance that exists is going to determine whether or not you can let out a seam. However, sometimes a small change can make a lot of difference. If you can restitch a seam ¼" inside the current seam on both sides of a garment, you're actually adding 1" to the diameter of the garment. The main thing to remember is to taper the new seam into the old. In other words, if you want to let out the seams on a dress or blouse, begin stitching on top of the old stitches below the sleeve seam and gradually taper your stitches into the seam allowance over perhaps 1" of stitching.

If you are letting something out clear to the hemline, remove the hem along the seam area, stitch the seam, remove the old seam stitches, press the seam flat and repair the hem.

Taking in a seam is a lot easier because you have more to work with. Begin by putting the garment on inside out. Place pins along the lines where you want new seams. Shaping seams can be lengthened the same way. Carefully remove the garment. Shift the pins to make side seams match.

To be sure the garment will fit the way you want it to, first stitch the seams with long basting stitches. These can be machine basting stitches or running stitches done by hand; the idea is to use easily removable stitches. Try the garment on again right side out. When it's right, stitch by tapering out from the existing stitches as described for letting out a seam. Trim or finish the seam allowance edge, copying the existing treatment as closely as possible. Press and repair the hem if necessary.

The amount you can correct a bad fit by taking in the seams is limited. Deeper side seams are not going to change the width of the shoulders or the size of the waistband. To correct these, the garment might have to be taken apart entirely, and then the project would no longer be a matter of simple alteration.

Mending Simple Tears

It's going to be impossible to mend a tear in such a way that it completely disappears. If the tear is in a piece of dress clothing and is located where it will show, it may not be worth the trouble. If the garment is comfortable enough that it can have a second life as at-home work clothes, mend the tear while it's still small. Tears in work clothes can catch on things, making them potentially dangerous as well as annoying.

Patching Tears in Woven Fabrics

For very small tears, iron-on patches might be the best solution. They are available in a few colors. Choose the one closest to your fabric or slightly lighter, and cut it just slightly larger than the tear. Follow the package directions to apply it to the underside of your garment. They adhere better to some fabrics than others. Cotton takes them very well.

If the fabric can't take the heat needed to iron on the patch, you can't use them and must try another solution.

Cut a piece of scrap fabric the weight of your garment fabric or lighter and slightly larger than the tear. Weight is going to be more important than color, although a close color match is nice. Back the tear with the fabric, pinning it carefully so the fabric around the tear is lying flat on the patch. With thread that matches the garment, sew along the tear with a wide, close-together zigzag stitch. If the tear closes entirely, one row of stitches might hold it together. More likely it will take two or three overlapping rows. Carefully trim the backing fabric away close to the stitches.

Darning Tears on Woven Fabrics

If the tear is at a barely noticeable place, like under the arm, and you want a more professional-looking mend so you don't have to reduce the garment's use, you can try darning the tear. Placing the area around the tear in an embroidery hoop might make it easier to keep it flat. Using a darning needle and two strands of thread or the heavier darning thread, begin about ½" beyond and above the tear. Do not make a knot. Simply leave a tail and trim it off later.

Choosing the direction that most closely runs perpendicular to the tear, weave the needle in and out of the fabric in line with the grain, taking about eight stitches per inch. Extend the stitches about ½" past the tear. Turn and weave another row of stitches parallel to the last row. Continue this weaving pattern over the area, treating the tear as if it weren't there.

Do not wash a garment before mending it. Washing will cause the raw edges of the tear to fray, making it more difficult to repair. The broken strands in torn knitted garments can cause runs that are much more difficult, if not impossible, to mend.

If the tear is on the grain line, which is likely in woven fabrics, you won't need to go in the opposite direction. However, if the tear is diagonal or an L shape, darn in a crosswise direction weaving in and out over the first set of stitches.

Tears in Knitted Fabrics

A very fine knit like a T-shirt can be mended with a zigzag stitch, in the same way you would mend woven fabrics, as long as you are careful not to stretch it out of shape. The hand-darning method will work, though it isn't quite as effective, because it won't stretch with the fabric.

Heavier knits—ones on which you can easily see the rows of knit stitches—will need to be mended taking the knit stitches into account. To make the tear disappear entirely, you will need some yarn to match the garment and some knowledge of knitting. If you are dealing with an expensive sweater that came with extra yarn wrapped around a piece of cardboard, hire an expert knitter to mend it for you.

However, if this is an inexpensive garment, or one that has already gotten a lot of wear, mend it simply to close the hole before it gets larger. Find a similar weight yarn if possible and, using a blunt tapestry needle, try a little free-form darning. Be sure to catch any loops that do not have yarn running though them. These will run if they aren't anchored.

Mending Holes

Holes in garments are treated pretty much like tears except that they are more difficult to hide. Assume the garment is now at-home work clothes and patch or darn it to stop further damage.

Patching Holes

To mend a hole on the sewing machine, begin with a scrap of fabric of similar weight. Cut it slightly larger than the hole. Trim the loose thread away at the edges of the hole. Pin the patch to the underside of the fabric. From the outside, zigzag-stitch around the edge of the hole. From the inside, zigzag around the outside edge of the patch.

If you have a very small hole, especially in lightweight fabric, the round of zigzag stitches at the hole will probably be enough. Trim the patch fabric away close to these stitches.

If you are patching some place that will rub, like the knees of a child's pants, put the patch on the outside, but otherwise stitch it the same. You can, of course, turn under the edges of the patch and straight stitch them in place, but they will be bulkier and will not give as much as the zigzag stitches.

If you don't like the outline of the hole showing on an outside patch, zigzag around the empty hole to keep it from fraying and then apply the patch.

Darning Holes

Darning a hole works pretty much the same way as darning a tear except you'll always have to go in both the lengthwise and crosswise directions. Don't try to darn any holes that are larger than a quarter. Also, if a spot on a garment is wearing extremely thin, darn it before it wears through entirely. This is easier than putting your own fabric over the hole.

The verb "to darn" is related to the Middle Dutch *dernen,* meaning to stop up a hole in a dyke. This suggests that darning is a task that's better to do while the hole is small and manageable.

Darning gourds or mushrooms might help you keep your darning stitches smooth. Center the hole over the smooth top, and gather the fabric around the handle to hold with your off hand while you darn. These darning tools work better for holes than for tears. They tend to pull a tear open rather than help you hold it closed.

Buttons and Buttonholes

There are several problems that can arise with buttons or buttonholes. Most of them are easily solved, if you simply take the time to do it. Here's what you need to know to handle these minor problems with ease.

Buttons

Not being able to sew on a button is the sewing equivalent to not being able to boil water. No one actually believes you when you say it.

The only tricks are to match the button if the original is lost, match the thread used to sew the other buttons, and sew it on with approximately the same amount of thread.

First, check the lower seam allowances. Sometimes manufacturers will sew on extra buttons there. Other clothes come with one button in a tiny plastic bag with the label. If you saved it and can find it, you're in luck. If your button was lost and you can't quite match it, see if you can't move a button from the least conspicuous place and put your almost-match in its place. Avoid the problem of matching buttons as often as possible by noticing loose buttons and restitching them before they come off.

If the button has torn the fabric beneath it, mend the hole with an iron-on patch or by darning, then replace the button. If you have darned it, reinforce the area by holding a small square of twill tape behind the mend and sewing the button through it as well as the fabric.

Reducing Buttonholes

Sometimes a button will not stay buttoned, even though there is no particular pressure on it. The fault is probably the buttonhole. Check to see if the buttonhole stitching has started to come out. If it has, replacing it will most likely solve the problem.

FIGURE 4-8

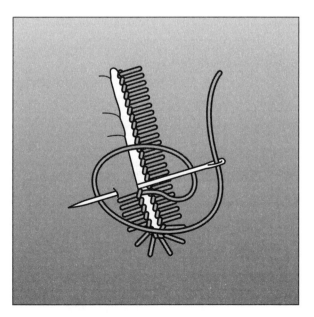

◀ Buttonhole stitch.

Cut any loose threads. Line the exposed raw edges of the buttonhole with tiny buttonhole stitches, using thread that matches the other buttonholes as closely as possible. Also, use the other buttonholes or the needle holes from the lost stitches to determine the depth of your stitches. Refer to **FIGURE 4-8** and follow the steps below.

1. Hide a small knot on the underside of the garment, or take three stitches on top of each other to anchor your thread.
2. Bring the needle and thread to the outside through the buttonhole to begin.
3. Insert the needle back through the buttonhole and out at the end of the stitching line.
4. Loop the thread around the needle going behind the eye end and under the point.
5. Pull the needle through, adjusting the thread so the "knot" you've just made is at the raw edge.
6. Repeat steps 3 through 5 very close to the last stitch.

Other Suggestions

If reworking the buttonhole isn't enough to keep the button from slipping out, or if the original stitches are still in place, the buttonhole may have just been made a little too large. Reduce its size by taking a few looping stitches over one end of the buttonhole. Test it as you go so you don't end up making the buttonhole too small.

If you have a sweater, blouse, or dress that tends to separate between the buttons, see if it can't be sewn closed. Try pulling the garment off and on with only the top one or two buttons undone. Determine exactly how many buttons you actually need to use. If the buttonhole band has a row of topstitching, that would be a natural place to stitch. Heavier sweaters will be better if you stitch them loosely by hand using a hemstitch along the edge of the button band. Begin even with or just below the first button, and stitch down until you are even with the last button. Don't stitch clear to the hemline if you want it to appear as if the buttons still work.

Congratulations! Now you know the basics, and you're ready to tackle some projects from scratch. (E)

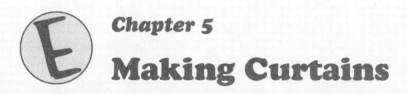

Chapter 5
Making Curtains

Making your own curtains will be more economical than buying ready-made ones. You'll also have a much wider range of colors and textures to choose from. If you have unusually shaped or proportioned windows, making your own might be the only practical choice. Check catalogs and magazines for ideas. Different fabric combinations, lengths, trims, and shapes might inspire you to greater creativity.

Planning Your Curtains

Before you rush to the fabric store to buy your fabric, you need to make a few decisions. Will the room benefit from having the curtains extend beyond the window, or should the outside edge of the woodwork be visible around the curtain? Do you want the curtains to hover just above the sill, hang to the bottom of the lower edge of the woodwork or apron, or hang clear to the floor? Perhaps they belong somewhere in between.

Do you want sheer curtains to diffuse the light, or heavier ones to block it? Or are you more interested in a window treatment for its decorative value? Should they be a solid color to bring out a color in the room or a print to tie several colors or neutral tones together? Your answers to these questions will help you determine the type and location of your hardware and the type of fabric and style of curtain you choose.

Begin with the simple shirred curtains. Shirred curtains are the most basic type of curtains. The top of the curtain is hemmed with a casing through which the curtain rod is inserted, gathering the curtain along its length. Shirred curtains will not slide open and closed easily, though they are often tied at the sides, framing the window with a graceful draped effect. They are also not appropriate for very heavy fabrics because of the difficulty of gathering them on a rod. Most other curtains use some of the same construction techniques as the shirred.

FACT

Café curtains are short curtains that cover only the lower part of a window. They provide some privacy while allowing light in. Usually they are used in combination with a valance, which is a short curtain at the top of the window.

Estimating Yardage

Your first consideration is the weight of the fabric. The more sheer the fabric, the fuller the curtains should be. Usually the width of the curtain or curtain pair is twice the width of the curtain rod. Heavier curtains might only be 1½ times the width, and sheer curtains can be three times as wide.

Decide whether you want one straight curtain that hangs over the window at all times or is pulled to one side for an asymmetrical look, or if you want two panels that meet in the center and are tied back or dropped into place as desired. Curtains on doors or casement windows are often shirred at the bottom as well as the top. Determine the placement of the lower rod and use it when figuring your measurements.

Next, decide on the length of the curtains. To this length, add 4" for a top hem and casing, or 7" if you want a 1½" heading. A heading is a small ridge of ruffled curtain above the casing. Add more if you have a wide, flat curtain rod. Also add 6" for a bottom hem. You could make narrower hems, but the extra fabric inches add crispness to the top and weight to the bottom. If you are using a bottom rod, add the length for its casing instead of the lower hem.

Bring all your measurements and figures with you to the store, not just your final yardage estimate. You may find fabrics that make you want to change your plans. In that event, a pocket calculator will come in handy, too. Do not be embarrassed to ask for help with your figuring.

If piecing is necessary, the seams should be on the vertical to hide among the folds. The width of your curtains in relation to the width of your fabric will tell you how many of the figured lengths of fabric you will need. Since selvages sometimes shrink, you will be trimming them away, reducing the fabric's width by at least ½". Another ½" of width will be lost if you are piecing two; 1" will be lost from the width of a middle length if you are piecing three. There will be 2" used on each side of each curtain for hems, further reducing the width of your fabric lengths.

If you need just under 1½ times the width of the fabric to make each of two curtains, you will need three times the total length of your finished curtains, plus 10" for the hems. In other words, plan to use a length for each curtain and a third length to split between the two. Add 1" or so per yard for possible shrinkage, and you have an approximation of the yardage you'll need.

If you choose a fabric with a print that will need to be matched, take the distance from one repeat of the pattern to the next. Multiply that measure by the number of lengths of fabric, and add that to the total yardage.

Choosing Curtain Fabrics

You'll have a wide variety of fabrics to choose from. However, besides the fabrics that are too heavy to shirr, there are a few things to avoid.

Pure cotton fabrics are sensitive to the sun and fade rather quickly. If your curtains will catch any direct sunlight, cotton polyester blends will last longer. They have a crisper look as well. If you like the rustic look of cotton, choose linen or undyed muslin.

Also avoid prints that have any kind of noticeable horizontal design unless it is woven in. If a printed design is off grain, it will make your entire window treatment look crooked. And if you try to cut your curtain with the print rather than the grain, your curtains will never hang in straight folds.

Cutting Out Your Curtains

If your curtain fabric is washable, preshrink it as described in Chapter 3. A great many yards of fabric will be difficult to straighten all at once, so pull threads to cut your fabric into lengths and straighten them individually. If you have a pattern to match, simply start each length at exactly the same place in the pattern, cut it to the correct length (the finished curtain plus your hem and heading allowances), then cut away the fabric to the next pattern repeat.

With the lengths cut out and straightened, cut away all selvage edges. Split any lengths that are wider than necessary. You can usually pull lengthwise threads to make a straight cut.

ALERT!

If you want curtains that open and close easily but don't want the trouble of pleats and hooks, make your curtains as if to shirr them only without a heading. Use curtain rings with tiny clamps to hang your curtains. They are available from home decorating catalogs and from some well-stocked department stores.

Sewing Your Curtains

If your fabric is the right width for your curtains, you are ready to hem them. If not, begin by piecing the lengths together.

Piecing Your Curtains

The best way to seam your lengths together is with a French seam. Begin by deciding where these seams should be. Typically the narrower length should be toward the outside of the window to be less noticeable. Take care to keep all printed designs, naps, and one-way shines in the right direction.

To make a French seam, pin your two lengths of fabric together with the *wrong* sides together. Sew a narrow ¼" seam along the edge. Press the seam open, then turn the fabric right sides together and press the seam again. If the fabric wants to slide, pin the seam. Sew a second seam ⅜" from the first seam to hide the raw edge within the seam. Press the seam flat against the curtain.

Hemming the Sides

Press the sides of each panel under 2". A sewing gauge is very helpful here. Fold the raw edge under to the fold line. If you are after a country or rustic look, you can straight-stitch the side hems close to the fold. For a more formal curtain, either use the hemstitch on your machine or do the hems by hand. Refer to Chapter 4 for instructions on hemstitches.

Making the Casings and Headings

If you didn't include extra fabric for a heading, press the top of the curtain panels under 4", and then press the raw edge under in line with the crease. Pin the hem carefully so the corners of the top casing's hem don't extend beyond the side hems. Hemstitch with your machine or by hand.

If you added extra fabric for a heading, press the raw edge under 5½". Then press the raw edge under 2". Sew close to the hem edge with a straight or hemstitch. Sew another row of stitches 1½" from the top edge. This will define the heading, and the casing for the rod will be below it. Either set up a temporary guide on your machine for sewing 1½" from the edge, or mark the stitching line with pins or chalk.

If you are pressing a double fold for a hem, you can press the edge under and fold it over again, but it won't be as accurate as folding the full amount under first. It's hard to see exactly what you're doing with the second fold.

Hemming the Bottom

Before you hem the bottom of your curtains, compare the panels. Put them wrong sides together to compare the center and outside lengths. Trim one if necessary. Compare again after the hem is pressed under and before you stitch it. If you are anchoring your curtain with a rod on the bottom, make the bottom casing the same way you did the top.

If you allowed 6" for the bottom hem, press the raw edge under that amount then press the raw edge to the fold line. This hem can be stitched the same way the upper casing was. Or, to be sure the hem allowance doesn't stick out beyond the sides, you can fold the corners under. To do this, fold only as far as the side hemstitching as shown in **FIGURE 5-1**. Be sure the lower corner is still sharp. Blind-stitch along the diagonal crease to keep it from coming out.

FIGURE 5-1

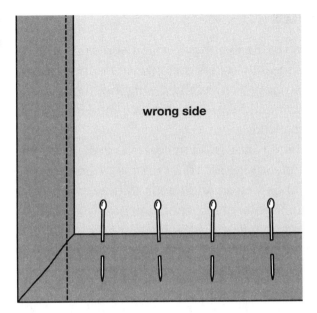

wrong side

◀ **Hemmed corner:** Turn under the end, but keep the corner sharp.

In some situations, such as when an air vent is directly under your curtains, you might want to add more weight to the lower hem. There are chain weights made for this purpose, or you can use a length of ball chain like that used for light pulls. Run them through the hem and stitch them at each end. You could also use metal washers in the corners. Plan to remove them when you wash the curtains, or they might rust and stain the curtain. Be careful also that you don't use weights so heavy that they stretch your curtains or tear the hem.

Making Ruffles

Ruffles on curtains may seem too frilly in certain applications, but in bathrooms, breakfast areas, or kitchens, they can add a cheerful touch. You might find a ready-made eyelet or cotton ruffle that works perfectly with your curtain plans, but generally you'll need to make your own from the curtain fabric or a coordinating one.

Measuring the Ruffles

Ruffles often run along the inside edges and across the bottoms of a pair of curtains. Sometimes the ruffles are only on the bottoms. Another row of ruffles can be sewn just below the casing, but more often a valance is made to mimic the fullness of the ruffle and shirred onto the outer portion of a double rod.

When you decide how to use your ruffles, take their width into account when you are measuring for your curtains. A bottom ruffle will take the place of a hem as well as add length to the curtains. The ruffle itself can be from 3" to 8" wide and, depending on the weight of the fabric, anywhere from double to triple the length of the curtain it's gathered against. Consider, too, if you want your ruffle to have a heading. This would be 1" of ruffle fabric above the gathering stitches, making a small decorative head to the ruffle.

If you will be making your own ruffle instead of buying it ready-made, consider the weight of your ruffle fabric. Lighter-weight fabric is usually cut twice the width of the needed ruffle, plus 1". Include the heading, if any, in this measurement. Stiffer, heavier fabrics are usually hemmed on both sides and only need to be cut 1" wider than your ruffle and heading will be.

Don't try to guess how much ruffle fabric you'll need. Figure out how many strips of fabric with a width of 42" you'll need, and multiply that by the width of fabric needed for the ruffle. Remember to account for piecing seams and trimming off the selvages. If, at the store, you discover your fabric's width is much different than 42", do some refiguring.

Cutting and Hemming Ruffles

Cut your ruffle fabric into the strips as you calculated. If you are folding your ruffles double, you can stitch the strips together with ½" straight seams and press the allowances open. Fold the entire ruffle, right sides together and stitch ½" from the raw edge. Turn the tube right side out. A large safety pin fastened to the seam allowance can help with the turning if your ruffle is narrow. Iron the ruffle flat with the seam running along the center of one side. Turn the raw edges of the ends ½" inside the tube, press, and stitch the ends.

If you are hemming your ruffle, piece the strips together with French seams as described for piecing the curtain panels. Press these seams to one side. Hem the bottom edge of the ruffle lengths using ½" of fabric, or with a hemming foot attachment for your sewing machine. If your machine came with this type of presser foot, here's your chance to try it. If you have allowed for a heading, hem both long sides of your ruffle.

FACT

You can make tie-backs for your curtains using the same stitch-and-turn method described for making ruffles. Cut your fabric twice the width of your desired ties plus 1". Cut one long strip that equals the length you want each of your ties to be plus ½", times the number of ties. Stitch and turn, then cut the ties apart.

Gathering the Ruffle

Make two rows of long machine stitches ¼" apart where your ruffle needs to gather. If your ruffle does not have a heading, these rows of stitches will be ¼" and ½" from the edge. If you are making a ruffle with a heading, these rows will be just under and just over 1" from the edge.

Attaching a Ruffle with a Heading

Hem the side or sides of your curtain that will not have a ruffle as described earlier. Press the casing hem under, but do not stitch it. The edges of the curtain that will be decorated with a ruffle need to be turned and hemmed. This can be done toward the front if you want, because the ruffle will cover it, thus giving the back of the curtain a more finished look.

Pin the ruffle to the curtain, wrong side of ruffle to right side of curtain, with the rows of gathering stitches running along or just above the hem. Distribute the extra ruffle fabric as evenly as possible over the curtain edge. If the ruffle is going around a corner, allow extra fullness so the ruffle doesn't turn under. Extend the ruffle only to the point where the curtain will fold for the top casing.

Use a pin to pull the ruffling stitches, and gather the fabric until it lies flat between the pins. Topstitch along both rows of gathering stitches.

If you are running a row of ruffles along the top of your curtain, either above or below the casing, stitch the casing down as described earlier. Gather the ruffle onto the width of the curtain, and attach the same as was described above.

Pleated drapes and lined curtains are not projects that should be tackled by beginners. The problems aren't so much the techniques as the unique sewing problems caused by heavy drapery fabric, heat-resistant lining, and crinoline or other stiffening products needed for the pleats.

Attaching a Ruffle Without a Heading

If your ruffle is folded double, the gathering edge is finished, and your ruffle can be attached just like the ruffle with the heading, except that you'll be stitching close to the edge. However, if your gathering stitches are along the raw edge of a single-thickness ruffle, you'll need to attach the ruffle in such a way as to cover the raw edge. This same method can be followed for a folded ruffle if you want a more finished look.

For ruffles accenting the bottom or side edges of the curtains, begin by pressing the raw edge of the curtain ¾" from back to front, then press the raw edge under ¼". Do not stitch. Lay your ruffle on the curtain, right sides together, with the bottom edge of the ruffle pointed toward the center of the curtain. Line the raw edge of the ruffle up with the inside fold on the curtain edge. Gather and stitch as described for the headed ruffle, being sure to allow extra fullness if you are gathering around a corner.

Turn the pressed edges of the curtain up over the gathers and stitch close to the edge. There's no perfect way to do this around the corner, so just try to be sure all raw edges are tucked under. The ruffle should fall into place. Iron the curtain away from the ruffle. You may want to topstitch the finished ruffle end to the curtain.

If you are attaching a row of ruffles to the surface of your curtain, cut a length of extra-wide double-fold bias tape ½" longer than the width of the curtain. Open out the first fold, and stitch the ends under ¼". Pin your ruffle to the tape, lining the raw edge up with the center fold on the bias tape. Gather and stitch, then turn the bias tape over the gathers and stitch. Sew this tape-edged ruffle along the casing after it has been hemmed in place.

QUESTION?

Why not finish the top edge before you gather it?
The three layers of fabric at the edge of the ruffle created by turning it under will not gather the same as the single layer of fabric below it where the other row of gathering stitches will be. In fact, it won't gather well at all.

Making Valances and Flounces

Valances are generally a separate curtain shirred onto the outer portion of a double curtain rod. The straight-bottom ones are made just like the curtains, but there are other possibilities.

Some elaborately draped window valances are actually made with no sewing except the hems. The trick is to give yourself the right fullness and length to drape them the way you want. Also, be willing to do a little hand sewing from the top of a stepladder to keep them that way.

Swag or Scalloped Shaped Valances

Swag-shaped valances extend far down the window on the outside edges and angle dramatically upward to a narrow valance at the center. These are made simply by cutting the fabric into the desired shape and adding a narrow hem, or finishing the edge. Make your pattern on heavy tissue or on the brown paper you can find sold in a roll (usually in the aisle with packing materials).

Pin your pattern to the fabric and cut both sides at once. Be sure your fabric is lying with either right sides or wrong sides together so you get a right side and a left side for your curtains. If you are using fabric that is exactly the same on the front and back, you may be able to cut your curtain the desired length and top width, then cut it in half diagonally to get both sides. If you are doing two identical windows and your fabric has no one-way effect, cut one from lower right to upper left and the other from lower left to upper right.

The more complicated scalloped, curved, or pointed valances are done with lining. Design your shape to fit your window, and cut out the shape from your fabric. Cut out a second identical shape from a neutral fabric that will not show through your curtain fabric. Put the lining right side down on the right side of your curtain, and stitch around the lower curves and the sides.

FIGURE 5-2

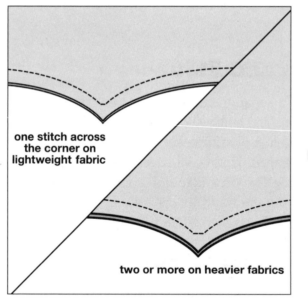

one stitch across
the corner on
lightweight fabric

two or more on heavier fabrics

◀ **Points:** Stitch across a point rather than into it.

To make sharp points, stitch across the corner (see **FIGURE 5-2**). Thin fabrics will only require one stitch across the point while thicker fabrics will require two or even three. Trim the seam allowance away close to the stitches so there is less bulk inside the point.

Grade the seam allowances by cutting the lining's allowance to one half the allowance of the curtain. Clip inward curves almost to the stitching line and the outward curves with a V. Turn the curtain right side out, and press the lower edges and sides. Rolling the edge between your thumb and finger can sometimes help you turn the seam completely. Treat the two layers as one when you make the top casing.

ALERT!

Valances that have a draped or pulled look are made by curving the top edge. It's difficult to guess exactly how such a valance will hang. It can also be a bit tricky to sew the casing on a curve, but the gathers when it's shirred on a rod will hide the puckers.

Mock Valances and Flounces

Sometimes a valance is actually part of the lower curtains but is made to appear as if it's separate. This is generally done by making the casing part of the valance then gathering the valance onto the top of the curtain just below the casing. If your window is large enough for an even fuller look, consider overlapping the curtains under the valance. Both sides can be pulled back with ties once the curtains are hung.

Flounces are made similarly to the mock valances, except the lower edge is caught up to the curtain close to the casing, leaving a loop of fabric to puff out. This seam is actually sewn to the curtains proper before the top of the curtains are attached to the valance.

Tab Curtains

Tab curtains are hung on decorative rods by loops or tabs made from fabric or ribbons that are attached to the top of the curtain. They are usually not as full as shirred curtains, so they take less fabric. Different tabs will give your curtains a different look. How many tabs you use and their widths will determine how far you will be able to slide the curtains open.

To make your own tabs, cut a strip of fabric to the desired width times two, plus 1" for the seam. The length will depend on the size of your curtain rod and how much drop you want between the rod and the top of your curtain. Take the desired distance from the top of the rod to the curtains times two, plus 1" and the approximate diameter of the rod. This will give you the length you need for each tab. Take this measurement times the number of tabs for the length of fabric you need to cut. .

The tab strip is sewn and turned the same way as the doubled-over ruffle was. Press the strip flat with the seam down the center of one side, and cut it to the proper lengths. Fold the tabs in half, and space them on the right side of your curtains after the side seams have been hemmed. Line the raw edges of the tabs up with the raw edge of the curtain top and the loop ends toward the center of the curtain. Stitch them in place ¼" from the edge. Cut a facing piece the width of your curtains plus 1" for side hems and approximately 4" long. Put narrow hems on the sides of your facing, using ½" on each side.

Stitch the facing to the top of the curtain, right sides together about ½" from the raw edge. The tabs will be between the two layers. Trim the seam allowance of the facing to about ¼". Turn the facing to the wrong side and press. Fold the bottom edge of the facing under, and hemstitch it to the curtain.

Scalloped Topped Curtains

Some curtains, usually café curtains with tabs or with peaks clipped to rings, will have scallops between the tabs or rings. To make scallops, cut the curtains allowing an extra 6" or so at the top to fold back for lining. The amount you need to allow will depend on the depth of your scallops. Also, if you plan to fold the top back for tabs, remember to allow the total length of the tab in both the curtains and the lining.

After the side hems are sewn, turn the top down toward the front the amount you allowed for your lining. Pin it both at the bottom edge and across the fold to hold it securely.

Make a pattern for the scallops. These can be a half circle if you are attaching your curtains to rings or much deeper for tabs. Space them evenly across the top of the curtain, perhaps 1" apart. Mark the scallops with a pencil or chalk.

Being sure that the fabric stays flat on the fold, stitch along the marked scallops. Cut away the half circles to within ¼" of the stitching and clip the curves. Turn the lining to the back and gently push out the peaks or tabs. Press. Turn tabs under the appropriate length, and hand-stitch them to the lining.

Congratulations! You've finished your first set of curtains!

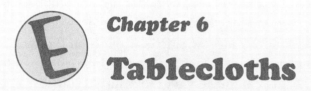

Chapter 6
Tablecloths

Tablecloths can show off your good china or set the theme or tone for a gathering. On accent tables, cloths can protect an antique from scratches or hide an already marred surface. The right fabric choices can help give a room of mismatched furniture a more coordinated look.

Measuring and Shopping

It's easy to measure square and rectangular tables—add twice the drop or overhang and 2" for the hems to the dimensions of your table. For round tables, measure the diameter, add twice the drop and 1" for the hems. For oval tables you will need to measure the diameter at the widest point as well as the narrowest width. When buying fabric, you will treat these diameters as if they were the lengths and widths of rectangular tables.

If the measurement for the narrow side is wider than the width of your fabric, which is generally 42" to 45", the tablecloth will need to be pieced. Since bulky seams can make your table surface uneven, it is preferable to avoid them or at least place them in the overhang, if possible. One possible solution is to buy extra-wide fabric, generally sold for quilt backing. Unfortunately, extra-wide fabric doesn't come in a very wide variety of colors. Another more expensive possibility is to buy a bed sheet and remake it into a tablecloth. If you decide to piece your tablecloth, plan on making two seams, one on either side, rather than one down the middle, and allow $5/8$" on each side for each seam.

Another thing to keep in mind while shopping for your fabric is the care of your finished cloth. A dining room tablecloth will need to be washable. Cotton blends are more resistant to stains than pure cotton. Print fabrics will hide minor stains better than solids. Accent tables that are in direct sunlight shouldn't be covered with pure cotton because it will fade.

ALERT!

Fabrics with obvious stripes or plaids are not recommended for round or oval tablecloths because any inaccuracies in cutting or hemming the curves will show up against the straight lines.

Piecing Larger Cloths

Believe it or not, two seams an equal distance from the opposite sides or ends of a table are going to be less intrusive than one down the center. Split the length of fabric you've bought for piecing and sew the two pieces on either side of the whole length. As with the curtains, cut away the selvage.

You can piece a tablecloth using a French seam as described in Chapter 5 for piecing curtains. Sew a narrow seam with the wrong sides together, turn, and sew with the right sides together. The drawback to this method is that it creates a fairly thick ridge of six layers of fabric with one layer on either side.

If the pieced seams are going to end up on the tabletop, an alternative is to sew the seam with right sides together the full depth of your allowance. Press the seams open, turn each raw edge under to the seam, and topstitch. This creates a wider ridge that is only three layers thick and less of a problem for tippy glasses.

Cutting an Oval Cloth

To avoid having corners of your tablecloth resting in your guests' laps, you will need to cut your tablecloth into an oval the exact shape of your table.

Piece the cloth if necessary. Place the cloth wrong side up on the table and center it exactly. Pay particular attention to where the piecing seams are in relation to the edge. Weight the tablecloth down around the edge of the table to keep it from shifting. Using chalk or other washable marker, outline the edge of the table.

Remove the cloth from the table and fold the cloth in half with right sides together. Use pins to be sure your marked outlines on the two layers are lining up exactly. Do this by running a pin in and out on the line then checking to see if the visible center portion of the pin is on the line on the bottom layer.

If you have sufficient space, you can lay your cloth out flat to measure from the marked table's edge to the cutting line. With slippery fabrics that will not stay accurately folded or heavy fabrics that will make cutting through four layers difficult, this is probably the best method.

Fold the cloth again, being sure this time that the marked diameter lines up on all four layers. Pin the layers together and lay it out flat. Mark the distance of the drop plus hem allowance from the first mark. Cut through all four layers along this second mark.

Cutting a Circle

A round tablecloth can be marked and cut the same way as an oval one. If you are making a cloth for a dining room table and planning on a drop of only a few inches, this is probably the easiest way to measure. However, if you are making a cloth for an accent table with a drop to the floor, it will be difficult to measure this distance from your chalked curve with any accuracy.

Begin instead by folding your square cloth in fourths, as you did for the oval. Match the pieced seams, if you have any. Calculate the radius (half the diameter) of your table plus one drop and hem allowance. Make a loop on one end of a length of string that measures a couple of inches more than your calculation. Be sure your string won't stretch. Tighten your loop around a pin and insert the pin close to the folded point that is the center of your tablecloth. Putting a small pad of paper or a sponge under the corner for the tip of the pin to penetrate will help keep the string and cloth anchored.

Using a measuring tape, trim the string so it equals the calculated radius of your tablecloth. Holding the string taut, use the end of the string to help you mark your cutting line. Cut through all four layers.

Stitching the Hems

Because the hems on tablecloths are so narrow, a straight machine stitch is normally used rather than a hemstitch. There are a few distinct differences between hemming tablecloths and hemming curtains.

Straight-Sided Hems

Square and rectangle tablecloths look easy to hem. You simply press the edges under and stitch. The corners, however, may cause you problems. Be sure you measure accurately when you fold up the hem allowance and that you don't allow the fabric to slide or stretch as you stitch. These are the two leading causes of extended, misshapen corners.

Mitering the corners will help even more. "Miter" is a carpenters' term referring to a joint made by cutting the edges of two pieces of wood at an angle and fitting them together to make a beveled or mitered joint. In sewing, it refers to edges of cloth that are joined together with a fold angling in from a corner (to resemble a mitered joint).

Easy Mitered Corners

On curtains, we expect to see the stitches of the side hems extending clear to the bottom of the curtain. It's part of the vertical lines that we associate with curtains. The bottom hem is usually wider than the sides anyway. On a tablecloth, we expect all the sides to be the same.

FIGURE 6-1

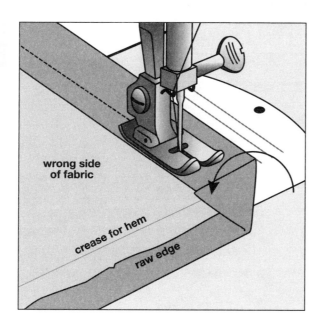

wrong side of fabric

crease for hem

raw edge

◀ **Easy mitered corner:** Fold under the corner as you hem.

The easiest way to miter a corner, and the most practical method with narrow hems, is to fold under one corner as shown in **FIGURE 6-1**. With the hems pressed under, pick any place on the middle of a side to begin stitching close to the folded edge. Stop stitching a couple of inches from the edge so the hem of the next side is not yet under the presser foot. Stop with the needle in the cloth.

Open out the hem allowance of the next side, but keep the side you were stitching folded to the edge. Fold the corner of the folded hem allowance over, lining up the outside edge with the fold line of the second side. Fold the hem allowance into place. Finish stitching the first side, and pivot with the needle in the fabric to begin stitching the next side.

If you are concerned that the folded corner may work loose, secure it with a couple of blind stitches.

Stitched Mitered Corners

Another method of mitering a corner is shown in **FIGURES 6-2** and **6-3**. This method is recommended for slightly deeper hems or bulkier fabrics because part of the fabric is trimmed away.

FIGURE 6-2

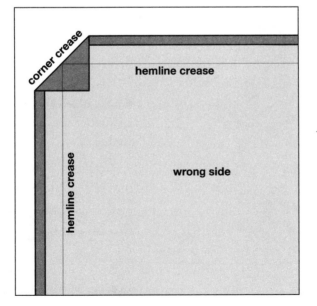

◀ Stitched mitered corner.

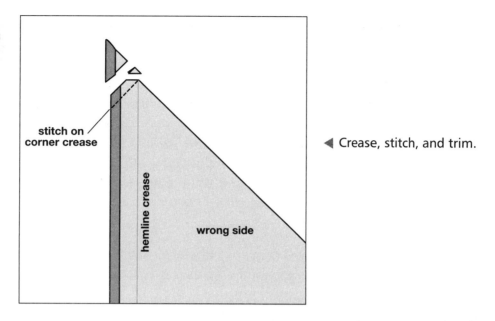

FIGURE 6-3

stitch on corner crease

hemline crease

wrong side

◀ Crease, stitch, and trim.

When you press your hems, press each corner under, matching the hemline creases as shown in **FIGURE 6-2**. Before you stitch the hem, fold the corner diagonally with right sides together, and stitch along the diagonal crease as shown **FIGURE 6-3**. Trim away the excess at the corner, and trim close to the stitching at the point. Press the seam open. A point presser comes in handy here. Without one it might be necessary to finger press the tiny seam allowance open and iron it from the right side when it is folded flat and ready to hem.

If you are accurate with your folding and stitching, the hem allowance should fit exactly. Stitch the hem all around, making square corners with your stitches.

Curved Hems

Stitching curved hems can be a bit of a challenge because they need to be eased into place like the flared hems mentioned in Chapter 4, only more so. The narrower the hem allowance, the easier this is going to be. That is why ½" is recommended for curved hems.

Press the edge of your tablecloth under ½". Open it out, and press the raw edge up to the crease. Stitch close to this outside fold using a long machine stitch. Pin the hem allowance in place with pins every 4 to 6". Ease the allowance to fit by pulling up threads to gather it. Stitch over the gathering stitches.

The smaller the tablecloth, the more gathering will be necessary. If, when you press your hem under the ½", you discover what seems like excessive puckering of the allowance, trim away ¼" of the allowance. Use lace binding to help ease the hem allowance into place. Stitch one edge of the lace close to the raw edge of the tablecloth, stretching it slightly as you go. Hemming by hand will give you the neatest hem, but you can stitch it by machine if you prefer.

FACT

Picnic tablecloths will blow out of place with the slightest breeze. Putting curtain weights in the hems is one solution. Turn the corners of square tablecloths under the table and pin or customize with buttons or snaps. Run a piece of elastic through the hem of a round tablecloth for an exact fit.

Binding Alternative

Narrow bias binding can be used to cover the raw edge of a tablecloth, eliminating the need for a hem. It can also lend an interesting accent to the tablecloth. However, loose-weave fabrics will fray and pull away from the binding and should be hemmed instead.

The fastest way to attach binding is to simply lap it over the edge of your cloth and stitch. You will notice that one side of your seam binding is deeper than the other. Put that side on the back and sew close to the edge of the shorter side of the binding with the front of your tablecloth facing you. Turn the ends of the binding under ¼" or so at the beginning and the end. Use a few blind stitches to stitch the two folded ends together where they meet.

The binding can pull away even on the tightest of weaves after repeated washing. To prevent this, instead of simply lapping the binding over the edge, open out the center fold of the binding and tuck the raw edge of your tablecloth under the edge fold on the deeper side of your binding. The right side of the tablecloth should be against the unfolded inside of the binding and the wrong side facing you, as shown in the top portion of **FIGURE 6-4**. Stitch along the edge fold of the binding.

FIGURE 6-4

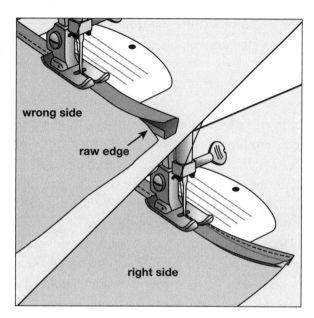

wrong side

raw edge

right side

◄ **Bias binding hem:** Secure the raw edge of the hem inside the binding.

Fold the binding along its center crease and press the edge of the tablecloth under along with it. Now, with the right side of the tablecloth facing you, stitch close to the edge of the binding.

Reversible Tablecloths

Another way to eliminate the need to hem a tablecloth is to make it reversible. To do this, you will need to cut two tablecloths the same size out of coordinating fabrics. Test your fabric choices before you buy them to check that when they are placed wrong sides together, neither fabric shows through the other.

Piece your tablecloths if needed and cut them to the proper shape. You will only need to allow ½" for the lower seam, which will replace the hem. Carefully arrange the two tablecloths together with the right sides together. Be sure the piecing seams match, if there are any, and that both layers are smooth.

Stitch around the tablecloth ½" from the edge, leaving 6" to 12" open for turning. The larger the tablecloth, the wider this gap should be. Backstitching at the beginning and the end of your stitches will keep them from pulling out with the stress of turning. If you are making a square or rectangular tablecloth, take a diagonal stitch or two across the corners to make the points sharper.

Grade the seam allowances by trimming one to half the depth of the other. Clip the corners and cut Vs close to the stitching along curves, including the allowance of the gap. If your fabric has a tendency to fray, stitch along the seam lines inside the gap before you clip. Turn the tablecloth right side out. Use the blunt end of a seam ripper or something similar to poke the corners out of the points. Don't use anything sharp like scissor points, or you might poke a hole in your fabric.

Press the tablecloth flat. Blind-stitch the gap closed as described in Chapter 4. Topstitching around the edge might keep the edges sharp. Topstitching is a row or sometimes two rows of straight stitches taken on the top of the fabric close to a finished edge. It is sometimes done with contrasting thread.

If you want to put a ruffle on a reversible tablecloth, be sure it is attractive from both the front and the back. Sew it to one circle, matching the raw edges with the bottom edge of the ruffle pointed toward the center. Sew the circles together, turn, press, and blind-stitch.

Decorating Ideas

The possibilities for decorating your tablecloth are limited only by your imagination and budget. Consider the use of the table as well as its appearance when you choose your fabrics.

Adding Trims

Decorative trims can be very effective and are easily added. Consider adding ruffles to the edge of a table. Refer to the section on ruffles in Chapter 5 and add them to your tablecloth in the same way. Fold the ends of the ruffle inside if it's double, or under if it isn't, and blind-stitch them together where they meet.

Lace or other ready-made trims placed in the overhang can add interest. Be sure to mark the distance from the edge so the trim is straight and even. Depending on the type of trim, corners can be overlapped or folded under. For heavier trim, sew it across two opposite sides of a rectangular table. Turn under the raw edges of the trim for the other two sides, and use them to cover the raw edges of the trim sewn to the first two sides. If you are adding lace that you want to see through, sew the lace as described here, then carefully cut the tablecloth fabric away from under it, leaving ½" of fabric along the stitches. Tuck the raw edges under to the stitching, and sew them down and to the lace.

ALERT!

It would be easy to accidentally cut your lace when you are trimming away the fabric. To prevent this, once you have started enough to have an opening, slip a piece of cardboard between the lace and the tablecloth fabric and move it ahead of your scissors.

For lightweight trims, begin in the center of one side by turning the raw edge of the trim under and stitching the lower edge along the markings for the trim. Just before you reach the corner, fold the trim to fit around the edge, adjusting the visible fold so it resembles the mitered corners described for the hems. Pin the upper edge of the trim in place at this fold and continue stitching, pivoting the needle when you turn the corner. Just before you reach the place where you started, turn the raw edge of your trim under so it bumps up against the folded edge. Stitch the upper edge of the trim. If the spliced edge or the corner folds look as if they might separate, secure them with a few blind stitches.

Trims added to the overhang of round or oval tablecloths will need to flex and be easily gathered. Avoid any that are stiff or heavy. Run a row of stitches along the top edge of the trim to help you ease it into place. On the tablecloth, mark the lower line for the trim with chalk. Sew the trim along this line with a straight stitch close to the edge. Ease the upper edge of the trim into place using the gathering stitches.

Coordinating Fabric for Trim

To add a stripe of coordinating fabric to a square or rectangular tablecloth, cut the tablecloth to the size inside or above the trim. Cut the coordinating fabric into the desired width, and sew strips to two sides of the tablecloth using French seams. Press the seam allowance in the direction of the trim and stitch it down. Repeat the process with the other two sides, again with strips of the main tablecloth fabric, and then hem the edges.

The same process doesn't work for round or oval tablecloths because of the difficulty of cutting curving fabric to fit exactly.

Double Cloths

Using two tablecloths can be very effective. This is generally done by covering a round accent table with a floor-length tablecloth and topping that with a short, square one. For a Victorian look, use a lace cloth for the top cloth. Two coordinating fabrics of equal weight might have a more country look, depending on the fabric. Don't dismiss it as a possibility for a small dining table.

Table Accessories

Since you are making your own tablecloths, it's an easy matter to make matching accessories for the table. Plan ahead, and buy your fabric all at once.

Napkins can be hemmed with a narrow version of the tablecloth hem. Consider making them out of linen or other soft fabric and trimming them with a strip of your tablecloth fabric. Simply turn the long edges of the strips under and sew them to the linen napkins before you hem them. Cloth liners for breadbaskets can be made the same way.

Place mats, centerpieces, and runners can be made like the reversible tablecloth or edged with seam binding. A piece of batting or heavy flannel between the layers will add some shaping.

Breadbasket cloths made by layering coordinating fabric are particularly effective because both sides show as the corners stick out of the basket. Consider using a basket lined with your two-sided cloth and filled with fruit for a centerpiece.

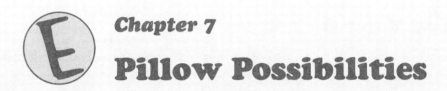

Chapter 7
Pillow Possibilities

Pillows can make a room look comfortable and inviting. They are an easy way to add color accents and, since they are small, they are an inexpensive way to introduce luxurious fabrics into a practical décor. You may, at first, think of square accent pillows, but they can be any size or shape that suits your tastes.

Learning the Basics

Pillows can be made from nearly any fabric. Consider what use the pillow will get when you are choosing between washable and nonwashable fabrics and stuffing. Allow extra seam allowance for fabrics that tend to fray.

Stuffing Material

For best results, use polyester pillow stuffing or ready-made forms. If you want to use a form, purchase it before you cut your pillow fabric, because they are available only in a limited number of sizes. Foam rubber can be cut to order if you can find it available. Cut it about 1" larger than your finished pillow's dimensions. You'll want the edges and corners to compress, or your pillow will have a boxy look with empty seams.

Other possibilities for stuffing include shredded foam rubber, which will look fine for decorative pillows but will be uncomfortably lumpy for a pillow for sleeping or sitting on. You can get fair results by recycling women's hose. Be sure to cut away all elastic and seams, including reinforced toes. Stuff the pillow tightly so the individual hose don't separate into lumps.

Cut and Stitch

When your pillow is stuffed, it is going to appear smaller than the seam-to-seam measurements. For a pillow to look 12" square, you will need to cut your fabric about 16" by 16", allowing for ½" seams and about 3" total for thickness. Cut your pillow on the grain of your fabric to assure that it will keep its shape.

If you've chosen a stretchy fabric or one with a very loose weave, or if you need to cut your fabric off-grain in order to get the desired effect, make a casing or lining out of muslin or other firm fabric that won't show through your pillow fabric. Make the casing the same size as your pillow, stuff it, and use it to stuff your pillow once it is together, or use the fabric as lining, stitch the muslin pieces to the back of your pillow fabric pieces, then treat them as one fabric.

The back of your pillow can be identical to the front, or it can coordinate. If your front is odd-shaped, pin it to the back fabric—right sides together—and trim the back to fit after they are sewn together.

Stitch ½" from the cut edge all around, leaving a gap of a few inches similar to the gap left in the reversible tablecloth described in Chapter 6. If possible, leave your gap in a straight line for easier blind stitching. If you've chosen foam rubber or a pillow form, leave nearly all of one side unstitched to make it easier to insert the stuffing.

Remember to take a stitch or two across the corners to make sharper points as described in the section on valances in Chapter 5. Clip the curves and corners. Ironing one seam allowance toward the pillow can sometimes make it easier to get the seam to open out when it's turned.

Turn and Stuff

Turn your pillow right side out through the gap. Poke out the corners with something blunt and press. Be as accurate as possible when pressing the seam allowance under at the gap so it won't look different from the rest of the pillow edge.

If you want to have a tiny lip around your pillow, a sort of mock piping, topstitch ¼" from the edge after you've turned your pillow all the way around except at the gap. Topstitching is stitching done on the outside that is expected to show. Finish the topstitching after you've stuffed the pillow.

Stuff your pillow thoroughly. If you are using bagged stuffing, a wooden spoon can be helpful to get the corners and the rest well packed. Don't skimp on the stuffing. It will compress a little with use, and you don't want your pillows getting that floppy, sunken look.

Blind Stitch

Pin the gap closed, and use the blind stitch to close it. (The blind stitch is described in Chapter 4.) This is done the same way as shown in **FIGURE 4-2**, except you are holding your two pieces together instead of having them flat like the opened seam in the illustration. The main thing to remember is to do all your movement across the gap under the fold so you enter the stitching line of one fabric straight across from where you left the other.

Even if you are going to topstitch your pillow, blind-stitch it closed first. The two folds will separate and look different from the rest of the edge if you rely on the topstitching alone to close the gap.

Adding Ruffles and Piping

Ruffles or piping can dress up a pillow and are easy to include before you sew your pillow front and back together. Visit the trim section of your fabric store to see what's available, but remember that you can make your own if you can't find just what you want.

Ruffle Review

If you want to make your own ruffle, refer to the ruffle section in Chapter 5. The doubled-over ruffle is recommended for pillows. When you are putting ruffles on a pillow, you want your ruffle to go all the way around without a break. To accomplish this, sew the ends of your ruffle strip together as you would if you were piecing it, creating a hoop. Press the seams open, and fold it in half the long way.

Stitch one row of gathering stitches ½" from the raw edge. Divide the ruffle at even intervals by folding and marking with pins. Make the same number of divisions around the pillow top.

Pin the ruffle to the right side of the pillow top, lining up the raw edges. Provide extra fullness to the corners. Avoid putting any piecing seams at the corners, if possible. They won't gather well, and you need tighter gathers in the corners. Also, seams will be more likely to show at the corners.

Pull the gathering threads to make the ruffle fit between the pins and stitch around the pillow on top of the gathering stitches. Sew the back to the front and stuff as usual.

To make a double ruffle, sew flat lace to the ruffle strip before you sew the ends together. Look for unruffled edging that is slightly narrower than your ruffle. If you can't find what you want that hasn't already been gathered, you can trim off the ruffled edge or take out the stitches and iron the edging flat. Gather the two ruffles together onto the pillow top.

Piping

Piping is a fabric-covered cord that can be used to add a dressy, finished look to seams. It is often added to pillow tops instead of ruffles and helps to define the edges.

Piping is available ready-made in a few colors and sizes. You can expand your choices by making your own, either with bias binding tape or by cutting your own bias strips. You will need cording a couple of inches longer than the circumference of your pillow. Cording is available in several thicknesses. Consider the size and style of your pillow when choosing your cording.

To cut bias strips, fold a selvage edge up to a trimmed on-grain edge of your fabric. The diagonal fold will be on the bias. Cut along this fold line and cut your strips from either side of this cut. A measurement of 1½" will probably be wide enough for these strips. Make them wider if you've chosen one of the heavier cords.

The ends of your strips will be on grain, but they will be diagonal to the strips. To piece your strips, line up two of these ends, right sides together, forming a right angle between the two strips. The edges of each strip should meet ¼" below the ends rather than at the actual corners. The reason for this is to keep the strips in line at the seam edges. You could trim the edge perpendicular to the strip and sew the seams, but you would be stitching on the bias, which will make both pieces stretch. Also, you would have the entire bulk of the seam concentrated at one place instead of spread out over a few inches of the piping. Sew the strips together with a ¼" seam. Press the piecing seams open.

If you are using bias tape, open it out and press it. Fold your bias strip over your cording. Using a zipper foot, sew the binding as close to the cord as possible.

Piping is sewn to the pillow top much the same as a ruffle. Gather a little extra at the corners if possible. Overlap the ends of the piping and curve them off the fabric as shown in **FIGURE 7-1**.

FIGURE 7-1

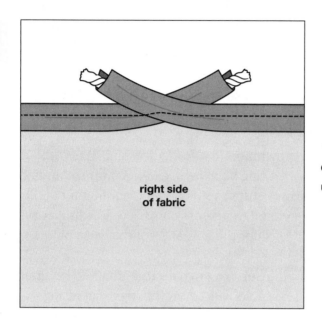

right side
of fabric

◀ **Piping ends:** Overlap the ends so the piping appears unbroken.

Making an Appliqué Top

You can make a simple appliqué pillow top using a method called chintz appliqué. This involves cutting a single motif out of a print fabric and sewing it onto a coordinating fabric. This is especially effective when you are decorating with several fabrics including a print.

Cut one motif out of your print fabric, leaving a ¼" border around it. Pin the motif in the center of a pillow top cut from a coordinating fabric. You can measure in from the sides to be sure your appliqué is centered, but if the pillow has an irregular shape, the focal point may not be the physical center. Looking centered may be a better gauge than the measured center. Using thread that matches the pillow top, zigzag slowly all around the shape, turning the fabric as you go. If you need to stop stitching to turn the fabric for a tight curve, stop with the needle to the outside of the curve. Overlapped stitches will show up less than gaps will.

FACT

In the early 1700s, the English textile industry influenced the British Parliament to ban the importation of cotton fabric from India. This made popular print fabrics called chintz or Persian prints very expensive. Rather than give them up entirely, women bought a yard of the fabric, cut out the motifs and appliquéd them on less expensive fabrics. The technique was called Persian embroidery or chintz appliqué.

Making a Handkerchief Top

A pillow with a bit of a Victorian look can be made from four identical embroidered handkerchiefs. You will need a square of fabric for the pillow back and a top square of that same size that will show as a border around the handkerchiefs. Two rounds of ruffled lace are optional.

Planning Your Pillow

Your pillow can be any size you want. The amount of the top that is covered by the handkerchiefs will depend on the size of the embroidered design on them. Fold the hankies into squares that are a little larger than the embroidery, and place them together in a square with the embroidery at the outside corners. Move them together or farther apart until you like the effect. Determine the size you'll want each hankie to be, adding seam allowances.

If the edges of the hankies are shaped, making it difficult to use as seam allowances, or if the embroidery is too close to the edges to allow for seams, consider putting the embroidery toward the center instead of the outside corners. The curved edges of the hankies will expose some of the border fabric between them at the center.

You will need the hankies to be connected before they are sewn on the border fabric so you can turn the edges under as one piece or ring the hankies with ruffle. To do this, sew two of the hankies next to each other to a piece of waste fabric from the hankies. Stitch close to the finished edging, but stop before the edgings curve away from each other. Trim the waste fabric so it doesn't show. Repeat with each joint.

FIGURE 7-2

◀ **Handkerchief pillow:** Use embroidered hankies for a Victorian look.

Sewing Your Pillow

Once the four embroidered corners are sewn into a square, either with seams or by stitching them to backing pieces, you can ring this center square with lace or ruffle if you want.

Next, press the seam allowance under. If you have added a ruffle, this will be easy to do. Pull the ruffle out into place and the seam will turn under.

Center your hankie square on the top square. Topstitch close to the outside of the hankie square and along the edges of each hankie if they were not seamed. Add another round of lace to the outside edge, and finish the pillow as usual.

Quilting and Other Options

If you seamed your four hankies together, you can put quilt batting between your hankies and a backing piece before you add the first round of ruffle. Pin the layers together, and topstitch in the ditch. This means you machine-stitch right on the seam. It will give a little more dimension to the hankies. Rows of stitching ¼" on both sides of these seams will dress it up even more. A walking foot is recommended to keep the layers from shifting and giving your pillow top a twisted look.

Stitch around the outside edge, and trim the batting away before you add the round of ruffle or turn the edge. Eyelet beading, which is flat eyelet lace with slots for threading ribbons through, can be sewn along the seam allowances in place of the quilting.

You may also want to use satin ribbons. These can be tied into bows leaving long tails and stitched to the corners of your finished pillow. Try cutting four ribbons about 15" long. Put them together and, treating them as one ribbon, tie them into a bow. Separate the loops and sew the bow to the center of your pillow. You might want to treat the ends with a fray retardant.

Making a Quilt-Block Top

Pillow tops made using the old quilt designs give a room a homey, country look. Quilting is becoming quite popular now and patterns are readily available. The Lemon Star, shown in **FIGURE 7-3**, is the basis for many star and lily patterns.

Making the Pattern

Begin on paper with a circle with a diameter half the length of your desired pillow top. If you don't have a protractor, use a plate or anything else that will let you make a perfect circle. Cut out your circle, and divide it into eighths by carefully folding and creasing it. Cut out two of these wedges.

Glue one wedge to a piece of cardboard, then glue the second to the first, matching the points on the circle, so one rounded edge will cover the other, forming a diamond shape. Accuracy is important or your eight diamonds won't fit together.

Add ¼" around your diamond for seams. An acrylic ruler makes this job much simpler. Cut out your template.

FIGURE 7-3

◀ **Lemon Star:** Give yourself a taste of quilt piecing with this pillow top.

QUESTION?

Why is the pattern called a Lemon Star?
The name comes from a mispronunciation of the LeMoyne Star, a pattern named after the LeMoyne brothers, early settlers and governors of France's Louisiana Territory.

Cutting the Pieces

You will need the following materials for your Lemon Star pillow:

Four diamond pieces, each of two contrasting colors
A third fabric for the background
Fabric for the back of the pillow
A piece of batting the size of your pillow
Fabric scrap the size of your pillow to use as quilt backing
Piping or ruffles (optional)

To cut your star pieces, place your template on the wrong side of your fabric and mark around it with a hard lead pencil or fabric marker. Cut out your pieces.

You will discover that the angle between the points of your star will be ninety degrees. To fill in the background around your star, you will need four squares for the corners and four right triangles. The easiest way to make these is to measure a side of your diamond to cut the corner squares. Add about 1" to that, and cut two larger squares. Split these squares in half on the diagonal. They may be a little large, but you can trim them down later.

Never mark your cloth with ink, even within a seam allowance. There is too much of a chance that it will dissolve enough to spread and cause a stain. If you do use ink to mark a cutting line, be sure to trim it all away.

Piecing Your Pillow Top

Mark a dot on all four corners of your diamonds where the ¼" seam allowances cross. Mark a similar dot on one corner of the squares and the right-angle corner of the triangles. These points are the places where you will begin and end your stitching.

With right sides together, pair up one diamond of each color. Use pins to match the corner dots. Stitch from one side corner dot to the dot at the point, backstitching at each end to reinforce your stitching. Continue in this manner all around your star. Match the corner dot of one square piece with the side dot on one star point. With the star on top, stitch from the side dot to the dot at the point. Repeat this process with the adjoining point and with the squares and triangles around the star.

Press the seam allowances. The easiest way to do this is to press all the seams in a counterclockwise direction. Trim the outside edges of your pillow top to ¼" beyond the star points.

Quilting the Top

Since this is a traditional quilt block, it is appropriate to quilt it. Layer it with batting and a backing and top-stitch as described for the handkerchief pillow. Stitch in the ditch and/or ¼" inside each diamond and ¼" outside the points. Add piping or ruffle if you want, and complete as usual.

Making a Woven-Ribbon Top

A pillow top made by weaving ribbons together makes an interesting accent pillow. Make it from ribbon scraps, or choose identical satin ribbon in different widths for a more elegant pillow.

To make a small pillow that will appear to be about 10" square when it is stuffed, you will need the following materials:

13" by 13" piece of fabric for the back
13" by 13" piece of fusible interfacing
Pillow stuffing
4½' of ruffle, if desired
13" lengths of ribbon

The number of lengths of ribbon you will need will depend on the width of the ribbons. You would need approximately 10 yards of 1" ribbon.

Cut your interfacing and determine the horizontal and vertical center. You can do this by folding and finger pressing a crease along the center lines. Place the interfacing, fusible side up, on a padded surface such as an ironing board or folded blanket.

Begin at the vertical center with one length of ribbon. Pin the ends in place. If you are using satin ribbons, be sure to keep the pins within the seam allowances, or the hole might show later. Pin a ribbon across the horizontal center. Add two more ribbons, one on either side of the vertical ribbon. These will go over the horizontal center ribbon.

Add more ribbons as shown in **FIGURE 7-4**, weaving them in with the ribbons that are already in place. You can thread the new ribbons over and under, or remove the pins on alternate ribbons and fold them out of the way. Continue weaving until the interfacing is covered. Make any necessary adjustments to ensure that the ribbons are lying flat.

FIGURE 7-4

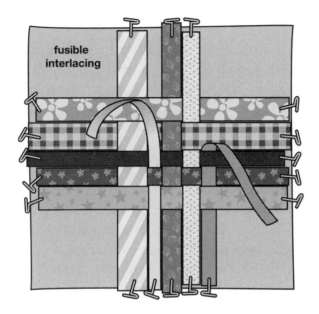

fusible
interlacing

◀ **Weaving ribbons:**
Add your ribbons from
the center outward.

Press the ribbons to fuse them with the interfacing. If you are using satin ribbons, a pressing cloth would be a good idea. Stitch around the outside edge of your pillow top to be sure that the ends of your ribbons stay in place. Complete your pillow as usual.

FACT

You can tuft your pillows by sewing shank buttons to each side—use a long needle and extra strong thread such as carpet thread. Leaving a tail of thread when you start, run the thread through the pillow, through the shank of one button, through the pillow again, and through the other button shank two or three times, then tie the threads securely.

Making Chair Cushions

Solid wood chairs may be charming, but they aren't always comfortable. To make your table one that family and guests want to linger at, add cushions to the chairs. These can match your curtains or tablecloths, or each one can pick up a different color in the room.

Figuring Yardage

Begin by measuring your chair seat at the widest and deepest points. These dimensions, plus 1" for seam allowances, multiplied by two for top and bottom, and multiplied by the number of chairs, will help you determine your yardage.

Suppose your chair seat is 18" wide and 16" deep. You'll only be able to get two seat pieces out of one width of fabric, or enough for one chair. Take 17" (depth plus 1) times the number of chairs, divided by 36" for the number of yards of fabric you'll need.

If you don't mind piecing the bottom side of about half of your cushions, you can save on fabric. Take twice the number of chairs divided by 2½ to get the number of 17" lengths you'll need.

You will also need enough foam rubber to cut one 19" by 17" square or an equivalent amount of fleece. If you are having difficulty finding either of these, you could use three or four layers of heavy flannel.

Making a Pattern and Cutting Your Pieces

To make your cushions fit perfectly onto your chairs, place brown wrapping paper or some other large piece of paper on the seat and mark the outline of the chair. Fold the outline in half and correct it so the sides are the same. Add ½" all around for seam allowances. When your cushion is stuffed, it'll be just smaller than the seat—the right fraction to look great.

If the chair seat extends behind the backrest post, make your pattern so it fits in front of the post only, or cut out the back corners to accommodate the posts. Otherwise your cushion will extend over the front of your chair, making it look like it doesn't fit. Worse, the front edge will wear out quickly.

Cut out two of your pattern for each seat. If you are piecing the bottoms, fold your pattern in half and add ½" to make a pattern for the bottoms. Stitch the halves together, and press the seam allowance open.

If you are adding ruffle or piping, do it next.

Ties and Stuffing

Use scraps of fabric to cut 2" by 16" strips for ties. You will need two per chair. Fold the strips lengthwise, right sides together, stitch, and turn. These will be too narrow to try to iron the seam along one side as described for the curtain ruffle in Chapter 5. Press the seam along one edge instead. Zigzag-stitch across the ends.

Put your pattern on the chair once again and mark on it the location of the backrest posts. With your pattern on your seat top, use a pin to mark these positions.

Fold the ties in half and pin the folded end within the seam allowance of the top. With the ends of the ties pointed toward the center of the seat cushion, stitch the ties in place along the seam line.

If you are using fleece or flannel for stuffing, stitch the layers to the wrong side of your cushion bottom at ¾". Trim the stuffing close to the stitching. This will mean that your stuffing will be stitched to your cushion cover so it won't bunch, yet it will not be part of the seam allowance when the top and bottom (and ruffle if you're adding one) are stitched together.

If you are using foam rubber, use your pattern again to cut it in the shape of your chair seat.

Finishing

Put the bottom piece on the top piece, right sides together. Stitch around the seat, encasing the ties and any edgings inside. If you are using foam rubber for stuffing, leave nearly all of the back open. Turn right side out, and press. Smash the sides of the foam rubber in, and insert it through the gap in your cushion cover. Blind-stitch the gap closed. (E)

Chapter 8

More Stuffed Fun

All stuffed crafts are made essentially the same way that pillows are. Odd shapes can create a few problems, but they can be overcome with a few tips and some practice. Soon you'll be able to create your own stuffed toys and decorations, limited only by your imagination.

Fashioning a Fabric Wreath

Wreaths make fun decorations all year, not just at Christmas time. Choose spring green or autumn colors. Decorate with flowers or lightweight objects that symbolize a particular holiday or season in place of, or in combination with, ribbons and bows.

You will need to cut your wreath fabric into two equal circles. An 8" radius is a good size. To mark the circle, you may want to use the string and folded cloth method described in Chapter 6 in the round tablecloth section. Cut a circle with a 1½" radius out of the center of both circles.

Add any piping or ruffle you want for the outside of the wreath. Keep any ruffle narrow so it doesn't overshadow the wreath. Also, because of the curve of the circle, a wide ruffle would have to be gathered very tightly to still be ruffled at the outside edge. For this pattern, do not overlap the ends of your trim. Fold ruffle ends up as you sew them on the circle, leaving a ½" gap. Taper piping off the seam line into the allowance when they are about ½" apart.

Put the right sides of your two circles together and stitch narrow seams around the outside edge and around the inner circle.

FACT

You can appliqué your last name or a business name on your wreath front before you sew the circles together and hang it on your front door. Or you might consider some other friendly word or phrase, like "Welcome" or "Peace," instead.

Clipping and Turning

Clip the curve on the center circle with straight clips, and cut Vs in the outside curve. To turn, cut your wreath through both layers from the center of the gap left by the trim straight through to the center hole. Turn the broken circle, and press the seams open.

Put the cut ends of the front fabric of your wreath right sides together and stitch a ¼" seam, adjusting the wreath as you sew in order to cross both edge seams. Press this seam to one side, pressing the still open allowance of the back in the same way.

Stuff your wreath through this cut in the back. Blind-stitch the cut closed. Sew a small loop on the back to hang your wreath from a hook.

FIGURE 8-1

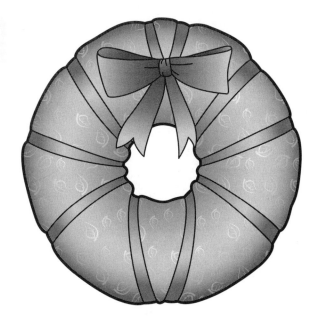

◀ **Fabric wreath:** Decorate your wreath for any holiday season.

Decorating Ideas

You can add a large bow to your wreath, placing it to cover the seam. Consider turning your wreath so the seam is to the side for an asymmetrical look. You can wrap your wreath in narrow ribbons, either one long ribbon that wraps around and around the wreath or ten or twelve short ribbons that tie around the wreath at regular intervals with knots in the back or small bows in the front. You can sew on or use a hot glue gun to attach silk or straw flowers, plastic decorations such as hearts or clovers, or felt shapes like black cats and orange pumpkins.

Consider a bouquet of six or so silk flowers tied together with narrow ribbons with long trailing tails. Curve the bouquet around one lower side and stitch it in place. A white satin wreath with white ribbons would make a lovely wedding shower decoration, especially if the guests tucked money under the ribbons.

To make a heart-shaped pillow, exaggerate the curves at the top, compared to the point at the bottom. More of the width will be lost to stuffed depth there than at the point.

Making Gingerbread Dolls

Gingerbread dolls make fun toppers to Christmas gifts or autumn decorations. Make your own pattern by folding a paper in half and cutting out one side of the shape like a paper doll. Make the head a bit larger than it looks like it should be. More of the stuffing here will compress than the arms, legs, and body will. Trace around your paper doll on another piece of paper and add ¼" seam allowance.

Cut out two pieces from this pattern. Sew white rickrack across the wrists and ankles of the front piece to represent frosting.

Sewing Button Faces

White buttons will show up better on dark fabric, but little black buttons might look more like the traditional cookie's raisins. Try several different ones out, and move them around to decide on their placement. Remember, the head is going to be smaller once the seams are sewn and the head is stuffed.

Because of the choking danger that buttons pose, buttons on dolls—even on those that are intended for decorations and not for toys—must be sewn on very securely. Your doll could end up in a little child's hands sometime in the future. Don't count on your stitches being enough to keep the buttons safely in place. The fabric itself could tear away with the button. Reinforce the button with twill tape or seam binding.

To do this, cut a piece of whichever tape you have available just a little longer than the distance between the eyes. Baste this tape to the wrong side of the gingerbread doll's face along the line where the eyes will be. If you are adding buttons for a nose or mouth, sew a piece of tape there as well. Sew the buttons in place through the fabric and the tape. Remove the basting stitches.

Learning Embroidery Alternatives

If your doll is for a child under three, abandon the buttons entirely. Draw circles for eyes and a curved smile on your doll's face, and embroider the face on instead. The three most basic stitches are all you'll need.

Outline Stitch

Often called the stem stitch, the outline stitch will be useful to give your doll a smile. Since the back of your doll's face will always be hidden inside your doll, you can begin with a knot. Refer to **FIGURE 8-2**, and follow these steps:

FIGURE 8-2

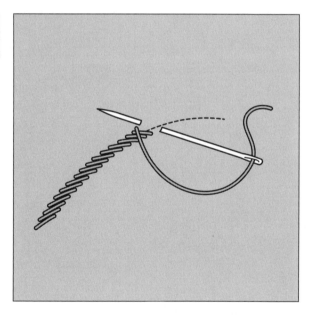

◀ Outline (or stem) stitch.

1. Bring the thread through to the front at one end of the marked smile.
2. Insert the tip of your needle just below the line about ¼" away from your beginning point.
3. Bring the needle back out halfway between the beginning point and the entrance point of the needle.
4. Keeping the loop free of tangles, pull the needle and thread through.
5. Repeat steps 2 through 4, making sure the needle always exits on the same side of the line and of the loop.

At the end of the marked line, push the needle through to the back and take three tiny stitches on top of one another on the row of stitches where they won't show. This will secure the end of the thread. For most embroidery, you would weave your end among the stitches on the back, but this might not hold once your doll's in a child's hands. Cut the thread off, and your doll has a smile.

Though it's more expensive, you can use fabric paints and inks to decorate your dolls. Some will not show up well on dark fabrics, but many will. Experiment with different types that you find in crafts stores.

Satin Stitches

Satin stitches are used to fill in small areas with color. If it's done right, the stitch gives the area a smooth satiny finish. Refer to **FIGURE 8-3**, and follow these steps to fill in the eyes of your doll:

FIGURE 8-3

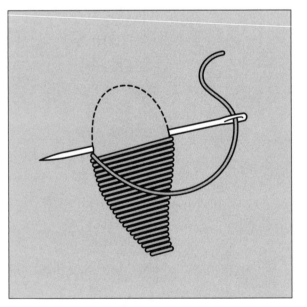

◀ Satin stitch.

1. Anchoring your thread with a knot, bring the thread through to the front along the bottom of the marked shape, just to the left of the center.
2. Insert the tip of the needle at a corresponding point to the right of the bottom center.
3. Bring the point of the needle out a thread or so above the beginning point.
4. Repeat steps 2 and 3, keeping your stitches close together but not overlapping.
5. Secure the thread on the back where the stitches will be hidden by the satin stitch.

If you want, you can use the satin stitch to make a nose. An alternative, however, would be the smaller French knot.

French Knot

The French knot takes a little practice. You might want to try it out a couple of times on a scrap. Refer to **FIGURE 8-4** and follow these steps:

FIGURE 8-4

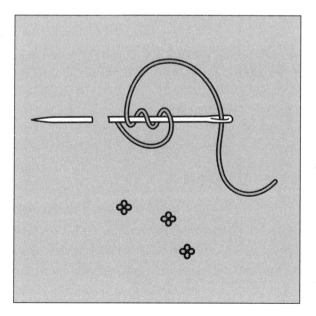

◄ French knot.

1. Bring the thread through to the front at the point you want the French knot.
2. Wrap the thread that is between the cloth and the needle around the needle three times.
3. Insert the tip of the needle into the cloth right at the beginning point.
4. Gently take up the slack in the thread so the loops are close to the cloth and fairly snug around the needle.
5. Pull the needle and thread through to the back and out again at the mark for your next knot (if you are doing several).
6. Secure the end of your thread by tying it in a knot or taking the overlapping stitches if you can hide them.

If your knot followed your needle through the cloth, your loops weren't pulled tightly enough around the needle. If the whole knot popped through, they were pulled too tight. Try again. It just takes practice.

You might want to use French knots in the center of the satin-stitched eyes as pupils or maybe accent them with two French knots to make them look more like buttons.

FACT

You can make small, decorated pillows and stuff them with potpourri and hang them in your closets. Consider making tiny pillows the size and shape of strawberries. Decorate them with black French knots and stuff them with potpourri. Add leaves that you cut from felt.

Finishing the Gingerbread Doll

If you want to include a loop at the top for hanging your gingerbread doll, cut the loop and sew it to the seam allowance at the top of the doll front. Put the decorated front piece and the back piece together, right sides facing, and stitch around the outside edge. If you need to raise the presser foot and pivot the cloth, be sure to stop stitching with the needle in the cloth so your stitches will be even. Leave one straight side unstitched. Clip the curves. Turn, press, stuff, and blind-stitch the gap closed.

Making a Jingle Kitty

A quick gift for a baby that combines pillow making and embroidery skills is a stuffed kitten face with a bell inside. You will need scraps of flannel or other soft cloth, pillow stuffing, embroidery floss, and one small jingle bell.

Cut two circles about 6" in diameter. From the leftover scraps, cut four ear shapes about 1½" high. Remember to add seam allowances. Sew the ears together in pairs, right sides together, leaving the bottom end open. Clip, turn, and press the ears, and set them aside.

Sew the bell to the center of the *wrong* side of the front piece. This will put the bell inside where there is no chance of it being chewed off. Cover the stitches left from this with a satin-stitched triangle for a nose. Add satin-stitched eyes and an outline-stitched mouth. Add whiskers using a single strand of yarn and the outline stitch.

Make a small pleat in the raw edge of the ears to give them some shape and sew them along the seam allowance of the front, with right sides together.

Position the back piece over the front and sew them together, leaving a small gap along the top of the head. Turn and stuff as usual.

It's easier to do the embroidery stitches before the pieces are all put together because you have access to the back of the fabric. However, until the toy or craft is stuffed, occasionally it's difficult to tell where the embroidery ought to be. If you are unsure where to position a face or other decoration, add it last. Bury your knot in the back by going in between stitches in the nearest seam.

Trying a Turtle Shape

If you want a bit more challenging pillow/toy, try making one with a turtle shape. It uses the same pillow-making skills you've already learned, plus a little imagination.

FIGURE 8-5

◀ Create a turtle pillow and test your new skills.

Making the Pieces

Begin by cutting out three circles the size you want for the turtle's shell. These will be the top, the backing for the quilted top, and the bottom of the pillow.

Design a leg pattern that is appropriate for the size of your shell. Something with a bend, a little like a sock, will be more authentic than straight pieces. See **FIGURE 8-5** for one example. Cut four pairs of these pieces, keeping the need for right and left, bottom and top in mind. Design a head pattern that tapers in at the neck, and cut two of these.

Pair the legs up and stitch around them, leaving the end next to the body open. Clip, turn, press, and stuff. Sew the open end closed at the seam line. Do the same with the head, but don't stitch it closed yet. Set it aside.

Mark a turtle-shell pattern on the top piece. Layer it on top of the batting and backing, right sides to the outside. Sew the layers together near the edge and machine quilt along the marked lines. Use contrasting thread so it shows up.

Putting Them Together

With your shell piece right side up, try out several positions for the head and the legs. Mark the head position with pins that extend beyond the raw edge, allowing a little extra space. Flip the legs over onto the top and pin them down, lining up the stitching lines of the legs and the shell. Sew the legs in place.

Cover the shell with the bottom piece, right sides together, and stitch around the circle, leaving the area open that you marked for the head. Clip the edges, turn, press, and stuff.

Position the neck of the head piece through the hole, and blind-stitch the shell and bottom piece to it. This gives you an opportunity to tip the head slightly upward. Embroider on some eyes, and he's done.

Stitching Block and Box Shapes

Three dimensional shapes like blocks or soft boxes are made, in part, the same way. Only instead of cutting a top and bottom and relying on the stuffing to provide the height, there are side pieces to sew as well. Begin with the basic cube and make toddler blocks.

Toddler Blocks

Cut six squares of whatever size you want for your blocks plus ½". These can be made from fabric scraps or can be appliquéd with numbers and letters if you want. Begin by sewing the side pieces to the bottom piece. Start and stop your stitches ¼" from the edge, similar to the way you stitched the Lemon Star in Chapter 7. This will make it much easier to do the stitching on the adjacent sides. Sew the top piece to the outside edge of one of the side pieces the same way.

Fold the bottom piece so you can line up two of the side pieces, right sides together, and stitch between them. Repeat with each pair of sides. Do the same thing with the top. It can be a bit tricky to adjust the block to let you get to the seams but don't worry about how much you scrunch the fabric; simply keep everything but what you are sewing out from under the needle.

Leave one edge open to turn and stuff. A cube of foam rubber will make the blocks more square than stuffing, but stuffing will make it easier for a child to hold. Finish by blind-stitching the open edge.

FACT

You can buy fake fur and make your own fuzzy dice. Cut circles in felt and hot glue them to the sides to represent the dots on dice. Felt will fade faster than the fur, so bright dice with white dots will look nice longer than pale dice with black dots.

Soft-Sided Box

A box doesn't need to be made in a perfect cube. The bottom and top can be rectangular and the sides only an inch high, as long as the sides fit the bottom and the top. The box is begun essentially the same as the block until you have the four sides stitched to the bottom. Next, stitch the back side of the lid to the top of the back piece. Press the seams open.

Make a button loop out of ribbon a couple of inches long. Sew this to the seam allowance at the center front of the lid piece. The length of the ribbon will determine where your button is eventually placed on the front piece.

Cut a piece of fabric for the inside lining that matches the shape of your box pieces as they are now. This should be a sort of cross shape. Cut a piece of batting the same size. Layer them as follows: batting on the bottom, lining piece next with the right side up, box pieces with the wrong side up. Sew around the outside edges, leaving the edge of the front piece, or top of the cross, open. When you stitch with batting it is usually between two layers of fabric. When it is on the outside, it's better to stitch with it on the bottom as the presser foot tends to catch it if it's on top.

Trim the batting close to the stitching and clip the corners. Turn so the batting is to the inside and press the edges. Top stitch in the ditch along all the seams. Blind-stitch the top edge closed and hand-stitch the sides together. Add a shank button to the front piece.

Batting isn't going to hold up more than a couple of inches, so keep the sides of your boxes shallow. You can insert cardboard between the layers instead of batting but if it gets bent, there's no straightening it back out.

Different Shaped Boxes

Suppose you want to make a box that is round or oval or even heart shaped. Instead of cutting separate sides, cut one long piece to fit all the way around the box. Remember to fit this side piece to the seam line rather than to the outside edge of your box bottom and top.

Cut four pieces of your box shape, two for the bottom and two for the lid, and two pieces of quilt batting the same size. Begin by layering the bottom with pieces in this order: box bottom with the right side down, batting and lining with the right side up. Stitch them together with a ¼" seam all the way around. Trim the batting close to the stitching. Set it aside.

Put whatever ruffle or trim you want on your outside lid piece. Layer it and the lining as follows: batting, lining with the right side up and decorated lid top with the right side down. Stitch, clip, turn and blind stitch the opening closed. You can add quilting stitches if you want, then set the lid aside.

You will need two side strips and a batting piece the same size. Layer them with the batting on the bottom, the outside piece with the right side up and the lining piece with the right side down. Stitch along one side of the strip. Trim the batting in the seam allowance and press the seam open. Sew the batting to the outside piece along the other seam allowance, trim the batting and press the seam allowance under. Run a line of stitches along the seam allowance of the lining piece as well. Fold the piece the long way and sew the ends together, leaving the side and lining still opened out. Press this seam and trim away the batting in the seam allowance.

Clip the lining edge at close intervals along the seam allowance. Pin this edge to the bottom piece. Stitch along the seam allowance. Clip Vs in outward curves and straight cuts in inward curves of the bottom piece.

Fold the seam allowance from the box bottom up, and fold the outside strip with the batting over the lining. Blind-stitch all around the box bottom.

Connect the lid to the box with a short ribbon, hand-stitched to the inside of the box and the underside of the lid.

Making a Child's Ball

A child's stuffed ball illustrates how easily different shapes can be made using basically the same techniques. Copy the pattern shown in **FIGURE 8-6**, enlarge or reduce it as you choose, and cut twelve pieces from scraps.

FIGURE 8-6

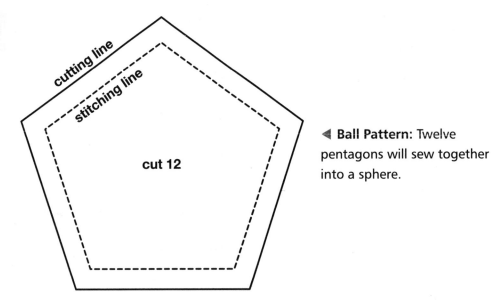

cutting line

stitching line

cut 12

◀ **Ball Pattern:** Twelve pentagons will sew together into a sphere.

Because of the difficulty of manipulating your pieces under the needle of your sewing machine, the last steps of construction will have to be done by hand. In light of this, you may want to do all the piecing by hand. If so, begin by pressing the seam allowance under on all the pieces. Blind-stitch six pieces together, five pentagons around a center one. Do the same with the other six pieces. Blind-stitch the sides as shown in **FIGURE 8-7**.

FIGURE 8-7

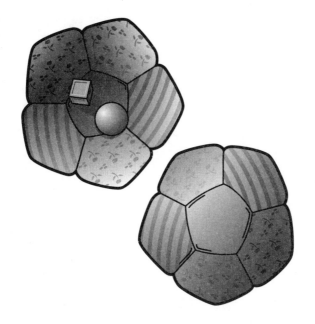

◀ **Forming "bowls":**
Sew pieces together in
two groups of six.

Fit the two "bowls" together to make a ball and blind-stitch across
nine of the ten short sides. Stuff the ball and stitch the last side closed.

If you want to try to machine-stitch the ball, do not press the edges
under. Stitch the pieces together the same as you did the block, forming
the two "bowls." Next, press the seam allowances under, and stitch the
two halves together by hand. Ⓔ

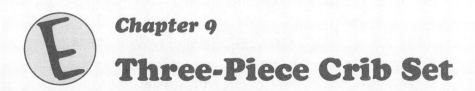

Chapter 9

Three-Piece Crib Set

Nobody's more fun to sew for than baby. A crib set consisting of a fitted sheet, a comforter, and bumper pads makes a practical choice. Whether you are sewing for your own baby, making a gift, or preparing for a grandchild's visit, you'll want the crib to be as comforting and safe as possible.

Taking the Measurements

A standard crib mattress is 52" by 27½" by 6". If you are making a set for a portable crib or other crib that's not of standard size, measure the mattress's width, length, and height carefully. The bumper pads and sheet should fit exactly. If they are loose, they can become hazardous if the baby gets entangled in them. If they are too tight, they might tear, becoming just as hazardous.

To make a fitted sheet, you will need one piece of fabric the width of your mattress, plus twice the depth, plus another 4" for the hem, which will also serve as the elastic casing. For a standard mattress, that comes to 43½", or approximately the width of most fabrics. The length of this piece will be the length of the mattress, plus the same as was added to the width. This comes to 68" for a standard crib. Since you will lose 1" or 2" at each end of your new fabric when you straighten the edges, buy 2 yards of fabric for your sheet if it's a standard crib mattress.

For a 42" by 34" comforter, you will need 1 yard each of two coordinating fabrics. If you want to add a 2½" homemade ruffle around the edge of your comforter, you'll need an additional 1¼ yards.

FIGURE 9-1

◀ **Crib set:** Coordinating sheet, bumper pad, and comforter.

To make the bumper pads for a standard bed, you will need 2¾ yards of fabric. In addition, you need an optional 1½ yards for a ruffle and either ½ yard for ties or 4²/₃ yards of woven ribbon that's ¾" wide. These ties will be lined with self-gripping fasteners, usually called Velcro. If you want to tie your bumper pads in place with bows, you will need about half again as much fabric or ribbons.

Unless your crib is a great deal smaller than standard, you will still need to get the 2¾ yards for the bumper pads. You should be able to cut your ties from the leftover fabric and get by with 1¼ yards for the ruffle.

ALERT!

As fun as it might sound, resist the temptation to make a matching pillow for the crib. Pillows are a suffocation hazard and should never be placed in an infant's crib. An older child might also use it as a step and fall over the rail.

Buying Special Supplies

There are a few extras you'll need to make the crib set and a few decisions to make. Plan a little in advance and try to get everything at once.

Fabric

Do you want the entire set to be from one fabric? Should the sheet and one side of the comforter be a lively print, while the bumper pads and the other side of the comforter are a coordinating plaid? All the ruffles might be of a solid color, possibly ready-made. The necessary materials are the following:

2 yards fabric for sheet
1 yard each of two fabrics for comforter
2¾ yards for bumper pads
1¼ yards for optional ruffle on comforter or 8½ yards pregathered ruffle
1½ yards for optional ruffle on bumper pads or 4²/₃ yards pregathered ruffle
½ yard for bumper pad ties, or 4²/₃ yards ¾" ribbon

You will want to buy washable, soft fabrics like cotton or cotton blends. Flannel would be good for the sheet and one side of the comforter for cold weather. There are some delightful juvenile prints to choose from, so shop when you have time to browse. When you get it home, wash and straighten your new fabric as described in Chapter 3.

Quilt Batting

You will need quilt batting for the comforter and for the bumper pads. A medium weight is recommended. Extra loft will be hard to work with in the bumper pads and will be a smothering hazard for the comforter. Thin batting will not give enough padding to the bumper pads, but it may be what you want for a comforter in warm weather.

Foam rubber can be used in the bumper pads, but it isn't recommended because it isn't washable. Also, it would be difficult to stuff into the panels without a lot of hand sewing.

You will need one piece of batting measuring approximately 43" by 1 yard and eight pieces measuring 41" by 12". One double-bed-sized bag would be more than enough. Perhaps one crib size and one craft size will give you enough and be cheaper. Check the dimensions on the packages and make some comparisons. You may also find batting sold by the yard. Find out the width of the batting and see if you can figure out exactly what you'll need.

Notions

Besides the optional ribbon or ruffles you might want to buy, you will need a few things from the notion section. Get a package of ¼"-wide elastic that contains at least 1²/₃ yards. Be sure it is stiff enough to spring back inside a casing. Avoid lingerie and baby elastic because they are too soft to provide the cling needed for this project.

You will need 49" of self-gripping fasteners, unless you plan to tie the bumper pad in place with bows. You will actually only need 17½" of the hook half of the fasteners since size adjustment will be made along the longer soft half of the fasteners. However, they are usually sold together, so you will need to buy 49".

You will need some yarn or embroidery floss to "tie" the comforter. Don't get these confused with the ties for the bumper pads. These yarn ties are what give a comforter its tufted look. Baby yarn, if you can find it in the right color, will be the easiest to work with. You will also need a tapestry needle to fit the yarn. The smallest needle possible that the yarn can still be threaded through is what you're after.

Making Fitted Corners

Let's begin with the fitted sheet. From the trimmed edge of your fabric, measure 67". Pull a thread, and cut across the width of your fabric. Measure from selvage to selvage to be sure your width will still be 43½" after the selvages are trimmed away. Trim them away if you can, and cut down the length of the fabric to make a piece 67" by 43½".

This is one project in which it won't matter if you have to leave a selvage along one edge. The reason you should normally cut it away is because it will sometimes shrink. In this case, that won't really matter. You will still need to hem the edge so you have a casing for the elastic.

If your bed is not a standard size, cut the fabric to the calculated dimensions.

FIGURE 9-2

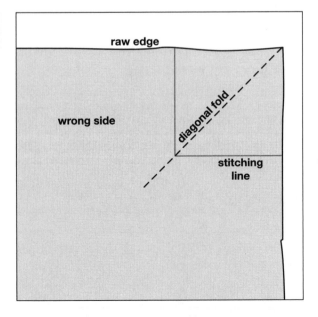

◀ **Fitted corners:** Mark the stitching line.

FIGURE 9-3

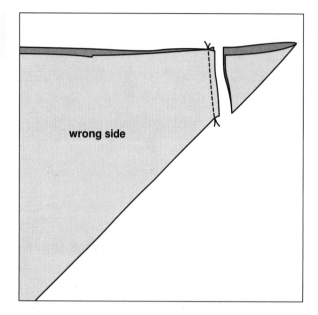

wrong side

◀ Fold, stitch, and turn.

To make a fitted corner, mark off lines that define an 8" by 8" square at the corner of the fabric (as shown in **FIGURE 9-2**). If your mattress is other than 6" deep, mark off a square equal to the depth of your mattress plus 2". This should equal half the amount you added to the width and length of the mattress.

Fold a corner on the diagonal, match the marked lines, and stitch along them. Trim away the corner ½" from the stitching (see **FIGURE 9-3**). Zigzag-stitch along the raw edge of the seam allowance and press to one side. Repeat with the other three corners.

ALERT!

You shouldn't put plastic sheets on an infant's bed because of the smothering hazard. Most crib mattresses are waterproof, anyway, but if yours isn't, protect your baby from the plastic with a quilted mattress pad *over* the sheet. You can find already quilted fabric and can make the pad just like a fitted sheet.

Encasing the Elastic

All your sheet needs now is a hem and something to hold the elastic in place around the head and the foot of the bed. The easiest way to do this is to hem the sheet and use the hem as a casing. Fold the entire edge of the sheet under ¾". Open this out, and press the raw edge under so it meets this first crease line. Stitch the hem all the way around the sheet close to the inside fold.

Cut the elastic into two 30" strips or the width of your mattress plus" 2 or 3". You will be threading one through the hem at each end of the sheet. Begin by locating the points on the long sides of the sheet 3" from the corner seams. Mark these points on the hem allowance.

With a seam ripper, take out about three stitches in the hem at these points. Fasten a safety pin to one end of a piece of elastic. Thread it through the hole in the hem and toward the corner seam. Be sure to secure the tail of the elastic to the sheet with a pin before you lose it inside the hem/casing.

Pull the pin and the end of the elastic out of the hole in the hem beyond the second seam. With the fabric adjusted so the elastic won't pull away, line up the end with the 3" mark. Machine-stitch and back-stitch across the hem and elastic ¼" from the end of the elastic and again about ½" from the end. Do the same to the other end of elastic, and then repeat with the other elastic strip at the other end of the sheet.

Repair the hem by stitching over the gap and about ½" or so on both sides of it, and your sheet is done.

Making a Comforter

Comforters, by definition, are quilts that are tied instead of quilted. They make excellent gifts and are great for fund-raising bazaars. You can make them any size you want, with or without ruffles. These directions will make one comforter that is approximately 38" by 46" including the ruffle.

Sewing the Pieces

Cut *one* of your two fabric pieces to 34" by 42". This piece will be the cover or top of your comforter. The other piece will be the backing, and you will trim it and the batting to fit when you put the layers together.

The ruffle will go on easier if the corners are rounded. Use something perfectly round as a guide to cut the first corner, and then use the removed remnant as a guide for the other three.

Cut the 1¼ yards of ruffle fabric into 6" strips. Cut away the selvages, and sew the strips together into one large loop. Press the seams open, and fold the ruffle in half the long way, wrong sides together. Sew a round of gathering stitches ½" from the raw edge and another ¼" from the edge, giving you two rows of stitches for smoother gathering. To make it easier to gather such a large ruffle, stop stitching at each seam, cut the thread, and start again, leaving long tails. This will give you thread ends to use when you are gathering the ruffle.

Divide the ruffle into eight equal sections. Divide the edge of the top comforter piece into eight equal sections, too. Use these to space the ruffle around the comforter top. Gather, pin, and sew the ruffle in place as you did ruffles on pillows.

It doesn't matter which fabric you think of as the front of your comforter, but if one of your comforter pieces has a stripe pattern, sew it on as the top. It will be difficult to align the backing piece exactly when you sew it to the top, and offset stripes are going to show. You can turn the comforter the other way when you tie it so your "backing" becomes the front.

Turning and Tying

Put the untrimmed backing piece, right side up, on top of the batting. Place the top piece, right side down on top, centering it. Beginning in the center, pin the layers together with safety pins, smoothing the layers outward. Pin the outside edge with straight pins.

Stitch around the comforter, leaving a gap for turning. Remove all the pins. Trim the batting close to the stitching and the backing to match the edge of the cover. Turn, press, and blind-stitch the gap closed.

Smooth out the comforter and safety pin the layers together again. Mark a pattern of dots for ties an equal distance apart—5" is a suggestion. The fabric print or stripe may lend itself to this pattern. Using your tapestry needle and, leaving about a 2" tail, pull your yarn through all the layers and back to the top about ¼" away. Making a second stitch back through the same holes is recommended. Tie the yarn in a double knot, and trim the ends to ½". Repeat with all the dots in your pattern, and the second piece of your crib set is done.

Cutting and Stitching the Bumper Pads

Bumper pads are intended to protect a tiny baby's head from hitting against the hard slats of the crib. They are not intended to protect against the dangers of slats that are too far apart (slats should be no more than $2^3/_8$" apart). Nor are they intended to make up for a mattress that doesn't fit the crib; you shouldn't be able to fit two adult fingers between the mattress and the side of the crib. Bumper pads aren't even necessary, but they make us feel so much better about leaving the little one alone in the crib.

Cutting the Main Pieces

You will need to cut eight pieces 41" by 12". If you are making bumpers for a crib that's not standard in size, consider the difference between its dimensions and the 52" by 27½" standard mattress. Take one half the sum of the width plus the length, and add 1" for seam allowances to get the length of one panel. The width should probably stay at 12".

You will also need eight pieces of quilt batting the same size. Pin a batting piece to the wrong side of each of the pieces. Machine baste ½" from the edge all around the pieces. This simply means sewing the batting on with your machine's longest stitches.

Measure just over 13¼" inward from the end stitches and mark a stitching line from top to bottom. This will divide the panel into thirds. Baste the batting to the panel along these lines. Do this to all eight panels.

Sew four of the panels together, end to end, right sides together. Cut the batting close to the seam line, and press the seams open. Do the same with the other four panels.

ALERT!

Remove bumper pads from a child's bed as soon as he is able to pull himself up to stand. The bumper pads become a step that might make it possible for the child to go over the top of the rail. He won't need them anymore, anyway.

Ruffle

Cut the ruffle fabric into 6" strips. Cut away the selvages, and sew the strips together into one long strip. When the bumper pad is installed, the ends of the ruffle will stick up above the bumper pad where the two ends of the pad meet. To finish these ruffle ends, fold one end of the ruffle strip in half, right sides together, and stitch with a ¼" seam. Clip the corners, turn, and press. Do the same with the other end. Press the ruffle in half with wrong sides together. Stitch the raw edge for gathering as you did the ruffle for the comforter.

Next, gather the ruffle onto the right side of one of the bumper-pad panels. To do this, divide the ruffle into eight equal parts, and match these to the seams and the centers of each piece on the panel. While the raw edges of the ruffle and pad line up, the ends of the ruffle will line up with the *stitching* line rather than the raw edge at the sides of the panel. Gather the ruffle, and stitch ½" from the edge.

Adding Ties

Ties are intended to keep the bumper pad firmly in place. Wedging the pad between the mattress and the slats will accomplish part of this, but you don't want the top sagging downward. You will need to secure the pad at the top as well as the bottom. That is why this pattern calls for fourteen pairs of ties.

Cutting the Ties

To make the ties with self-gripping fasteners, cut fourteen strips of cloth 12" by 2½", or cut your woven ribbon into 12" lengths. If you want your ties to actually tie, cut fourteen 18" by 2½" strips, or cut your ribbon into 18" lengths.

Fold the fabric strips in half, the long way, right sides together, and stitch ½" from the long edge. Clip a safety pin into the seam allowance, and use it to turn the strips right side out. Press them flat. Tuck the raw edges at the ends inside, and blind-stitch them closed.

Adding Self-Gripping Fasteners

If you have 12" lengths, either fabric or ribbons, you will need to add the self-gripping fasteners next. Separate the loop side from the hook side. Cut the loop half, or soft half, into fourteen 3½" pieces. Pin one loop half to one end of each of the ties or the wrong side of the ribbons. Sew all around, close to the edge.

Cut the hook or stiff side into fourteen 1¼" pieces. Sew these to the *right* side of the ribbons on the end opposite the other fasteners or on the opposite side of the opposite end from the other fasteners on the cloth ties. In other words, if you fold your ties in half, both of the fasteners will be either up or down.

Sewing Ties to the Pads

Fold the fastener ties in half so the inside edges of the two halves of the fasteners are even. In other words, the soft-sided end will extend a couple of inches below the other end. Pin the fold of your ties to the right side of the bumper pad, even with the raw edge. These will be on top of the ruffle on the top edge. Place one tie at each of the four corners of the pad, keeping them inside the side seam allowance on the ends. Place one tie on the upper and one on the lower edge of every other basted line or seam, evenly spacing the ties across the top and across the bottom. Stitch them in place along the seam line.

If you are not using the fasteners, fold your longer ribbons or cloth ties in even halves and place them the same way.

It is considered unsafe to have ties on bumper pads that are more than 9" long. Anything longer than that can get wrapped around an active infant's throat. If you are rejuvenating an old set of bumper pads, measure the ties and cut them to 9" or replace them with the self-gripping fasteners.

Finishing

The only thing left to do is to sew your two bumper pad pieces into one. Place them together, right side to right side, matching seams and keeping all the ruffles and ties inside. Being careful that the ties and the side edges of the ruffle do not get caught in the stitching, sew the pieces together, leaving a gap to turn. Trim the batting close to the seam line, clip the corners and turn. Press, and blind-stitch the gap closed.

Top-stitch in the ditch at the three seams and along the basting lines. Your bumper pads are ready for the crib, and your set is finished. Ⓔ

Chapter 10

Appliquéd Tote Bag

Tote bags are handy for everything from holding your current handwork projects to carrying music to piano lessons or lotion to the beach. Since they are easily made in any size or shape, design one that will be perfect for your purposes and decorate it with something that identifies its use.

Designing the Bag for Your Needs

There are two basic styles of tote bags—flat and box. Flat bags are made from two same-size pieces of fabric sewn together. While the bottom corners of the flat bag can be tucked, or boxed, slightly to give it more depth, to make a really wide-mouthed tote you will need to make all four sides for a box-style bag.

Flat Bags

Tote bags are generally square or rectangular, but they don't have to be. Consider the use of your bag—what shape and size will best suit its purpose? Remember you are working with fabric and, though you can find some fairly stiff fabrics, your bag will be pretty limp when it's empty. The larger it is, the more this will be true.

When you've decided on the shape you want, determine the exact dimensions. You will need either two same-sized rectangles or one that folds in half to become the size you need for both sides. Add at least ½" seam allowance all around. Also consider the thickness of its future content. As happened when you stuffed a pillow, your bag front will seem smaller once it's full.

FIGURE 10-1

◀ **Tote bag styles:** Just about any size or shape you could want.

If your bag is going to have a rounded bottom, make a pattern for your pieces. Remember to allow for depth with this pattern as well. Small tucks are possible in the sides of round totes as well as the square ones, and these will make the front seem smaller.

Box Totes

To make a more box-like tote bag, you will need sides separate from the front and back. For one piece, begin with the size and shape you want the bottom to be when it's finished. Extend the front and back pieces out from the bottom pattern to the height you want, and do the same with the sides. Add your seam allowances all the way around this cross shape, and you have your pattern.

It is a good idea to reinforce the bottom of this kind of bag, especially if you are making it large and expect it to carry fairly heavy loads, such as books or groceries. To do this, you can cut another piece the size of the bottom plus a seam allowance. You will turn under the seam allowances and stitch it to the bag either inside or out. If you will be putting it inside, it should be a tiny bit smaller than the bottom itself.

Or you can cut a piece that will extend 1" or so up the sides or up the front and back as well. This will probably need to go on the outside, or it will make the bottom spread.

FACT

Tote bags make fun gifts. Consider tailoring one to fit a loaf of homemade bread or other gift from the kitchen. Make a small one to fill with coloring books and crayons for a sick child, or a diaper bag for an expecting family. How about making a canvas grocery bag for an environmentalist?

Handles and Facing

You will also need to decide how long you'll want your straps. For most tote bags, the straps will be sewn on the top with the raw edges hidden under a facing. If your bag will be used for heavy items, your handles can be sewn down the entire front and back of the tote, meeting at the bottom. Consider making the handles long enough to go over your shoulder. Keep these possibilities in mind when you are planning and shopping.

You can buy heavy woven ribbon or make your straps by folding and turning strips of the same fabric you're using for your bag. You can even make a combination of both. If you are making top-mounted handles, allow about 1½" at each end for extension under the facing. This will reinforce the handles and help them stand up.

The facing is a 2" strip that will go all the way around the top of your bag. This strip may be pieced or cut from one length. Make it more narrow for a really small bag and wider for a larger one.

Fabric Shopping

You can make your bag out of anything you want, but heavy, tightly woven fabrics will give you a more satisfactory tote. Denim or canvas will probably be your best choices, but check for heavy twills or even upholstery fabric if they suit your project. The heavier the fabric, the more difficult it will be to turn for straps. Consider grosgrain ribbon backed with your tote bag fabric, or possibly backed with fabric you will use in your appliqué decoration. If you are planning to use fabric for handles or to reinforce the bottom, be sure to allow enough when you buy your fabric. You might not want to wash your fabric before you make your tote, because washing it might make it softer. You can treat your tote bag with stain-resistant spray and waterproofing to put off having to wash the finished bag.

ALERT!

If you are extending your handles down the front and back of your bag, mark their locations using a ruler and pencil before you plan your appliqué so you'll know what will fit. Marking the inside or outside edge of the handle will be easier to follow later than markings meant for the center of the handle.

Making Patterns for Appliqué

If you have a specific use in mind for your tote bag, you've probably already thought about how to decorate it. You can cut out a motif from a printed fabric or a single shape, but now might be a good time to try a more complicated design.

You can appliqué a picture by using several different fabrics. Think in terms of a child's coloring book for an idea of how detailed this should be. Children's coloring books are a good source of pictures for appliqué. You might want to simplify the images just a little or use only part of a picture and enlarge it. Line drawings intended for embroidery are another good source. If you have drawing skills, draw your picture the size that will fit your tote. If you need a little help drawing, you can photocopy a picture from a magazine or book, darken the key lines and trace it to make a line drawing. If it's the wrong size and you can't enlarge or reduce it to the right size with a copier, draw a grid over the picture or photocopy or trace it onto graph paper. Make a larger scale grid and use the grid lines to help you draw your picture.

You will be machine appliquéing your picture on your tote bag, so you won't need to add any seam allowances. However, to avoid having two rows of zigzag stitches at each internal line in your picture, some of the pieces should tuck under others. Look over your picture, and decide which of the internal lines should be tucked underneath. Mark dotted lines over the upper pieces to indicate these extensions.

Cutting to Order

Photocopy or trace a couple more copies of your picture. Keep one whole. Label each individual area in the other two so you'll know where it goes, and use these copies to cut out the patterns for these individual pieces. You need at least two so that you can cut out the extensions with the pieces. An alternative to copying the entire picture is to trace each piece one at a time, including its extension, from your original pattern.

Pick out fabric scraps you want for each part of your picture. Avoid fabrics with loose weaves as they will fray and pull away from your stitching. Slick, shiny fabrics may be difficult to keep in place when you stitch.

Pin the paper patterns right side up on the right side of your fabric. Cut out your pieces, leaving the labeled pattern on at this point.

Don't try to make every different shade in your picture out of a different piece of cloth. You can add details to your appliqué with embroidery, fabric paints, waterproof markers, buttons, or sequins. Add the details after the appliqué pieces are together on your bag.

Putting the Pieces Together

Now you need to put all those pieces together on your tote bag. There are several ways to do this and a couple of tricks that make it a little easier.

Simple Appliqué

If your appliqué is very simple, involving only a few pieces, simply arrange them in place on the front piece of your bag. Pin around them and, beginning with the pieces that are tucked under others, zigzag-stitch them into place as you did the fabric motif on the pillow in Chapter 7. You do not need to zigzag all along an edge that will be under another piece. Instead, simply pull back the upper piece and take a stitch or two beyond the overlap line.

With Dressmaker's Carbon

If your picture is more complex, you can use dressmaker's carbon. Locate the area on your tote bag front piece where you want the appliqué to go. Keep seam allowances and the eventual curve of a full bag in mind.

Pin your whole picture pattern to the tote bag. With the fabric on a hard surface, slip the dressmaker's carbon under the picture, and trace the picture onto the bag. Now you have a guide to use to pin the pieces in their proper place on the bag. Begin with pieces that will be under others and zigzag around the edges.

You can pin a few pieces on at a time, stitch them, and then add more. Or you can pin the whole picture in place before you begin stitching. Your choice might depend on how large your pieces are and how many pins are going to interfere with the stitching. You can match your thread to each individual piece, use a neutral tone such as gray or tan, or use one color to accent each line. The type of picture you've chosen and the look you are after will determine which you choose.

With Fusible Interfacing

An alternative to marking the picture on your bag is to trace it onto the fusible side of fusible interfacing. Put your pieces in place on the interfacing and press them down. Use just the tip of your iron to hold each piece in place until you can get them all where they belong, and then press them more thoroughly.

Trim the interfacing away around the outside edge of your picture. Place the picture on the front piece of your tote bag. Pin, then baste it in place. A quick X across the picture as well as some stitches around the edges will keep it from shifting.

Choose your thread as already described, and begin with the pieces that are under others. The overlap area will not be stuck down so you can easily bend them out of the way to take a stitch or two under them. Remove the basting stitches after everything is sewn down.

Making the Handles

By the time you have gotten this far, you have probably decided what you want to do for handles. You have sufficient fabric or ribbon to make them. All you need are a few hints on how to get them ready and put them in place.

Easy Handles

Grosgrain ribbon is fine for light loads, and it only needs to be cut to the right length. Fabric handles are stitched and turned like the ties in the last chapter. Since these will probably be 1" or more wide, try to press the seam in the center of the back. Topstitch the length of the handles ¼" from each folded edge to keep them flat.

QUESTION?

What if my fabric's too heavy to turn?
Press the sides of your handle strip under ¼", then fold it in half lengthwise, wrong sides together. Stitch the edge, closing up the two turned-under edges. Stitch along the other side as well.

Fabric-Backed Ribbon

If you want your tie to be a combination of fabric and grosgrain or other ribbon, cut a strip of fabric 1¼" wider than your ribbon. Press ½" under on each side of the fabric strip. Center your ribbon over it and stitch close to the ribbon's edge. The fabric should show approximately ⅛" on each side of the ribbon.

Handles for Heavy Loads

If you want handles that extend down the front and back of your tote bag, you can prepare the two handles in one long piece. If you are making a box, it will measure four times the height, plus twice the width of the bottom, plus twice whatever you want for the extension at the top of the tote. You can make this in two equal lengths if that is easier to work with. Zigzag across the raw edges at the ends of the handles.

Sewing It All Together

The order of construction will vary a little depending on whether you are adding your handles only to the top or if you are sewing them clear to the bottom. Also, the box-type bags are constructed somewhat differently than the flat type. But all of them go together quickly.

Bottom Seams

For flat styles, begin by sewing the bottom seam. Since this raw edge is going to be inside your bag and could catch on things and fray, the allowance should be finished. A French seam is one option and can be used for lighter weight fabrics. Other suggestions are zigzag-finishing the edge or using pinking shears.

A flat felt seam is another possibility. To make this seam, sew it as usual with right sides together. Trim one allowance, probably the one toward the back, to ½ the depth of the other. Fold the deeper allowance over the shorter one and sew them both flat to the back piece, stitching close to the fold.

A variation on this is to press the seam open and turn each seam allowance under. Stitch them on their respective sides of the seam, as described for a seam in a tablecloth in Chapter 6.

If you are making the box style and did not cut it as one piece, sew the front and back pieces to the bottom piece, and finish the seams in some way as described above.

ALERT!

If you are planning to reinforce the bottom of your *flat* bag with a piece that you'll add to the inside, you don't need to finish the seam allowance. The reinforcement will cover the seam when you add it at the very end.

Reinforcing the Bottom

A small reinforcing piece intended to be sewn inside of a box-style tote can be added at this point. Turn the edges under, and sew it to the bottom section of your tote bag.

If you have chosen a reinforcing piece that extends up the sides and front and back, it can be added now. Turn under the top edges, pin it right side up to the right side of the still-flat tote bag piece. Stitch close to the folds.

If you are using handles that extend to the bottom and you would like them to disappear under this reinforcing panel, simply wait and add this piece after the handles are in place.

Handles to the Bottom

If you are adding handles that go clear to the bottom, add them next. Lay your tote bag out on a flat surface. If you have not marked where your handles should go, do so now, making sure they are equal distances from the center on each end.

Pin your handle piece or pieces along these marked lines. Have the ends meet in the center of the lines as they cross the bottom section. Be sure the loops are even on both sides where they extend beyond the top edge. If your handles are made from one long piece, pin the ends where they meet. Pin both sides to the top, then adjust the other half until the loops are equal.

You should pin the handles clear to the top, but you will not be attaching them to the bag's edge. The straps need to go over the facing, and the facing goes on after the side seams. The handles would be next to impossible to sew on after the side seams are done. Therefore, sew along both edges of the handles beginning and ending about 3" from the top edge. Leave the tops for after the facing's in place.

Side Seams

Next, sew the side seams. If possible, use the same method to finish these seams as you did the bottom. This can get tricky when a flat felt seam of the bottom seam is in the seam allowance of the side. You might overcome the difficulty by making it the side that is trimmed. And remember, this is the inside of a bag. The seam allowance doesn't have to look perfect.

Top Attaching Handles

Mark where you want your handles to be, being sure they are all equal distances from the center. Pin the handle edges to the front and back, right sides together, extending the ends of the handles 1" beyond the raw edge of the tote bag. Sew the handles to the bag at the ½" seam line.

Facing

Sew the ends of the facing piece together so it forms a hoop the size of the top of your tote bag. Turn under one edge ¼". Put the hoop over the top of the bag, right sides together, lining up the raw edge of the bag with the unturned edge of the facing. Top attached handles should be under the facing, with ends extending beyond the edge. Handles that attach to the bottom should be unpinned and folded out of the way.

Stitch around the top edge of the tote bag. Turn and press. If you have top-attached handles, sew the extended ends to the underside of the facing. Stitch along both sides of the handle extensions, and stitch an X through it. Turn the facing to the inside, and stitch close to the turned edge. You might want to topstitch around the top edge as well.

Now you can finish sewing on your handles if you are using the ones that extend to the bottom. Pin them in place and sew them over the top of the facing. You might want to reinforce them by stitching across them at the top edge and at the line of stitching at the base of the lining.

FACT

When making a tote bag with handles that extend to the bottom, you don't need to cut a separate facing. You could cut the front, back, and sides longer, and hem the top instead. You would still have to do the handles in two steps so you could sew the side seams before you turned under the top hem.

Boxing the Corners

If you've made a flat-sided tote bag, but you want to give it a bit more depth, you can box the corners. It's easy with square corners, but you can do it with a rounded bag, too.

FIGURE 10-2

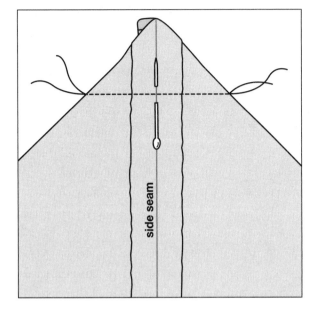

◀ **Boxed corners:** Stitch across the corner.

FIGURE 10-3

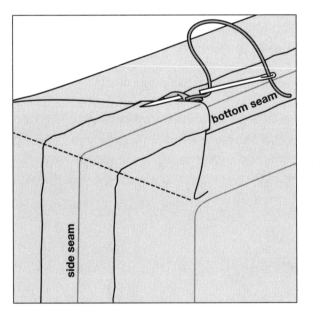

◀ Sew the point to the bottom seam.

Turn the finished bag inside out. Flatten a corner so the side seam is in line with the bottom seam; the point where they meet is at the point of your fold. Determine the amount of depth you want. Sew across the corner, perpendicular to the seams, as shown in **FIGURE 10-2**.

Fold this tuck down against the bottom seam, and hand-stitch it to the seam allowance with several large looping stitches, as shown in **FIGURE 10-3**.

Once this is done, you are ready to reinforce the bottom. Measure across your boxing stitches and from one line of stitches to the other. Cut your fabric to these dimensions plus 1". Turn the edges under ½" and sew this piece to the inside of the bottom. You will probably have to sew this entirely by hand. Depending on the size and flexibility of your bag, it could be difficult to get to it with the sewing machine.

For a tuck in a rounded bag, turn the bag inside out and take a small tuck in each side, near the bottom of the downward curve. Pin the tucks and turn the bag right side out to see if it gives you the effect you want. You might try different sized tucks at different locations. When you find the perfect spot, fold the seam so you can sew along the tuck in the seam. You will stitch just a few stitches on either side of the seam rather than stitching clear to a fold as you would with a square corner. Be sure to backstitch so the stitches don't pull out.

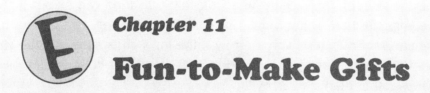

Chapter 11

Fun-to-Make Gifts

As you become more confident about your sewing skills, it's natural to look for ways to share them. Handmade gifts are always appreciated, and there's no danger that someone else will give another just like it. If you're still a little hesitant, you might start out by adding a personal touch to a store-bought item.

Trimming Infants' T-shirts

Infants' plain white T-shirts are inexpensive and easy to dress up. Mothers like the kind with the overlapping shoulders because they are easier to pull over a little one's head.

Begin by decorating the neck and shoulders of the little T-shirts. Narrow satin ribbon or narrow double-fold bias tape can be sewn around the edge, just below the hem. Zigzag stitches will help you fit your trim to the curves. Consider a very narrow ruffle for a girl's shirt. Put the ruffle pointing down instead of up, and be sure it's a soft cotton—such as eyelet—rather than a scratchy lace.

Turn the ends of your trim under, zigzag across them, or cover the ends with tiny bows.

Decorate the front of the shirts with a small appliqué. Craft stores offer a wide variety of embroidered or painted appliqué you can choose from. Two smaller, coordinating appliqués might be cute on the shoulders. Or make your own appliqué. A simple shape, like a heart or a star, looks great on such a tiny shirt. If you have trouble zigzag stitching on the stretchy T-shirt, try turned appliqué instead.

Easy Turned Appliqué

Turned appliqué only works with single fabric appliqué. Besides being good for decorating T-shirts, this method is handy if you want to add an appliqué to something that you can't manipulate under the sewing machine needle to zigzag, such as a ready-made tote bag or a jacket sleeve or pocket.

Draw your shape on the wrong side of your fabric. Place this piece on top of a second piece of fabric. This can be more of the same fabric, a neutral color, or something that matches what you plan to sew the appliqué to. Straight-stitch around the shape, leaving a small gap along the straightest edge available.

Cut around the shape, leaving ¼" allowance. Clip the curves, turn, and press. You can blind-stitch the gap or simply topstitch close to the edge. You might be able to follow your topstitching and machine-stitch the appliqué to the T-shirt. Or you can blind-stitch the shape in place.

One possibility is to make three small hearts (or stars or other shapes) out of a striped or checked material. For interest, cut two on the grain and, for the center shape, cut one on the bias so the stripes run on the diagonal. Another idea is to use the chintz appliqué you learned in Chapter 7 and cut a small motif from a juvenile print, leaving a seam allowance. Back and turn it as described above, and sew on the shirt.

Another idea is to use the same method to make a pocket pal for a toddler. Use a teddy bear, doll, or animal motif from a fabric, back and turn it, and sew it behind a pocket so it appears to be riding there. If the shirt or dress you are decorating doesn't have a pocket, make one using the same method. Sew the doll to the garment, and sew the pocket over it.

FACT

A lot of toddler clothing can lend itself to added decorations. Consider replacing bland buttons with fun shapes or adding trim to collars, hems, or cuffs. A little girl might like her big brother's hand-me-down overalls if you'd add some ruffle over the suspenders and maybe on the edge of the pockets. Be sure to secure charms and buttons so they don't pose a choking hazard.

Adding Snaps to Toddler Overalls

There is an abundance of cute little overalls sold for toddlers. Unfortunately, many of them don't include snaps inside the legs. If you've ever tried to change the diaper on an active toddler, you can understand why mothers love those snaps. Don't despair. You can buy those cute overalls and put the snaps in yourself.

Buying Supplies

The easiest thing to use is special snap tape that already has the snaps at regular intervals on the tape. If you can't find snap tape or you want sturdier snaps, you will need ½" twill tape and snaps. You have a choice between snaps that you stitch onto the tape or snaps with rivets that you will hammer into place.

Removing the Seams

Begin by ripping out the stitches on the inseams. If the seam is a flat felt seam, which it is likely to be, there will be two rows of stitching to remove. Don't be tempted to simply trim the seam away. You will need all the fabric or you will be reducing the size of the overalls. You will need to take out about 1" or 2" of the hem on either side of these inseams as well.

Press the seam allowance flat, and trim away any loose threads. If there are frayed areas, trim them away, cutting the allowance as straight as possible.

FIGURE 11-1

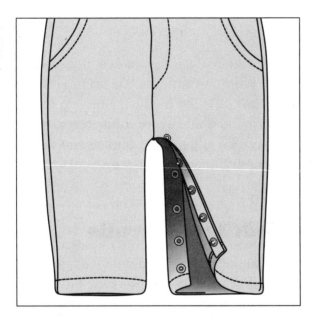

◀ Put snaps on the outside back and underside front.

Adding the Tape

Begin with the front of the overalls. You will want to use the tape to turn the raw edge of the inseam to the back. The twill tape will end up on the underside of the fabric. Place the edge of the twill tape on the edge of the right side of the inseam. They should only overlap about ¼". The tape should extend all the way to the raw edge of the hem allowance. If you are using snap tape, the side with the snap parts should be right side up as well. You may need to use a zipper foot to keep from hitting the snaps and making your stitches crooked.

Stitch close to the edge of the tape. Press the tape to the underside of the overalls and stitch along the other edge.

You will want the front piece to overlap the back to snap. Therefore, the tape and snaps on the back half of the overalls legs will need to be on the right side of the fabric. For that reason, you will need to overlap the tape along the seam allowance edge having the *wrong* side of the fabric facing you. Again, the business side of the tape should be right side up if you are using snap tape. Also, be sure you are starting at the same distance from the first snap as you started with the other half so the snaps will line up.

Stitch close to the edge of the tape. Press the tape to the front side of the fabric and stitch along the other edge. Repair the hem.

Adding Snaps

If you used snap tape, the overalls are done. If not, you must add the snaps next. Mark their placement on the tape. Putting one on either side of the crotch seam, even if they are only 1" apart, is a good idea. You will also want one at the very bottom of each leg. If you are riveting the snaps and are afraid the hem will be too thick, place them just above the hem. Place the rest evenly between these four snaps, at intervals of about 2".

If you are sewing on your snaps, sew them to the twill tape. If you are riveting, follow the directions that come with your kit. The caps or rings will be against the fabric, and the snaps themselves will be on the twill tape.

They may sound difficult, but rivet snaps are really fairly easy to use, and they stay snapped better than the regular kind. Once you get the hang of them, they also go in faster than the ones you sew. Read the directions on the back of the package, and see if they are something you want to try.

Learning Machine Monogramming

Another skill that makes personalizing gifts fun is machine monogramming. Add a single initial to handkerchiefs or two or three to shirts or bathrobes. Write entire names on the hems of pillowcases. How about using the same technique to add some witticism to an apron?

FIGURE 11-2

right side
of fabric

◀ **Machine monograms:**
Move the cloth to keep your markings under the needle.

Necessary Equipment

You will need an embroidery hoop to hold the fabric flat against the needle plate. Embroidery hoops intended for machine embroidery are not as deep as regular hand-embroidery hoops, making them easier to slide under the needle. The presser foot is removed, so you have more freedom to move your fabric to keep the design under the needle. If you are working with heavy fabric, such as canvas for a tote bag, you will have trouble getting it on the hoop. You might be able to embroider without the hoop. You will have to press down on the fabric as you move it to keep it against the needle plate.

An embroidery or free-motion needle plate will keep the fabric feeds from moving against the fabric. If you don't have one, don't worry.

Without the presser foot pressing the cloth against them, the feed can't really move the cloth anyway. You'll get used to moving against what little pull they create.

Getting Ready

Draw your desired monogram or other design on your cloth. You might want to include the width you'd like the stitching to be rather than just a center line to follow. Cursive or calligraphy-like letters will be easier to stitch than block letters, and your imperfections will be less noticeable. Practice on a scrap first to get the hang of it.

Put the cloth on top of the outside hoop, with the right side of the cloth facing you. Press the inside hoop on top, and pull the fabric tight. This is the opposite of the way you would use a regular embroidery hoop. The idea is to keep the fabric stretched tight and flat against the needle plate.

Set your machine for zigzag stitching and to the width you'll want at your beginning point. You can adjust the width as you go or move your fabric at an angle to create narrower stitching in some places.

Move the needle to the highest position and slide the hoop under it. Use the hand wheel to lower the needle into the cloth where you want to begin. Lower the presser-foot lifter, even though the presser foot isn't there. Lowering it engages the tension discs. Otherwise, the thread won't stay taut enough to pull up the bobbin thread.

Embroidering

Make the first couple of stitches, then backstitch over them before moving on. Stitch slowly, moving the hoop as you go. If you need to skip from one place to another, raise the presser-foot lever, slide the hoop to the next place, and lower the needle again. Remember to backstitch so the embroidery won't pull out. You can clip away the thread between the different stitching areas when you are finished.

If you're having trouble, set your machine on a basting stitch, if it has one. The pause between stitches will give you more time to position the hoop.

When you get the hang of monograms, try your luck at some simple embroidery, using the machine stitching in place of the hand-embroidery satin stitch.

ALERT!

If your machine is new to you, check the owner's manual. You may have attachments or settings that make machine embroidery even easier. Don't be afraid to try out all your machine's features.

Toddlers' Quiet Books

They're called quiet books because they can keep a child quiet for a few minutes, and in some situations it's nice that the pages are quiet when they turn. This is only part of their charm, however. The pages won't tear or crease or cause paper cuts. They can even tolerate a certain amount of tasting. And, if you are careful about the supplies you use, they are washable.

Basic Book Construction

The easiest books are the ones made from picture print fabrics. The "cheater's quilts" prints are particularly suited for this project. These print fabrics are designed to be cut into quilt blocks. They often feature children's teddy bear or farm animal prints.

The size of the printed block will determine the size of your book. Buy enough to have eight complete blocks. Cut out these eight blocks, leaving ¼" for seam allowances. Sew the blocks together in pairs, side by side. Press the seams open.

Layer the pairs with quilt batting or heavy flannel. To do this, put two pairs together on top of the batting, right sides facing. Stitch around the edge, leaving a gap. Trim the batting, clip the corners, turn, and blind-stitch the gap closed.

Do some topstitching if you want. The border decoration on the prints might suggest some rows of stitching. Remember, what you do on one picture will show on the picture that's behind it, so outlining characters is probably not a good idea. Put the two sets of pages on top of each other, and stitch along the center seam.

FACT

If you buy extra fabric, you can cut out the characters just like the ones in the quiet books. Use some of the bright-colored border print of the same fabric as a back, and stuff the characters to go along with the book. You could even make a little tote bag with the child's name embroidered on the front just for this special book and the stuffed-toy characters.

Some Variations

If you want more than eight pages in your book, leave additional seam allowances on the side that will be toward the center. When you are sewing all the pages together, make two rows of stitching spaced on either side of the center seams, thus creating a "spine."

You can make the front cover distinctive by cutting out the motif and appliquéing it to a bright-colored background. Or you can cut the center motif into a smaller square and sew borders around it.

If your fabric blocks are large and you like to quilt, layer each pair of pages with thin batting and a backing cloth. Quilt around the center motif of each block. You can even add some stuffing behind a shape or two by cutting a slit in your backing fabric and adding pillow stuffing. Put two of these pairs together, sew, and turn as usual.

Activity Book

Another idea is to make a cloth book that gives a child something to do on each page. Some suggestions include funny shaped flaps that either button or snap closed. Make the flaps using the turned appliqué method and sew one side securely to your page.

You might use the same turned method to make a pocket. Stuff a tiny figure cut from printed fabric and put it in the pocket. You might want to tether it to the book with a ribbon or a piece of elastic. Or you could put a tiny handkerchief in the pocket instead.

A stiff, wide ribbon decorated with a buckle can stick in place with self-gripping fasteners. Or maybe you want to make it an actual working buckle. Ribbons or shoestrings that tie and teach children about knots are another possibility. Look over the accessories in the sewing department. You may find large hooks and eyes or decorative buttons and snaps that will give you even more ideas for activity pages.

Making a Zipper Page

Zippers are fun for children, so be sure to include one. Choose a jacket-weight zipper so it's easier for tiny fingers to zip and unzip. Don't worry if you don't know how to install a zipper. You can simply sew it flat to the page.

You will probably have trouble finding one that fits your book exactly, so you will need to shorten it. To do this, hand-stitch over the teeth as shown in **FIGURE 11-3**, and cut off the excess. The stitches keep the zipper pull from sliding off the zipper.

FIGURE 11-3

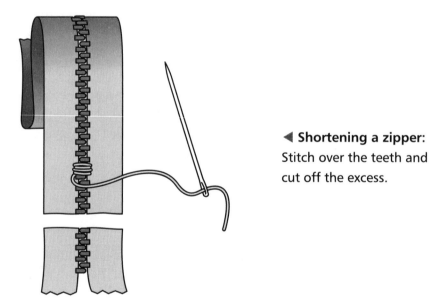

◀ **Shortening a zipper:** Stitch over the teeth and cut off the excess.

Lay the zipper flat on your page, and sew along both side edges. Because cutting the end may leave some sharp edges, you might want to cover it with a flap of cloth to protect your reader from scratches. You might simply use a piece of the same fabric as your page. Cut it large enough so you can turn under one side. Sew it over the end of the zipper, and extend the rest of the edges off the page.

This is the same method you would use in garment construction if you needed to shorten a zipper. Be sure to leave at least ½" below your stitches when you cut the excess off so the teeth don't work open from that direction.

Adding a Window or Door

If you're feeling really creative, try making a window or door that opens to reveal something behind it. These are easiest to do if you can find an appropriate picture print for behind the door.

Because your door will be cloth, it will be limp. This is all right when it's open, but you want it to stay in place when it is closed. You could line your door or window with crinoline, which is used to stiffen pleats on draperies. Another option is to use self-gripping fasteners for the entire length of the open side. This will allow it to close completely without sagging.

In order to have all raw edges finished, you might cut your doorway, leaving ¼" seam allowances. Cut a facing piece with an equal-sized hole. Cut two pieces for your door (or window), adding ¼" seam allowances.

The door pieces will actually be 1" wider and 1" longer than the hole cut in the outside piece. It will get smaller (by ¼" each side or ½" each direction) when these pieces are sewn together. The hole will get larger (by ¼" each side or ½" each direction). If your hole is 2" by 3", cut your door 3" by 4".

Sew the two doors together, right sides facing, leaving the hinged side open. Turn and press. Sew the door to the doorway, right sides together, lining up the raw edges at the hinged side. Sew the facing on top of the doorway and door. Clip to the corners, turn, and press. If you've measured accurately, the door will fit exactly. Sew this over the top of your picture print. (E)

Chapter 12

Lined Baskets and Pincushions

Baskets are cheap, plentiful, and fun to use for sewing projects or supplies, for storing all manner of things, or for decorating. Linings make them more colorful, and linings with pockets make them more useful. Pick out some baskets, and give it a try. Baskets also make great gifts!

Measuring Your Basket

As with anything you sew, it's important that your measurements be accurate. As the carpenters say, measure twice, cut once. Drawing a diagram and labeling it with the measurements of your basket will help you identify any possible difficulties in advance so you can plan around them. Be sure to take the measurements *inside* your basket.

Determine first where you want the top of your lining to be. If there is a decorative top edge on your basket, you may want the lining to attach just below it. Measure the depth in several locations, and use the deepest as your measurement. When you attach your finished lining, you can fold the top edge under a bit more to make it fit in the shallower spots.

You will need a good measurement of the circumference of your basket. This needs to be at its largest point, generally the top edge. Remember to take it inside the basket.

The dimensions and shape of the inside bottom will determine the shape of the bottom piece of lining. Taking paper slightly larger than the bottom and pressing it into the basket, smoothing the bottom and creasing it at the side edges might give you a good pattern. Remember to add seam allowances.

FIGURE 12-1

◀ **Lined Baskets:** You can line any size or shape of basket.

QUESTION?

How do I know how much to allow for seams?
The standard seam allowance for garment construction is ⅝".
When you make your own pattern, ½" is easier to figure. Straight
seams can be done with ¼". It doesn't usually matter as long as
you remember what you allowed and leave enough so the seam
won't pull out.

Cutting Pieces and Pockets

Any fabric you're comfortable working with can be used to line a basket. Imagine your basket lined with a bold cotton print, dark velvet, or, for a padded look, some prequilted fabric. Your intended use of the basket will help you determine what's best to use. You don't want items in the bottom of your basket disappearing on a busy print or fabric so dark it's hard to see to the bottom of a large basket.

Cutting the Lining

Even a basket that is basically square can be cut with one piece of lining to go around all the sides. Take your circumference and your depth, and add ½" seam allowance all around for the dimensions of this piece.

Once it is cut out, determine where your seam should fall in your basket. A corner is a logical place. Here, the seam will be least likely to show and won't interfere with any pockets you might be planning. Pin the seam as if it were stitched, and try the lining out in your basket. Mark the locations of the other corners on your lining with pins or chalk.

Planning the Pockets

Remove the seam pins, and spread your piece out flat. Determine what you'll want for pockets, if any. The marked corners should help you see the space available.

There are a lot of different ways to make pockets. You can hem the top and turn under the sides or use the turned method with a coordinating solid for the back, which will be the inside of the pocket. You can cut your fabric the width of your pocket plus seam allowances and twice as long as your pocket will be deep. Fold it over with the right sides together and stitch around it, leaving a gap. Turn, and the fold will be the top edge of the pocket. Topstitch it into place.

If you want your pockets to extend to the bottom of your basket, there's no need to turn the bottom edge. Simply line the raw edge up with the raw edge of the bottom of your lining.

If you want two side-by-side pockets of equal depth, make them as one pocket. After the pocket is attached to the side, you can separate them into two with a line or two of stitching. You can even cut a piece as long as your present lining and twice as wide as your pocket depth. Fold it in half, wrong sides together, and pin it to your lining. Separate it into a row of pockets that will go all around your basket. You will probably want to separate pockets at the basket corners.

If you want a pocket for scissors, make it narrow and deep enough that the handles catch on the top of the pocket before the tips of the blades touch the bottom, where they could cause damage to your lining.

If you are lining a sewing basket that you'll use to take your hand sewing on the road, consider making a pocket that will hold a small paper cup. This will serve as an easy place to catch the inevitable threads. Instead of sewing the pocket to the lining flat, cut it a little wider than the area it will cover. Either pleat or gather the bottom. You can also pin the pocket flat at the bottom but angle the top edges toward each other slightly, so the pocket flares out. The bottom will gather slightly with the taper of the basket.

Stitching and Gluing

Construct your pockets, however you've decided they should be, and pin them in place. Try out your lining in the basket to see that they work the way you anticipated. You may want to make some changes before you sew them to the lining.

Adding the Pockets

Sew the sides of your pockets to the lining. Sew the bottoms, as well, if they don't extend to the base of the lining. If you expect your pockets to get lots of use, reinforce the seams. To do this, after you've stitched the pockets down, pin a length of twill tape or seam binding to the back along the stitching line and stitch again. Sew the side seam of your lining and press the seam open.

Stitched-on Bottom

If your basket tapers even slightly, take a round of stitches on the side piece ½" from the bottom to use to ease or gather the lining to fit. Pin the side lining to the edges of the bottom, using the marks that indicate the corners to help you place it correctly. If you are uncertain if your pockets are going to come out where you want them, do a quick hand basting around the edge of the bottom. This way, you can remove the pins and try the lining in your basket. When it is placed to your satisfaction, stitch the seam. Your lining is ready to glue in place.

FACT

You can also make linings for the tote bags described in Chapter 10. Instead of cutting a facing for the top, make a lining just barely smaller than the bag itself. Turn under the top edges of both. Put the lining inside the bag, and topstitch around the upper edge.

Glued-in Bottom

If your basket tapers a great deal or is otherwise odd shaped, you might want to glue in the bottom instead of trying to stitch it to the sides. To do this, use your pattern to cut a piece of heavy cardboard the exact shape of the bottom of your basket. Try it in your basket, and do any necessary trimming.

Mark the wrong side of your fabric using your cardboard as a template. If your basket bottom is not symmetrical, be sure to place your cardboard upside-down as well. Cut around your mark, adding ½" all the way around. Clip the curves to the mark, and turn the edges under. You can use the cardboard as a pressing guide, holding it in the center of the fabric piece and ironing the ends up over it.

Use fabric glue or a hot-glue gun to attach the seam allowance to the underside of the cardboard. You will glue this to the bottom of your basket after you've attached the sides.

ALERT!

Do not try to use regular household glues unless they are recommended specifically for fabric. Regular glues like those intended for paper or for ceramic will turn your fabric very hard. Some of them will discolor it as well.

Attaching the Lining

If the top edge of your basket is fairly level, press the top edge of your lining under ½". If the edge dips, you will have to do much of your turning under as you go.

Position your lining inside your basket. Glue the corners down first, then ease each side to fit. If you are gluing in the bottom, allow the top to dry. Then, glue the bottom edge of the sides to the basket bottom, gathering them to fit. Glue your bottom piece to the bottom of the basket, covering the raw edges of the sides.

Adding Trim

Trim of all kinds can be added to the top edge of your pockets before they are sewn onto the lining or around the side itself before it is glued in place. You can also attach a trim to the turned-under edge of your lining before you glue it to the basket. Sometimes trim can even solve problems that arise when you are installing the lining itself.

If the top edge of your basket is so uneven you can't turn your lining to fit, or if your turned edge shows through your basket's loose weave, cut the top edge instead. Trim it as near to the exact shape of the top of your basket as possible. In fact, you may want to glue it first and trim it when the glue dries.

Cover the raw edge with a round of flexible ribbon or ruffle with a finished edge. If you want to make your own ruffle, sew it to bias binding as described in Chapter 5 or gather it onto the wrong side of a ribbon.

You can cover the point where the ends of the ribbon or ruffle meet with a bow, a small embroidered appliqué, or other decoration.

Removable Lining

The lining of a basket, especially one without a lid, is going to get dusty. The nozzle attachment to your vacuum cleaner can clean up most of it, but there's nothing like being able to remove the lining and wash it. If you're lining a basket that will transport food or a sewing basket that will set out, consider one of these alternatives to gluing.

Self-Gripping Fasteners

This particular method works best if your basket top is level. You will also have to sew the bottom on, rather than gluing it, of course.

Get a strip of self-gripping fasteners long enough to encircle the entire top of your basket. Glue the hook, or stiff, half to your basket top. Don't put the hook half on your lining or everything in your wash will stick to it when you put it in the washer. You can sometimes find adhesive-backed fasteners that will save the trouble of gluing. You will still have to sew the half to the lining since the adhesive may not hold in the wash.

Turn the top edge of your lining under. Sew the soft half of the fastener to the lining, leaving a little of the folded edge above the fastener. This will help to hide the edge of the fastener itself. Sewing a round of ruffle to the top before you add the fastener will help even more.

Tied-on Lining

Another alternative is to make an extension to your lining that comes over the lip of your basket and ties on the outside. This method works best with baskets that have level tops. You can make your lining to accommodate handles and lids.

Make your lining in the usual way, sewing the bottom to the side piece. Measure the *outside* circumference of your basket. If you have a bow handle on your basket, you will cut two extensions and tie them together beneath the bases of the handle. If your basket has a lid, measure around the basket up to either side of the hinge. Add ½" on each side of your extension pieces for hems. Two side handles will be dealt with later; measure your extension as if they aren't there.

Determine how far you want your lining to extend down the outside of your basket. Add 1" for a bottom casing, ½" for a top seam allowance and a little more for the thickness of the basket itself.

Sew narrow hems on both ends of your extension(s). Sew the bottom edge in a hem that can be used as a casing. Make a row of gathering stitches across the top. With the lining in the basket, determine the placement of the ends of your extension piece(s). If your basket has no handles or hinges to worry about, the edges of your extension piece will meet at whatever location around the basket that looks best to you.

With right sides together, pin the extension(s) to the lining, gathering it to fit. Sew along the gathering stitches. Make a narrow hem with the seam allowance along any part of the lining edge that isn't covered by the extension. Run a ribbon, cord, or shoestring through the casing, and gather the lining extension to fit.

FACT

You can make a laundry bag to fit a tall wicker clothesbasket. Make it large enough that the top folds over the outside of the basket. Make a pocket on the outside of the bag so when you take it out of the basket to take to the laundry, you can have a place to keep your keys, coins, or even small soap boxes.

Accommodating Side Handles

If your basket has two side handles, you have a couple of choices. If the handles are squarely on the top edge of your basket, simply leave that stretch of the top unsewn. Backstitch on either side of the gaps so the seam doesn't open up father. Press the seam open, and topstitch on either side of the gap. This will help the seam allowance lie flat, and the raw edges will be hidden.

If your basket is fairly thick and the handles are narrow, as is the case in bushel baskets, the handles may seem to be more under the extension than at the seam. In this case, mark their exact location with chalk or pins after the extension has been added. Cut along this line and then edge the cut with narrow double fold bias tape.

Another way to finish the edge for the opening is to make a lining square 2" longer than the handles and about 2" wide. Turn under the edge, and stitch it. Put the lining piece on the marked location for the cut, and sew ¼" on either side of the line and at each end, making a box. Cut the slit, and clip to the corners. Turn the lining through this hole and press it flat. Topstitch it to keep it in place.

If your basket is very big around, you might want to make your extension in two pieces simply to make it easier to pull the ties up around it. Hem both ends of both, and bring the ends together when you sew them to the lining.

Lining the Lid

Lids of baskets are often lined in a fashion similar to the glued-on bottom. This works fine, but a few little additions can make your lid more fun.

If you are lining a sewing basket, consider adding a pincushion to the lid. The entire lid can be made into a pincushion with a couple of layers of batting, or you might designate a small area for one.

To make the latter, pin a backing piece to the back of the lid lining and machine-stitch around the area you want for a pincushion. This might be a single motif of your lining fabric or a circle or a square. Make a small cut through the backing fabric and stuff with pillow stuffing. Finish as you would a glued-on bottom.

You can put pockets on the lid before you glue it to the cardboard, but don't plan to use them for anything but fairly light objects or they will pull the lining off. Adding ribbons to use to tie on a small pair of thread scissors is another suggestion.

Instead of using cardboard, the lining can be glued directly to the lid. If it's hard to get the edges turned correctly, cut the seam allowance off and glue the fabric directly. Or you might edge the piece with bias tape or sew a ribbon or ruffle around it. You can cover the edge with ribbon or ruffle after it's glued down, if you'd rather. Be sure your trim doesn't interfere when you close the lid.

Pincushion Basket

A variation on the lined basket is a pincushion made from a small basket. This is quick and easy, and it makes a perfect companion to the lined sewing basket.

You will need a small basket without a handle. Take one measurement of the distance across the top, down one side, across the bottom, up the other side, and across the top again. This will give you the diameter of the circle you'll need to cut to make the cushion. This circle doesn't have to be perfect. You can cut a square, fold it into fourths, and round off the four corners at once.

With a double thickness of thread, make running stitches all around the outside of the circle, close to the edge but not so close they will pull out. Gather the circle into a bag as you sew. Fill the bag with stuffing, packed as tightly as possible. Pull up the threads to close the bag, and tie them securely.

Push your little ball into the basket, gathered side down. You may want to glue your cushion into the basket or leave as it is. If you've had to remove handles on your basket, cover the stumps by gluing ribbon or lace or a round of each on the top edge of the basket. You may want to match the trim to your sewing basket. Cover the ends of your trim with a small bow or appliqué flower. Ⓔ

Chapter 13

Hanging Caddies

Hanging caddies can be used to keep supplies close at hand—like diapering supplies near a crib, shoes off the closet floor, or supplies together like gift wrap, craft supplies, or vacuum-cleaner attachments. A flat-pocket version can be used to sort mail or display greeting cards. They can be made to hang from rods, dowels, clothes hangers, or from straps to a rail.

Planning for Specific Uses

Your hanging caddy will store everything you expect it to, but only if you design it carefully. Begin by gathering together the things you hope to store in your caddy.

Decisions about Pockets

While you are taking inventory of the supplies you intend to store, consider the size of different items. The pockets on your caddy will be constructed in rows, and each pocket in a row will be of equal depth. They can be of different widths. Some can also be pleated for extra room while others can be flat, but the depth of all the pockets within a row will be the same.

Get very specific in your list of what pockets you'll need. Include space for items you don't currently have on hand. Consider putting really long items, such as rolls of wrapping paper or knitting needles, in pockets on the back of your caddy.

Decisions about Hanging

You can design your caddy to hang from a peg, a hook, or a clothes hanger. This is great for closet storage. You can choose a hanger with a rotating hook. A wooden coat hanger is less likely to break than plastic, but the curve designed for suit coats might not be what you want for your caddy. A hanger will limit the width of your caddy.

For caddies that will be heavy when they're full, it's a good idea to design the top to hold a rod supported on three hooks. To do this, plan to extend your top an extra 4". Later, you will cut a half circle about 6" across and 3" deep from the center of your top. The top 2" will be turned to the back and stitched, forming a casing with an opening for a center support.

For caddies that will have a permanent place on the wall, you can equip them with a sleeve on the back to hold a hidden dowel or a decorative curtain rod.

Another option is to put straps on the top of your caddy and equip the ends with fasteners that will snap or otherwise fasten to the caddy.

This will allow you to hang your caddy from some chair armrests, bedsteads, or crib railings. The fasteners can be on the back to be out of sight or in front to make the caddy easier to attach. Consider sewing decorative buttons on the front.

FACT

If you make your caddy with a clothes hanger for a top, it will be just the right size to cover with the plastic you get from the dry cleaners. This will keep wrapping paper and other supplies that aren't used often from getting dusty. Be sure the bag is *always* out of the reach of children.

Decisions about Design

Once you have decided how you will hang your caddy and what pockets you'll need, it's time to figure out your overall design. Generally, it's better to put the smallest pockets in the top row, progressing downward to the largest at the bottom. Use the dimensions in your inventory to determine what you'll want for each row of pockets. This will determine the overall dimensions of your caddy. A diagram will help you as you start actually constructing your caddy. Draw one as you plan, complete with dimensions of each pocket and how far apart you want the rows. Note which pockets will need to be pleated and how large these pleats should be.

Once you've decided on the layout of your caddy you need to think about fabrics. The weight of all the contents will determine how heavy your fabric should be. Corduroy for the hanging frame and lighter-weight cotton for the pockets might be perfect for gift wrap. Canvas or denim would be better for holding shoes. Prequilted fabric would work for greeting cards or baby supplies. Coordinating unquilted fabric could be used on the pockets.

Pattern and Pieces

Nearly all of the pieces of your hanging caddy will be cut by measuring and will not require a pattern. The one exception, if you are using a clothes hanger to hang your caddy, is the shape of the top.

Hanger Pattern

On brown wrapping paper or other pattern material, trace the sloping shoulders of your hanger. Indicate the placement of the hook. Add ½" around the slope if you've chosen a wooden or thick plastic hanger, ¼" for a wire hanger. From the end of the shoulders, draw straight lines downward the length of your caddy. Add ½" seam allowances all around.

Cutting the Pieces

Your plan should make it easy to cut your pieces. Remember to allow ½" seam allowances on all pieces. Begin with the front and back pieces. These should be exactly the same size, though they don't necessarily need to be of the same fabric.

You will cut each row of pockets in one long strip. You can cut your pockets twice as wide as the depth you want for the finished pocket, and then fold them in half. Or you can cut two pieces, for the outside and inside, sew the tops together, and turn them. A third option is to make your pockets out of a single layer of cloth and hem the top. Your decision will determine the width of the strips you cut for your pockets.

The length of the pocket strip will be the width of your caddy frame, plus whatever you need to add for pleats. Adding 2" to a pocket would mean that when your caddy is finished, you could flatten your pocket against the frame and hold a pinch of fabric that would be 1" deep. Use your fabric to help you visualize what you'll want to add.

If you design a caddy to hang from the front of a walker, be sure it is small and only used for fairly lightweight objects. Heavy objects could make the walker front-heavy and cause it to tip over.

If you are hanging your caddy from a dowel, you will need to cut a sleeve or casing. If you are using a ½" dowel, cut a strip 3" wide and plan to fold it in half for the casing. Cut it 2" shorter than the caddy's width if you want to hide the dowel.

If you are making fastening ties for the top of a detachable caddy, cut them twice the width you'll want for the finished ties, plus ½". You can cut one strip, fold it in half and stitch ¼" seam, turn, press, and cut it into your individual ties afterward.

Pockets and Trim

Now that you've decided how you are going to make your pockets and cut out the strips, go ahead and prepare them. Hem the top, fold them in half or sew them to a lining piece, turn, and press. The sides and bottom of your strip are still raw edges at this point.

Marking the Pockets

Carefully measure and mark off each pocket. Be sure to leave ½" at each end for the seam allowance. Flat pockets are easy. Simply mark where the stitches will divide the strip into separate pockets.

For pockets with pleats, there should be marks to indicate the pleats at the sides of each pocket. Fold the pleats in, and pin them at the lower edge. Be sure one pocket doesn't overlap with another. You will need to be able to stitch the pocket to the caddy front between the pleats of two side-by-side pockets. Test your row of pockets to be sure it fits your caddy. Adjust your pleats if you need to.

Sew across the pleats ½" from the raw edge. On all pockets except those that will be on the bottom row, zigzag stitch along the edge of the seam allowance. This will keep the edges from fraying. This edge will end up inside the pockets when you're done, and you don't want loose threads catching on the contents of the pockets.

Adding Optional Appliqué and Edging

You may want to decorate your caddy to reflect what you use it for or simply to make it more fun. The area in front of the hanger or above the top row of pockets lends itself to decoration. Remember to take the seam allowance and the contents of the upper pockets into account as you design your appliqué. Sew your appliqué onto the front frame before you sew the pockets on so there is less fabric to struggle with.

Another decorating possibility is some sort of edging on the pockets. A side benefit of this trim is that it adds a little stiffening and shaping to the pockets. A baby's caddy might look great with a narrow row of ruffles, either sewn on the back to stand above the pocket or sewn near the top edge and pointing downward. Rickrack can be sewn to the back of the pocket edge so only the top half shows, adding some decoration without becoming too frilly. Double-fold bias tape caught over the edge will add color as well.

ALERT!

Don't try to finish the top edge of your pockets with bias binding alone. After items are pulled out of the pockets several times the bias binding is likely to pull away, fraying the single layer of cloth in the process.

Attaching the Pockets

With your pockets pleated and trimmed and appliqués sewn in place, you're ready to sew your caddy together. Begin by attaching the pockets.

Your bottom pockets will line up with the raw edge of the front frame piece, but the location of the others needs to be marked. Draw a line on your frame ½" *above* the point where you want the bottom of your pocket to be. This will make it easier to get your pockets just where you want them. Measure from both ends of your line to the bottom or top of the frame to be sure your lines are straight.

Pin your pocket strips to the front frame, right sides together, so they line up the bottom edge of the pocket with the marked line. Sew across the pockets at the ½" stitching line that formed the pleats. Stitch again close to the zigzag stitched edge.

Fold the pocket row up, and press the seam. Sew along the side edges and sew between the separate pockets. Be sure to backstitch to reinforce the stitching at the top of the pockets. If you want, you can reinforce the stitching further with seam binding (as described in Chapter 12).

Sew the bottom row of pockets into place along the bottom and side edges. Sew between these pockets the same as you did the upper ones. If you are adding pockets to the back, sew them to the back frame in a similar manner.

Attachments for Hanging

If you are planning to hang your caddy from a rod suspended from three hooks, or if you are using a clothes hanger, you will be finishing your attachments later. Sleeves or ties that will be used for hanging your caddy should be added now.

Sleeve for a Dowel

There are any number of ways to attach a sleeve to the back of a hanging. Often these are sewn on by hand later. However, here is one suggestion for a sturdier sleeve.

Begin by folding your 3" wide strip in half the long way, with right sides together. Sew across the ends. Clip the corner at the fold, and turn it right side out. Fold and press the whole strip in half the long way to make a 1½" wide, double-thickness strip with finished ends. On the frame back, measure down from the top 1¼" and mark a straight line across the fabric there. Center your sleeve *above* this line with the raw edge lined up with it. This is sort of an upside-down version of the way you attached the pockets. Make sure the ends are within the side seam allowances.

If you are concerned that your caddy will want to sag or curl at the bottom when the pockets are full, you can add a second sleeve for a dowel at the bottom of your caddy. Attach it very close to the bottom seam allowance.

Sew the strip to the frame ¼" from the raw edge. You might want to reinforce this seam with twill tape or seam binding on the back. Turn the sleeve downward and press. Topstitch close to the lower edge of the sleeve.

Detachable Caddy Ties

If you want to be able to attach your caddy to something like a crib rail, you can add your ties to the frame on top of the pockets.

Turn under one end of each of the ties. Blind-stitch or topstitch them closed. If you are using self-gripping fasteners, put 1" or 2" of the stiff, or hook, half onto the finished ends of each tie. If you plan to attach your caddy with buttons, center a buttonhole in one end of each. Refer to your sewing machine manual for specific instructions.

Evenly space your ties across the top of your frame front, remembering to allow for the side seam allowances. Line the unfinished end of your ties up with the raw edge of the top of the frame. The self-gripping fastener should be lying face up on the frame. Sew across the ties ½" from the raw edge.

Add the other half of the fasteners to the back so they are spaced to match the ties.

QUESTION?

What if my machine doesn't have a buttonhole attachment?
Draw a line the length of your button's diameter. Work zigzag stitches along one side of the line. Widen the stitches to go across the end. Pivot and return to narrow stitches for the other side and repeat at the other end. Cut the buttonhole between the rows of stitches.

Putting Front and Back Together

There are two ways of putting the caddy frame together. One is to pin the front and back right sides together then sew around the edge like you would a pillow, leaving a gap to turn it right side out. This method is recommended for the detachable caddy and any other made with relatively lightweight fabrics. If you are using a clothes hanger, leave a gap near the top that's large enough to insert your hanger. If you plan to suspend your caddy on three hooks, leave the entire top open.

The other method, which is recommended for heavier fabrics that aren't going to turn easily, is to layer the front and back *wrong* sides together and sew around the edge. You will cover the raw edge with seam binding afterward.

If you choose this method for a detachable caddy, the ties will have to be sewn to the back after the edges are finished, though the soft half of the fasteners can still be sewn to the back in advance. Begin stitching on the clothes-hanger type at the center top, leaving space for the hanger hook. Just before you are ready to sew the other shoulder, slip the hanger between the layers, holding it out of the way of the presser foot but with the hook remaining outside.

FACT

If you are using the turned method to put your caddy together, you can add piping or ruffles to the edge. Sew them to the front of your frame before you attach it to the back.

Binding the Edges

If you've sewn your frame together with the wrong sides against each other, you will need to cover the raw edge with bias binding. You will probably want the extra-wide double-fold type.

Getting Started

Open out the center fold of the binding. You will be sewing one edge onto the back of your frame first. If you are binding a clothes-hanger type caddy, fold under one end of the binding and begin your stitching at the top next to the hole. You will not bind the top of the three-hook style caddy. You can begin binding it at the top of one side and, since you will be turning the entire top over later, there's no need to turn the binding under.

On a rectangular caddy, you will be sewing all the way around and ending with the binding overlapping where you began. There's no need to turn the beginning edge under for this type either. You'll do that with the end when you finish. Begin somewhere along the bottom edge.

Stitching

With the back of your caddy facing you and the binding right side up, line the edge of the binding up with the stitching. Stitch close to the edge of the binding. Since you will not want to round off the corners of your caddy, you should miter the corners. This will make them square and neat.

FIGURE 13-1

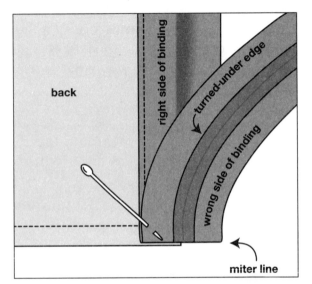

◀ **Mitered bias corner:** Pin the binding at the stitching line.

FIGURE 13-2

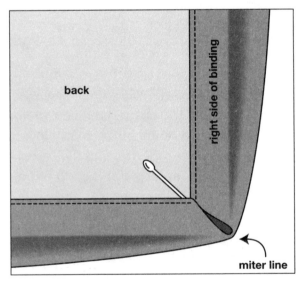

◀ **Mitered bias corner:** Fold the binding over the pin and stitch.

Refer to **FIGURE 13-1** and **FIGURE 13-2**, and follow these steps:

1. Sew along the edge of the binding clear to the edge of the caddy.
2. Cut the thread, and remove the caddy from the machine.
3. Fold the binding up with the fold on the fabric edge.
4. Pin the binding at the stitching line for the second side, as in **FIGURE 13-1**.
5. Fold the binding diagonally over the pin.
6. Line the edge up with the stitching line.
7. Sew the binding to the second side close to the edge.

When you get to the end, trim off the excess binding. Turn under the edge at the hanger hole or at the point where the binding overlaps. On the three-hook style, you'll only cover three sides and make two mitered corners. Cut the binding even with the top edge.

Turn your caddy over, and bring the binding to the front. Sew it down, covering the earlier stitching as much as possible. Try to stitch on the binding on the back as well. When you come to a corner, the binding will easily fold into a nice miter shape and you can pivot to the next side.

Final Details

Your caddy is nearly done. The gap in the turned styles will need to be blind-stitched closed. Buttons need to be added to a detachable style caddy, if that's how you're fastening it. The raw edge at the very top of the clothes-hanger style could be turned under and hand-stitched down.

Topstitching

The front and back pieces of your caddy frame are only connected around the edges. When the pockets are full, these two layers are likely to sag farther apart. Some topstitching is a good idea. A row directly under the pockets might be all that is necessary. For heavier loads, you might want to stitch over the lines that separate the pockets.

ALERT!

If you've put pockets on the back, you need to be very careful where you topstitch. You can try hand-sewing along safe lines in the back and inside the front pockets. Tacking them together—that is, taking a few looping stitches on top of each other at a few places—might solve the problem.

Finishing the Three-Hook Style

The top of the heavy-duty three-hook style caddy still needs to be finished. Begin by making a pattern for a circle with a diameter of 6". Identify the exact center of the top of your caddy, and mark 3" on either side of it. Fold your pattern in half, and use it to mark a semicircle on the top of your caddy.

Making sure both layers are smooth, stitch ¼" outside the circle. Cut out the circle on the marked line. Cover the raw edge with seam binding. Fold both sides of the top edge under 2". Turn the raw edge under ½". Sew across these two hem/casings close to the edge.

Your caddy is now ready for you to hang it and fill all those pockets with your supplies.

Chapter 14

"Welcome Spring" Wall Hanging

Quilting is a popular hobby, and small, decorative wall hangings are among the favorite quilting projects. They are easier to handle than full-sized quilts and do not require nearly the commitment of time or energy. This cheerful hanging, which will let you try your hand at piecing, is made mostly from scraps and will measure approximately 24" by 28" when completed.

Reading the Pattern

Often a quilt pattern will be simply lines on a grid, like the tulip and butterfly patterns illustrated in this chapter. The numbers, added here to indicate the order of piecing, are not present on most patterns. The piecing order is left to the quilter to determine.

FIGURE 14-1

◀ Wall hanging.

Small sections of a quilt, like this tulip and butterfly, are called blocks. The individual pieces that make up the block are sometimes called patches. Each block in a quilt may be made from the same pattern, which creates its own design as it repeats across the front, or cover, of the quilt. The blocks may also be separated by strips of cloth, which are called panels or sashing.

FIGURE 14-2

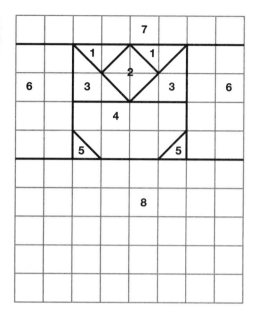

◀ Tulip pattern.

FIGURE 14-3

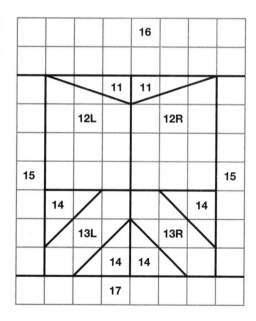

◀ Butterfly pattern.

Each square on the grid in **FIGURE 14-2** indicates 1 square inch. Piece #6, for example, will be cut 2½" by 4½". The extra ½" is the ¼" seam allowance added all around. But what about piece #2? You could use trigonometry to figure out its size, but the most accurate way to piece the tulip top is to cut all the triangles as full squares and stitch across the diagonal. This means piece #2 will actually be cut as if it were a 4" by 2" rectangle plus the seam allowances.

Similarly, the #13 pieces on the butterfly in **FIGURE 14-3** are cut 3½" by 3½", and all four #14 pieces are 2½" by 2½". Piece #11 is cut 1½" by 3½". This may seem confusing now, but it will become clear when you begin to sew the pieces together.

Planning the Message Blocks

Your wall hanging doesn't have to say "Welcome Spring." It can announce your name or any other message you want to share. You can make three tulips for the bottom row and have only one message panel if you like.

When you've decided on your message, you must decide how you want to write it. Hand embroidery, machine embroidery, or even appliqué are possibilities, as are fabric paints. Draw out your letters to determine the size of your blocks. You may want to add something else to the message block, such as dotting the "i" in "Spring" with a honeybee. This can also be appliquéd or embroidered.

Cutting the Pieces

Choose a white, blue, or pale green for your background fabric. The tulip and butterfly backgrounds need not be the same. You will also need background fabric for the message blocks, as well as batting and backing.

Cutting Pieces for the Tulip

Label your pieces as you cut them out with paper pinned to each piece, or lay them out like a puzzle. Taking the time now to keep things straight will save some confusion later. The numbers on the pattern will help you keep them in order. Choose two shades of red or yellow for the tulip and measure carefully. Cut the following pieces:

1. Two background pieces 2½" by 2½"
2. One darker tulip piece 4½" by 2½"
3. Two lighter tulip pieces 2½" by 2½"
4. One lighter tulip piece 4½" by 2½"
5. Two background pieces 1½" by 1½"
6. Two background pieces 2½" by 4½"
7. One background piece 8½" by 1½"
8. One background piece 8½" by 5½"

You will also need about 2' of green ribbon between ½" and 1" wide for the stem and leaves.

Cutting all these small pieces will be much easier with an acrylic ruler and a rotary cutter. Your pieces will be cut more accurately and therefore sew together more neatly. Consider investing in these tools, along with the necessary cutting mat, if you plan to do much quilting.

Cutting Pieces for the Butterfly

The butterfly pieces are also cut by measure. Choose a colorful fabric, perhaps a paisley or a Bali or batik print. Cut your pieces in the following sizes:

1. Two background pieces 3½" by 1½"
2. Two butterfly pieces 3½" by 4½"
3. Two butterfly pieces 3½" by 3½"
4. Four background pieces 2½" by 2½"
5. Two background pieces 1½" by 7½"
6. One background piece 8½" by 2½"
7. One background piece 8½" by 1½"

You will also need 7½" of ribbon for the butterfly's body. You can go with a traditional brown or black or choose a color from your fabric you want to emphasize.

Cutting the Rest

You will need two neutral or pale-colored pieces for the message blocks on your hanging. These will need to be 10½" high and whatever width you have determined. The sample wall hanging illustrated at the beginning of this chapter uses message blocks that measure approximately twice as wide as the pieced blocks, or about 16" finished.

You will need strips of cloth to use as the border of your hanging; 2½" wide is a suggestion. If your message blocks are 16" wide, you will need a strip about 8' long. Don't cut it the exact length for the sides, simply cut 2½" strips and piece them together until it is 8' long.

You will also need a piece of quilt batting and fabric for a backing somewhat larger than the finished hanging will be. Choose regular or low-loft batting. The extra-high loft will be too thick to quilt easily.

Piecing the Tulip

Piecing the tulip entirely from rectangles sounds more complicated than it actually is. Just take the steps one at a time, and the logic will become clear. It's less difficult than trying to cut the triangles while leaving enough room for seam allowances. You're also more likely to stretch a triangle when you sew across the bias.

FIGURE 14-4

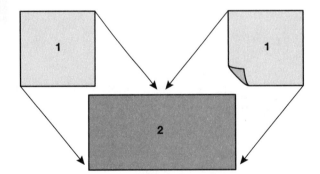

◄ **Squares to triangles:** Place the background squares on the tulip center rectangle, matching the outside corners.

FIGURE 14-5

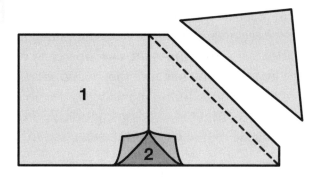

◀ **Squares to triangles:**
Stitch on the diagonal across the squares as shown and trim to a ¼" seam allowance.

FIGURE 14-6

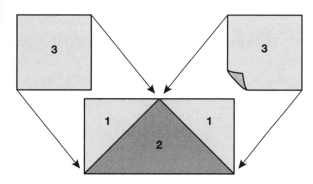

◀ **Squares to triangles:**
Place the tulip petal squares on the pieced rectangle, matching the outside corners.

FIGURE 14-7

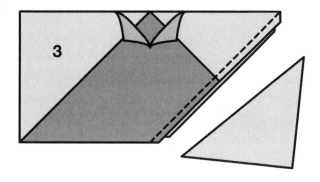

◀ **Squares to triangles:**
Stitch on the diagonal shown and trim to ¼" seam allowance.

The Tulip Top

Begin with background pieces #1 and tulip piece #2. Place one of the #1 squares on top of the #2 rectangle, right sides together, lining up the top, bottom, and outer sides, as shown in **FIGURE 14-4**. You can't actually do both the #1 pieces at the same time because they will overlap.

Sew diagonally across the #1 piece from the inside top to the outside bottom, as shown in **FIGURE 14-5**. Trim the upper corner off ¼" from the seam. Fold the remaining triangle out, and press the seam toward the darker fabric.

Repeat with the other #1 piece on the other side of the #2 piece. This seam will cross the previous seam. The point where the two rows of stitching cross should be ¼" from the top edge. When the #7 piece is sewn across the top later, it will put this point exactly on the seam line as shown in the pattern diagram.

Next, add the outside petal pieces labeled #3, as illustrated in **FIGURE 14-6**. Sew these pieces on the same way as you did the #1 pieces. In this case, the seams will cross from the upper outside corner to the lower inside corner of the petal squares (as shown in **FIGURE 14-7**). Trim, and press the seam allowances toward the #3 pieces.

ALERT!

Mark the diagonal on these pieces with a ruler and pencil or tailor's chalk before you try to stitch them to be sure your seams are straight. If your pieces are not straight, your block will not lie flat when it is finished.

The Tulip Bottom

Add the two #5 background pieces to the large tulip piece #4. These are simply pinned to the lower corners (as shown in **FIGURE 14-8**) and stitched as shown in **FIGURE 14-9**. Trim, open, and press the seam allowances toward the darker fabric.

Sew the two tulip pieces together and press the seam allowances toward the #4 piece.

FIGURE 14-8

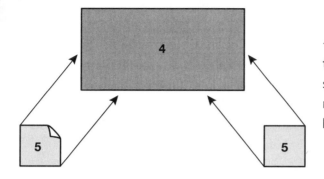

◀ **Corner triangles:** Place the small background squares over the tulip body rectangle, matching the lower corners.

FIGURE 14-9

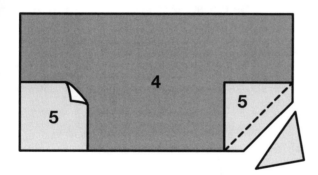

◀ **Corner triangles:** Stitch on the diagonal shown, and trim to ¼" seam allowance.

Adding the Background

The tulip flower itself is pieced, and all that remains of the piecing is to add the background. Sew the #6 pieces on either side of the tulip. Press the seams toward the background. The bulk of the fabric at the seams of the flower will be flatter that way. If it looks as if the tulip fabric might show through to the front, trim the seam allowance of the tulip fabric slightly shorter than the background seam allowance.

Add piece #7 to the top and press the seam allowance toward it.

Before you add piece #8, sew the ribbon stem to it. Determine the vertical center of piece #8 by folding it exactly in half and pressing a crease down the center. Run a piece of your ribbon along this line from raw edge to raw edge.

Sew the ribbon down by stitching close to each edge. If you stitch in the same direction on both sides of the ribbon it will lie flatter. Sewing down one side and up the other will likely result in diagonal wrinkles along the ribbon because it will stretch or slide slightly as you sew.

Add more ribbon diagonally from the base of the stem outward for leaves.

Piecing the Butterfly

Most of the butterfly is pieced much like the tulip. The exception is the way the #11 triangles are sewn onto the #12 butterfly pieces. Begin by drawing the diagonal stitching lines across the back of the two #11 pieces. One must be marked from lower left to upper right and the other from upper left to lower right. Mark the points on these lines where they would cross the ¼" seams.

On the back of the #12 pieces, mark the points where the side seam allowances would cross the top. Mark 1" below this top mark along the inside or center seam allowances. With right sides together, lay the #11 pieces on top of the #12 pieces, as shown in **FIGURE 14-10**. Using a pin through both layers of fabric, match the corner marks on the outside corner and the corner of #11. Place the mark 1" below the corner on #12, as shown in **FIGURE 14-11**. Stitch across the diagonal stitching line. Fold #11 up to be sure it matches the top of #12. Trim ¼" from the seam, and press the seam allowance toward the butterfly (see **FIGURE 14-12**). With right sides together, match the seams and sew the left and right butterfly wing pieces together.

The bottom of the butterfly is made the same way as the tapers at the bottom of the tulip. Refer to **FIGURE 14-13**. Put the #14 background squares at the appropriate corners of the left and right #13 butterfly pieces, right sides together, and sew diagonally across the smaller squares. Press the seam allowances toward the butterfly. Sew the two squares together, matching the seams.

FIGURE 14-10

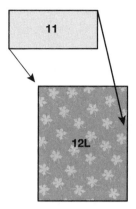 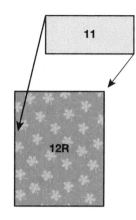

◀ **Rectangles to triangles:** Place the background rectangles on the butterfly wing pieces.

FIGURE 14-11

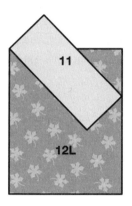 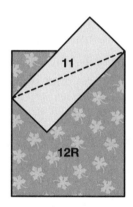

◀ **Rectangles to triangles:** Rotate the background rectangles and stitch on the diagonal.

FIGURE 14-12

 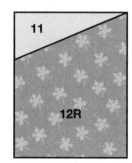

◀ **Rectangles to triangles:** Trim to ¼" seam allowance, and press.

FIGURE 14-13

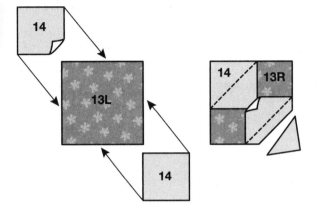

◀ **Corner triangles:** Place two background squares over each of the lower butterfly squares as shown. Stitch, and trim.

Sew the two halves of the butterfly together, and press the seam allowance toward the butterfly wings. Sew the body ribbon down the center of the butterfly. Add the two #15 background pieces, press the seams, and add #16 and #17. You might use the stem stitch described in Chapter 8 to embroider antennae on your butterfly.

Learning Reverse Appliqué

If you have decided to appliqué "Welcome" or some other message on one of your blocks, consider using reverse appliqué. The letters will actually be cut out of the background block with the appliqué fabric showing through from the back. The advantage is much neater lettering when you're done.

Mark, Stitch, and Trim

Begin by drawing your letters on the background piece. Your drawing needs to indicate the width of each line or curve of each letter as if you were cutting them out to appliqué. Remember the seams will take ¼" all around the piece.

Cut your appliqué fabric large enough to cover all the letters of your message. Pin-baste it to the background piece, with the right side of the appliqué fabric against the wrong side of the background fabric. A row of basting stitches through the letters will help keep your layers from shifting.

Zigzag-stitch just outside your drawn letters. The stitches should be fairly wide and close together.

Carefully cut the letters out of the background fabric. You don't want to cut the appliqué fabric, so short-bladed thread scissors might be the safest to use. If your appliqué fabric shows through the lighter background fabric between the letters, cut it away close to the zigzag stitching.

QUESTION?

How do you determine the direction in which to press the seam allowances?
The first rule is to press toward the darker fabric. The second is to press away from earlier seams. Sometimes, however, following one rule means you have to break the other. If that's the case, go with whatever will make the quilt cover lie flat, and trim any dark seam allowance that threatens to show through.

Some Alternatives

If you want your letters on top, draw them on your appliqué fabric and place this on top of your background fabric. The trick will be centering them unless you match your appliqué fabric to the size and shape of the background. Stitch around all the letters and cut away the excess. This is probably the easiest method for you to use for your honeybee, too. Stem-stitch the little wings after you've trimmed around the body.

If you want each of your letters to be of different fabrics, mark them on fabric scraps cut a few inches larger than the letters. Stitch, and then trim around them one at a time. The problem, again, is going to be placing them precisely on the background.

Another suggestion is to use some type of double-sided fabric bond. This will keep the letters stiff and in place while you stitch them.

What you *don't* want to do is simply to cut all those little letters out first and stitch around them. It will be nearly impossible to keep from stretching or twisting them while you stitch. If you have to redo even a small portion of your stitching, the fabric will fray apart. Backing the letters with fusible interfacing before you cut them out will help, but it won't entirely eliminate the problem.

Assembling and Quilting

With all your blocks finished, it's time to put the whole thing together. In quilter's language, putting the blocks together is called "setting your quilt." When it's all put together, this top piece is called a quilt top or cover. Sew the blocks together in rows. Press the seams, and sew the rows together. Press that center seam as well.

Attaching the Border

Next you need to sew on the border. With the border strip in your lap, begin with the bottom edge of your quilt cover. Sew the border strip on, and trim it even with the edge of the cover. Repeat the process with the top of your quilt.

Stop and press these two seams, then add the border to the sides of your quilt.

Marking Your Quilt

If you want to do any quilting that doesn't follow the seams or appliqué, you will need to mark it now. One suggestion is to stitch diagonally over the background, up to the letters, tulip, and butterfly. This type of stitching will help tie the quilt together visually, especially if the background fabrics are not the same in all the blocks.

Quilt batting is wrinkled when it comes out of the plastic bag. Spread it out a day before you intend to use it. Spray it with a bit of water and pat it out as flat as possible, and let it dry overnight.

An acrylic ruler is the best thing to use to mark these lines, since they have diagonal lines printed on them that you can line up with the edges of your quilt cover. With care, you can mark your diagonal lines with a yardstick. Make these lines anywhere from 1" to 4" apart—whatever looks good to you. Closer quilt lines will make the butterfly and tulip puff out more because the rest of the hanging will be flatter.

Consider marking matching lines across the other diagonal, forming a hatchwork design. You might want to end the lines at the seams of the border or continue to the edge.

Layering and Quilting

Smooth your backing fabric out on a flat surface, right side down. Spread the batting over it, and smooth the cover, right side up on top of that. Beginning in the center, pin the layers together at about 6" intervals. Flip the quilt over and see if the backing is smooth between the pins. Make any necessary adjustments.

Baste the layers together by hand. Again, it is best to start in the center and work outward toward the corners and the sides. Check the back again to be sure all the layers are smooth.

If you have a walking foot for your sewing machine, you can machine-quilt your wall hanging. Try to keep all the layers smooth as you quilt. Begin near the center, and work outward as much as possible. Stop stitching next to the butterfly and tulip, and resume stitching on the other side of them to avoid stitching across these figures. Stitch around them, either in the ditch, which means exactly on the seam, or stitch ¼" outside the figures.

You can hand-quilt your hanging if you would rather. Hand-quilting is properly done with a short needle called a between and quilting thread, which is stronger than regular thread and less likely to tangle. There are quilting hoops the size of embroidery hoops that will make it possible to hold your quilt flat while you sew. Make your stitches as small and straight as possible, or look for instructions on rocking the needle to quilt the traditional way.

When you have finished quilting your wall hanging, sew around the edges at about ¼". Trim away the excess batting and backing. If the sides seem uneven, trim them straighter using a ruler to mark a straight edge.

Preparing for Hanging

Generally wall hangings of this type are hung from a dowel and two level nails on the wall. The dowel is cut slightly shorter than the width of the hanging and the nails are concealed behind the hanging. If you sew your sleeve onto the back of your hanging before you bind the edge, it saves you some hand-stitching later.

Cut a sleeve about 2" wide and about 2" shorter than the width of your hanging. Fold it in half the long way, with right sides together. Sew across the ends, clip the corners, turn, and press.

Line the raw edges of the sleeve up with the raw edges of the top of your hanging. Be sure the sleeve is centered on the back of the hanging. Sew ¼" from this edge.

Let the folded edge fall naturally below this seam. Sew the fold of the sleeve by hand to the back of your hanging, carefully stitching through only the backing fabric so these stitches don't show through to the front.

Folded Binding

You can bind your wall hanging with double-fold bias tape, as described in Chapter 13. A much cheaper alternative is to make your own binding. Since you are not trying to bind around any curves, your binding doesn't need to be cut on the bias.

Making Your Binding

Cut your binding strips 2" wide across the total length of your fabric. You will only need three such strips from fabric 42" wide to bind your wall hanging.

Sew the strips together. To spread the bulk of these seams across a wider area, make the seams on the bias. To do this, place the ends of two of your strips together, with right sides facing. Instead of putting them directly on top of each other, move the top strip to form a right angle with the other. Sew diagonally across the ends. Trim, and press the seam open.

Press the raw edge of one end of your binding strip under ¼". Fold the binding in half the long way, wrong sides together, and press along the length.

ALERT!

While mathematically you will only need 6" of fabric to make your binding, you should still buy ¼ rather than ⅙ yard. By the time you have trimmed the ends straight, you will likely have less than 6" and will have to cut your strips narrower than 2".

Attaching the Binding

With the wrong side of your quilt facing you, find one of the border seams along the bottom of the quilt. Line up the folded end of your binding with this seam. This will make your joining point in the binding less noticeable. With the raw edges of the binding along the raw edge of the quilt, sew just over ¼" from the edge. When you come to the end of one side, stitch to the edge of the quilt and cut the thread, removing the quilt from the sewing machine.

Fold your binding over the stitching as if you were going to wrap it around the edge of your quilt. At the end of the stitching, fold the binding upward, much like you would to miter a corner with regular binding. Refer to **FIGURE 13-1**.

Don't pin the binding at this point, however. Simply fold it up, then fold it at an angle to position it along the raw edge of the second side. Your purpose in all this folding is to allow for enough binding to create a neat mitered corner. When you have the binding in a stitching position again, pin it near the previous side.

Begin stitching the second side by backstitching up to the pin. Continue on along the second side. The corner is not complete, but you'll take care of it later. Repeat the process at each corner. Just before you've gone all the way around your quilt, trim the binding to allow for a ¼" fold to the inside. Match the binding up with the beginning.

Finishing the Binding

Turn the quilt over, and wrap the folded edge of the binding around the edge of the quilt. If you extend the folded edge just barely over the stitching line and stitch close to that edge, your stitching should be on the binding on the back of the quilt as well. When you come close to a corner, see that the binding on both the front and the back have even diagonal folds. Stitch up to the point where they meet, and pivot on the needle to stitch the next side. After you've finished, blind-stitch the seam binding together where the two ends meet.

If you want a more perfect binding and you enjoy hand sewing, follow these same steps, except machine-sew the binding to the *front* of your quilt. Blind-stitch the binding to the back. At the corners, poke the needle through to the front, and finish stitching the corner there.

Now you know all the basics for making a full-sized quilt.

Chapter 15

Making a Simple Dress from a Pattern

Many people are afraid to try garment construction. They may worry that it's complicated or that the garment won't fit. Expense, too, may enter in. Patterns aren't cheap, and 4 or 5 yards of fabric to make a dress is considerably more than half a yard to make a tote bag. Try it once, however, and you may decide that making exactly what you want is worth the extra expense.

Choosing a Pattern

For your first try at sewing with a pattern, choose something simple. A dress with no waistline, sleeves, or collar is ideal. Look for a pattern that pictures a dress that gets its shape from vertical seams or from darts. If you don't like sleeveless dresses, choose a jumper you can wear over a T-shirt or blouse, or choose a pattern with cap sleeves. This means the sleeves are part of the dress's body piece rather than cut separately and set in. If you're having trouble telling from the picture how the sleeves are made, check the back of the pattern envelope. There is usually a line drawing of the back of the pattern that shows every seam.

You might want to look specifically for a dress pattern that includes several styles so you can use the pattern again and again without feeling like you're filling your closet with duplicates of the same dress. If you're worried, look for patterns marked as "Easy." These are often patterns that go together very quickly. They may even include some short cuts that you can use on other projects.

If you've never looked through a pattern book before, don't be overwhelmed. There are several pattern companies with large catalogs you can choose from. Go armed with your measurements and something to mark the pages with possible choices, such as a pad of sticky notes, and plan on spending some time.

Reading the Envelope

The front of the pattern envelope has an attractive drawing or a picture of a model wearing the dress you've chosen. There will usually be pictures showing all the pattern styles in the envelope. Also, near the top, you will find the sizes available in the envelope. Most of the information you need, however, is on the back.

Reading the Charts

At first glance, the back of the envelope may look too confusing to decipher. You will find a chart of body measurements and the corresponding size. Sometimes the size is listed both in American sizes—such as 8, 10, 12, and so on—and in the European sizes, like 34, 36, 38. There may also be a chart that gives the finished measurements of the garment itself. These will all help you decide which size to use.

As part of this same chart you will find a yardage chart. Find the style you plan to make, and read across to the row with your size to determine how many yards of fabric you will need. There will probably be a listing for fabric 45" wide and one for 60". Asterisks beside these widths will refer you to notes that indicate whether this amount will be enough for napped fabrics. If your fabric has a one-way print, use what is indicated for napped fabrics.

Shopping Information

Besides the number of yards of fabric you will need, the back of the pattern envelope will tell you the types of fabric that you might consider. This is not a complete list but simply some suggestions. It might also indicate what is not recommended for this particular pattern, such as stripes or stretchy fabrics.

The amount of interfacing, if any, will be indicated somewhere, perhaps as part of the chart or perhaps along with the notions. The notions are usually listed directly below the fabrics and include such things as thread, zippers, buttons, and so forth. Be sure to look over the list carefully so you can buy everything you need for your dress when you buy your fabric.

ALERT!

Male readers, don't feel excluded! If you don't want to make a dress as a gift, look for patterns for chef's aprons, tank tops, vests, or other simple patterns to help you get started.

Fitting the Pattern

Few of us are proportioned exactly the way the pattern chart seems to expect. Though you will have already decided which size comes the closest to your measurements, in order for your dress to really fit, you may need to make some changes.

Sizing

Refer back to the measurement chart on the back of the pattern. Use a highlighter to indicate which bust, waist, and hip measurement is closest to your own. Next, open out the folded pattern pieces and find the ones that are labeled for your style. Cut these pieces apart enough to separate them. You don't need to cut them all out exactly on the cutting line—that you can do when you actually cut your dress out.

You will notice that the pattern pieces have all the sizes on them. This makes altering a breeze. Simply use your highlighter to mark the cutting line of the appropriate size at the hips, waist, and bust. Gradually angle the line from one to the next, marking over the many cutting lines printed there.

Lengthening or Shortening

You can easily lengthen a hemline by adding to the bottom of each piece when you cut it out. Shortening's just as easy and can be done in the final stages of construction. However, among the body measurements listed on the chart is the distance from the back of the neck to the waist. If this is different from your own, you should alter the pattern.

Be sure to prepare your fabric as described in Chapter 3 before you cut out your garment. All your careful sizing will be for naught if your dress shrinks the first time it's washed.

You will notice on the primary pattern pieces there is a line marked "lengthen or shorten here." This is often a pair of lines about $1/8$" apart. To lengthen, cut along this line and splice in a piece of paper that adds the appropriate amount. Tape it to the pattern tissue. To shorten, measure the pattern up from this line the amount you need to shorten and draw a new line. Fold the pattern's line up to the new line and tape it in place.

Laying Out the Pattern

The pattern guide that comes with your pattern will probably have illustrations of several cutting layouts. These will be labeled as to which dress style and fabric width they are intended for. There may be illustrations for fabrics with and without nap. You can follow these illustrations, paying particular attention to fold lines and selvage edges. The usual way to lay out your fabric is right sides together with the selvages aligned. In some instances, however, this won't work. Your pattern guide's illustration will help you decide how this needs to be done.

Begin by pinning the largest pieces to the fabric. Be sure the fabric is smooth and folded properly. The long double-ended arrows on the pieces need to be straight with the grain of the fabric. Check by measuring to the selvage or center fold from one end of the arrow and again from the other end. If they are the same, the arrow is straight with the grain.

Also be alert to pieces that need to be placed on the fold. These are indicated by long arrows that curve toward the edge of the pattern.

Use straight pins to pin your pattern to the fabric. A pin every 10" to 12" is sufficient. Be sure your pins don't extend beyond the pattern's cutting line. Pin all your pieces in place before you begin to cut them out in case you discover a need to move the pieces closer together or rearrange them in order to fit them all to the fabric. Check for pieces, such as optional ties, or some types of facing pieces that call for more than two, and be sure you are leaving fabric scraps large enough to cut these out when the first set is cut.

Cutting and Marking the Pieces

Before you begin cutting out your garment, double-check to be sure all the pieces that you will need are pinned to your fabric. The pattern guide will have an outline drawing of each of the pieces and a list indicating which style uses each piece. Often the layout diagrams list all the pieces used for a particular style.

Cutting Tips

It's surprising how much time you can save by having really sharp scissors. Bent-handle shears are the best for cutting around your pattern because they allow you to leave the fabric on a flat surface while you cut it out. Keep the fabric as smooth as possible, and cut along the cutting lines of the pattern pieces through both layers of fabric.

If you have altered the pattern, cut from one size's cutting line to another. It is possible to save all the pattern sizes on a pattern by folding the tissue back and cutting only the fabric next to the lines, but it isn't as accurate. With anything except children's clothes, it is probably a waste of effort.

Notches

As you cut out your pieces, you will notice notch marks on the pattern. These are triangles drawn along the cutting line. They may be single triangles, pairs, or even three together. On old patterns they may extend beyond the cutting line, but in modern patterns, they are nearly always within the seam allowance.

These represent the points where you must match one piece to another. These notches will be represented on your cutout fabric pieces one way or another. The fastest way to mark them on your fabric is to make a straight cut from the cutting line to the inside tip of the triangle. If you are careful to center your cuts, you can use them to match the pieces exactly.

If you are worried about your fabric fraying, you can cut the notches outside the cutting line as you cut around your piece. Match the shape of the single triangles as closely as possible. Double and triple triangles, on the other hand, can be cut as larger notches. Match only the outside edges of the triangles, and cut straight across between them.

Marking the Pieces

As you cut out your pieces, leave the pattern tissue in place. There is still some information you need to transfer from the pattern to the fabric. If your dress has darts, these need to be marked on the wrong side of your fabric. Look for dots or small circles on the pattern. These indicate locations where things such as ties need to be attached or the location of fasteners.

FACT

You should leave the tissue pinned to the fabric until you are ready to sew each piece. This will help you identify the pieces and will keep them from getting mixed up with leftover scraps. Also, as you read the instructions for a particular piece, you might discover something else that needs to be marked.

There are several ways to mark these locations. Dressmaker's carbon and a tracing wheel will leave a dotted line. This is most effective on things like darts. Small dots can be transferred to the fabric with the same carbon and a pencil. If your fabric is folded right sides out, fold your carbon in half so the marking surface is on the outside. Slip the carbon between the layers of cloth removing only as many pins as is necessary. Mark both layers at once. If your fabric is folded wrong side out, fold the carbon the other way, and sandwich the fabric between the layers of the carbon.

If your fabric doesn't take the dressmaker's carbon because of its color or fabric content, you can take a contrasting color of thread and sew through the pattern and both layers of fabric at the marking dots. When you are ready to use the pieces, tear the pattern away from the thread. Cut the thread between the layers of fabric, being careful not to cut the fabric. Leave the threads in the fabric until you've used them to make the darts or whatever they are intended for.

You can also run a pin through the dots, gently tear the pattern away, and mark the pin's location with tailor's chalk. This only works if you've folded your fabric with the wrong sides out, however.

Stitching Darts and Seams

Your pattern guide will lead you through all the steps of making your dress. As with any project, you should read through all the directions before beginning. The guide will probably ask you to begin with stay stitching, which is never a bad idea. Stay stitching is most necessary with stretchy fabric or along curving seams. Be sure to sew in the direction indicated by the arrows or you will defeat much of the purpose of the stitching.

This will probably be followed by darts or shaping seams on the front of your dress. To sew seams, put the pieces right sides together, matching the notches. The pieces need to fit at the stitching line, not at the cutting line, so you may have to clip some seam allowances. This is where the stay stitching is important so you don't clip too deep.

Sew ⁵⁄₈" from the edge. Clip curves and press seams open. If your fabric tends to fray, use pinking shears to trim the seams or zigzag just beyond the seam. These zigzag stitches don't have to be as close together as they did for appliqué stitching. They can be about as far apart as usual straight stitches. Trim the seam allowance close to these zigzag stitches to finish the seams.

To make darts, fold the fabric, right sides together, bringing the two lines together. Be sure the fabric folds at the point of the dart and the lines or dots match. To check this, insert a pin through the marking on one layer, and check to see that it emerges at the marking on the other layer. The lines need to match at the seam line, too.

Sew from the outside edge toward the center point. Darts are generally pressed downward or, in the case of vertical darts, outward, away from the center of the garment.

Inserting a Centered Zipper

Before the back pieces of the dress are sewn to the front, you will probably need to insert a zipper. There are two basic ways to do this: centered or lapped. Centered is easier and a better one to start with. If your zipper is in the center back of your dress, you can center even if the guide suggests a lapped zipper.

Preparation

Begin by sewing the lower part of the dress's center back seam. There was probably a dot on the pattern to indicate where the zipper ends and the seam begins. If you didn't mark it, check the pattern piece or measure with the zipper. The seam should close just above the base of the bar stop of the zipper.

Be sure you backstitch at the beginning of this seam so it doesn't come open below the zipper. Stitch the seam to the bottom of the dress. Baste the upper part of the seam closed, using a long machine stitch. Overlap your basting stitches with the seam instead of backstitching. Press the seam open.

ALERT!

If your fabric tends to fray, press the very edge of your seam allowances under for the length of the zipper, and stitch close to this fold just through the allowance. This will leave you enough seam allowance to install your zipper. Zigzag the seam allowances separately down the rest of the seam.

Positioning

Lay the back section, right side down, on a flat surface such as the ironing board. Position your zipper, right side down, on the seam. The top of the zipper tape should be just below the raw edge of the neck of the dress. You will need $5/8$" above the zipper pull for a seam allowance. Try to center the teeth of the zipper exactly over the seam. Pin the zipper down as shown in **FIGURE 15-1**.

Stitching

Baste the zipper to the dress by hand, following a woven line close to the edge of the zipper tape. Stitch across the bottom of the zipper just below the metal stop. Use the zipper foot attachment to your sewing machine. With the right side of your fabric facing you, follow your basting stitches on one side of the zipper, across the bottom, and up the other side, as illustrated in **FIGURE 15-2**. Remove your basting stitches, and your zipper's done.

FIGURE 15-1

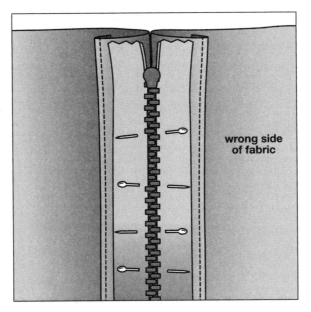

wrong side
of fabric

◀ **Centered zipper:** Pin and baste.

FIGURE 15-2

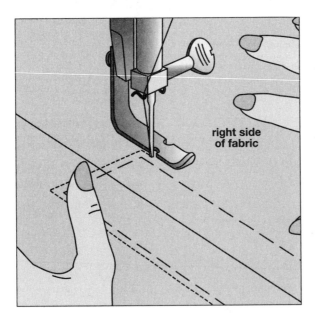

right side
of fabric

◀ Stitch the zipper along the seam.

Sewing Facing and Interfacing

You will probably have three facing pieces for the neck edge: one front and two back facings. You may have two facings for each armhole as well. Gather these pieces, and remove the tissue patterns. Your guide will probably suggest interfacing for these pieces, which will keep the neck and armholes from losing their shape.

Cutting the Interfacing

Your guide probably tells you how to lay these pattern pieces out on the interfacing. Here's a tip that saves a step. Lay the *fabric* pieces out on your interfacing. The wrong side of the fabric should be against the interfacing. If you are using fusible interfacing, have the fusible side up, toward the fabric.

Pin the facing pieces down, and cut out the interfacing. Your facing pieces are ready for the next step. For fusible interfacing, trim about ½" of the interfacing away from around the edges, then follow the manufacturer's directions to attach the interfacing.

For nonfusible interfacing, stitch ½" from all the edges. Trim the interfacing ¼" from the outside edge and close to the stitching the rest of the way around each piece.

If your fabric is very flimsy, and you are not sure you are laying the pieces out flat, use the pattern pieces to cut the interfacing, then pin the interfacing to the wrong side of the fabric pieces.

Sewing the Facing

Use the pattern pieces to help you identify the neck and armhole facings if necessary. Sew the neck facings together at the shoulders, and press these seams open. Turn the outside edge of the facing under ¼" or along the trimmed edge of the interfacing, and stitch to finish this edge.

Sew the front and back of your dress together at the shoulders, and press the seams open. With right sides together, pin the facing to the neck edge, matching the shoulder seams and the center front. The back of the facing will extend beyond the zipper.

Sew the facing in place, and clip the curves. Grade the seam allowance by trimming one layer shorter than the other. This will help the seam lie flat.

Finishing the Neck Edge

Turn the facing to the wrong side of the dress by first pressing the facing over the seam allowance. This will crease the facing at the seam, making the turn neater. Press the neck edge with the facing on the inside.

Turn under the ends of the facing, and hand-stitch them down on either side of the zipper. Tack the facing to the shoulder seams. That is, make a few small stitches through the facing and through the seam allowance where they cross. If the facing is lying on top of any shaping seams or darts, tack it down there as well.

Depending on the style of your dress, you may want to topstitch ¼" from the neck edge. Be sure you have pressed it smooth before you do this.

Armhole Facing

If your armholes are faced, they are done much the same way. Sew the side seams of the dress and sew the facing into a circle, turning the edge as described for the neck facing. Sew it on, clip, grade, turn, and press.

An alternative is to leave the underarm seam open and attach the facing first. Clip and grade the seam allowance, and press the interfacing away from the dress. Sew the side seam and the facing's underarm seam as one long seam. Press this seam open, and turn the facing to the inside. Tack it down to the shoulder and underarm seams.

Be sure to follow your pattern guide for order of operations since your pattern may have ties, pockets, or other things to add that are not described here.

Hem, and You're Done

With your dress nearly done, it's time to try it on. If you are making it for someone else, you can easily pin up the hem while it's on her. If it's for yourself, you might need to enlist the help of a friend for this step.

Fold the bottom edge under and pin it to the desired length. With the dress off, measure the underarm seams against each other to see that you've made the sides the same length. Make the necessary adjustments and press the hem. Trim to 2" below this crease, press under the raw edge, and hem. You may want to use a narrower hem if your dress flares a great deal. Refer back to the section on hemming in Chapter 4 for details. Ⓔ

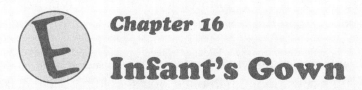

Chapter 16

Infant's Gown

Now that you've used a purchased pattern, try your hand at making one of your own. An infant's gown, besides being easy, is one of the most practical gifts new parents can receive. Once you have made the pattern, you'll find the gown goes together so quickly you'll want to make one for all the new babies you know.

Making a Pattern

The infant's gown illustrated in **FIGURE 16-1** is sized for newborns approximately three months old (or up to thirteen pounds or 24" long). It uses only two pattern pieces, which are illustrated together because over most of the pattern they are exactly the same. The only differences are that the center back is cut on the fold, while the center front has a $5/8$" seam allowance, and the front neckline scoops lower than the back neckline.

Use the diagram in **FIGURE 16-2** to make your own patterns. If you are going to make this gown more than once, you should probably make the front and back pieces separately rather than as one, as is illustrated here.

A yardstick and tool to make your angles accurate will make the drawing process easier. Be sure to mark the center back with the fold designation so you remember to cut that piece on the fold.

You can draw your pattern on brown wrapping paper, or, for something this small, cut off the bottom and split the side of a paper sack. A more permanent pattern can be drawn on interfacing with a fine marker. Choose the kind that is marked at regular intervals to make drawing the pattern easier.

FIGURE 16-1

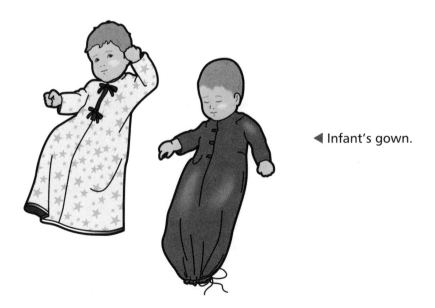

◄ Infant's gown.

FIGURE 16-2

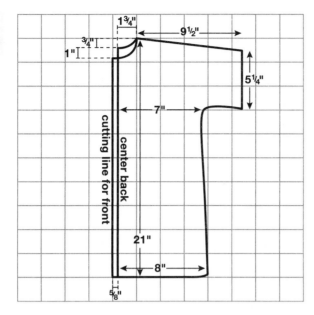

◀ **Infant's gown pattern:**
Make your pattern using the labeled dimensions.

ALERT!

These gowns are intended for either boys or girls. Think sleeping bags, not dresses. However, don't make either girls or boys wear them once they start to crawl. A long gown will frustrate babies who are trying to sit up.

Fabric and Notions

You'll want your infant's gown to meet the same federal flammability standards as commercial infants' sleepwear. Check the ends of the bolts of fabric; they'll say if the fabric is sleepwear approved. Pure cotton is naturally flame resistant and a good choice for baby clothes because it is also soft.

You will need ⅔ of a yard of fabric to make one gown. If you've chosen fabric with a directional print that is less than 45" wide, add an additional 6". You will also need a yard of narrow ribbon, twill tape, or lightweight cord if you want to tie the gown at the bottom. Narrow-fold bias tape or seam binding can be used to finish the neck edge. If you want to make your own bias binding, you will need ¼ yard of a coordinating fabric. You might be able to cut the binding out of the scraps left from your gown, if you want to use the same fabric, or add just a little more when you purchase the fabric. About a yard of ribbon or bias tape can be used as fasteners, or you can use two snaps or buttons.

Prepare your fabric by washing and straightening it. Cut out the three fabric pieces with your two pattern pieces.

Sewing the Sleeves

Begin by matching the shoulders of the front and back pieces. Stitch $5/8$" seams across both shoulders. Zigzag just outside of these seams and trim the fabric up to the zigzag stitches. Press the seam allowances toward the back.

Press under a narrow hem across the ends of the sleeves. Straight-stitch across these hems. While a little of the seam allowance may show at the wrist this way, it would be very difficult to sew around that narrow cuff after the side/underarm/sleeve seam is completed.

Sew the side/underarm/sleeve seams, and finish the allowance the same way you did the shoulder seams. You will need to clip around the curve at the underarm to keep the seam from binding. Reinforcing the seam by stitching it a second time—just around the curve—might be a good idea.

Next, sew the front seam, leaving the top 7" or 8" open. Do not zigzag this seam. It must be pressed open. If you are afraid the fabric will fray, zigzag each seam allowance individually.

ALERT!

If you're a perfectionist, you may want to hide the edge of the seam. You can leave the sleeve hem unstitched for 1" or so at each end. After the underarm seam is sewn, you can go back and finish the hem.

Making Bias Binding

There are several options for finishing the neck and front edge of the gown. One of these is to use bias binding to cover the raw edges.

Making your own is less expensive than using commercial binding and lets you match your fabric exactly.

Cutting the Bias Strips

You will only need about 28" of binding for this gown, plus an additional yard or so if you use it for the ties as well. Begin by finding the bias of your fabric. To do this, fold a selvage edge up to a line that you know to be straight with the grain. Mark the diagonal fold with chalk. Now cut out 1" strips of fabric along or parallel to this chalk line. If you are using scraps, you may have to mark the bias in several places to get enough strips.

Connecting the Strips

Trim the ends of all the strips so they are straight with the grain. This will put the ends at an angle with the strip itself. To sew the strips together, line up two strips at a right angle with the ends in line. Match the sides not at the corners but ¼" below them, where the seam will actually cross. This is very similar to the straight binding seams described in Chapter 14. Sew the ends together, and press open. Trim off the little tabs that extend beyond the sides of the strip at the seams. The beginning end of your strip should be cut perpendicular to the strip, instead of on the diagonal.

Folding the Strip

You will need to fold the sides of the strip in ¼". The easiest way to do this is to make a folding guide on your ironing board with a long pin. A long, glass-headed pin like the kind used to pin on a corsage works best, but any pin longer than 2" will work.

Begin by folding and pressing the sides of your strip under for about 2". Run your pin under your ironing board cover and out again about ¼" away to anchor it. Slide your folded binding under the pin as close to the anchor as possible. Run the tip of the pin back into the ironing board cover as close to the other side of the binding as possible without actually catching the binding.

You need to be able to pull the binding strip under the pin, but you should not be able to slide the folded strip back and forth crossways under it. As you pull the binding through your guide, the ends will turn up, and you can press them. This isn't going to be one smooth movement, but more a matter of pulling the strip 1" or 2" and pressing. You may need to occasionally adjust the binding so the edges continue to turn under evenly.

When you are finished, you will need to fold the binding in half and press again. You can change your pin guide to fit this smaller size and use it again, though it doesn't always work as well for the second fold.

FACT

While you will save money by making your own binding if you are making only one gown, you might actually save money by buying binding if you are making several. You can probably bind as many as three gowns with one package of bias binding, and the time you would spend folding that much binding might make it worth the added upfront cost.

Finishing the Neckline

The raw edges of the neckline and the front of the gown need to be finished in some way that will be comfortable for the baby. There are several different ways to do this. A narrow hem or seam binding could take the place of bias tape. Making facing pieces for the neck edge is also an option.

Covered with Bias Tape

One choice that adds a visible trim to the front and neck is to encase the edge with double-fold bias tape. Begin by stay-stitching ⁵⁄₈" from the edge around the neck and along the open edges of the front.

Open the bias tape out completely. Fold up the end of the bias tape, and begin close to the closed seam at the center front. With the binding *inside* the stitches and the right sides together, line a raw edge of the tape up with the stitching line. Stitch along the first fold of the binding to the neck edge. Repeat with the other side of the front.

Trim the seam allowances slightly so the raw edge won't show under the bias tape, but leave enough that it folds to the back along the stay stitching. Turn the seam binding to the back, and hand- or machine-stitch.

Do the same across the top. If you want to use bias tape for the ties, extend the bias tape no more than 9" beyond the front edge. Sew the layers together as you sew the last step of the binding in place. Make two more ties of the same length by stitching on top of the folded tape. Attach these ties behind the binding about two-thirds of the way down the open front.

Hemmed Edge and Faced Neck

You can use your pattern pieces to cut facings because the neck edge of the facings will be exactly like the body pieces. Remember to cut the back facing on a fold. Make them no more than 2" wide.

The facings are prepared in the same way as you did the facings for the dress in Chapter 15, except that here interfacing is not necessary. In fact, interfacing might make the neck edge a little too stiff for a baby.

Sew the facing to the neck edge. Instead of having facing hanging over the edge as you did with the zippered back of the dress in Chapter 15, you will have facings that exactly match the front of the gown. Sew down the length of the facing along this edge. Clip the curves and corners, grade the seam allowance and turn the facing. Tack the facing to the shoulder seams.

The front edge of the gown, from the bottom of the facing to the top of the center seam, can be hemmed with a narrow hem, similar to the way the sleeves were hemmed. When you stitch this hem, continue the machine-stitching over the facing and around the neck for a more consistent or topstitched look.

Turned Under with Seam Binding

You can use seam binding or single-fold bias tape to turn under the edge of the front and neck. Begin by stay-stitching on the $5/8$" seam line.

Place your seam binding *outside* these stitches, with one edge just over the stitching. Turn the binding's raw edge up, and begin at the lower front, stitching close to the edge that is along the stay stitching. Do the front edges separately, trim the raw edges of the seam allowance just shorter than the tape, and turn the seam binding to the back. Stitch close to the other edge of the seam binding, or hem it in place by hand.

Next, sew the seam binding to the neck edge, folding the ends up at the edges of the seam binding that encases the front. Stretch the fabric a little at the curves on the neck to give yourself a little more binding.

Trim the fabric seam allowance just shorter than the tape. You will need to clip the curves at the neck. Press the tape under. Stitch close to the other edge of the bias tape, or hem it in place by hand.

Stretch lace will be easier to work with than seam binding because of the curves in the garment. However, stretch lace will be scratchier for the baby. Single-fold bias tape, handled as if it were seam binding, will stretch as well, but it will be bulkier than seam binding. Weigh the benefits of each to make your decision.

Lapped Front

If you don't like the idea of the edges of the gown merely meeting in front and would rather see them overlap, this is possible, too. Instead of pressing the center front seam open, press it toward the right side (if it's for a girl) or toward the left side (if it's for a boy). This creates one over side and one under side. You can hem the over side or use either seam binding or bias tape to finish it as already described.

For the underside, you will want to use as little of the seam allowance for finishing as possible. Covering the very edge with bias tape is the best choice.

Finish the neck edge any of the ways already described. If you choose to make facings, don't sew down the front on the underside. Leave it loose until it's turned, and catch it in the bias tape with the rest of the front edge.

Front Fasteners

Bias binding ties that are a part of the neck binding have already been described. If you finish the front so the pieces overlap, you can put snaps or even small buttons in that overlap. But if you use any of the other options described, you still need a way to close up the top third of the front.

Ribbons are the easiest choice. Attach them to the back of the finished edges as described earlier for the second set of bias ties. Buttons can be added to one side and button loops to the other. The loops can be made out of stitched narrow double-fold bias tape, narrow ribbon, or yarn.

Snaps might be more practical. You can put the underside snap on seam binding. To do this, cut the binding to about 2" and fold it in half the long way. Stitch across the end, and turn. Sew the stitched end to the underside of the gown so the folded end extends beyond it. Sew one half of the snap to the seam binding and the other half to the back of the other side of the gown.

Another possibility is to use little embroidered appliqués that you can buy in stores. Choose a pair about 1" across. Stitch one edge to the edge of one side of the front so the center of the appliqué is along the center front edge. Sew one half of the snap to the underside of the appliqué and the other half to the other side of the gown.

Making a Casing for the Bottom Tie

The bottom of your gown still needs to be finished. It's no more difficult to make the hem into a casing for a tie than to simply hem it. The tie will make the gown more versatile and keep little toes warmer.

Begin by pressing the lower edge under 1". Press the raw edge under ¼". Before you stitch the hem, stitch the center seam allowance down to the gown within the hem allowance and ¾" above it. The purpose of this is to keep these allowances from working their way out the hole you are going to make in the seam for the bottom tie. Now you can straight-stitch the hem close to the hem allowance fold. Make a row of stitches along the bottom fold of the hem that extends for about ½" on either side of the center front seam. This is to keep the seam from opening up more than you want it to.

Now, on *either* the outside or the inside of the gown, use a seam ripper to remove the stitches of the center front seam within the hem area. The outside might be slightly handier for whoever changes the baby, but putting the opening on the inside might look a little better. Take your pick.

Fasten your tie (ribbon, twill tape, or lightweight cord) to a safety pin, and run it through the casing. Adjust the tie so it is distributed evenly. Tie the ends together securely. At the center back, stitch across the hem area, securing the center of the tie to the center of the back. This will ensure that the tie does not come out of the gown and become a strangling hazard. Pull the tie up, and tie the gown bottom closed by folding the loop as if it were two ties—instead of a loop—and tying in a bow.

Shirt Alternative

You can easily adjust your gown pattern to make little infant shirts. Simply cut them off 7" to 10" from the top. Hem the bottom, and finish the front and neck any of the ways already described. If you want, you can extend the front edges a little to make more of an overlap for buttons or snaps.

Another possibility is to cut both the front and the back on the fold. Use the shoulder/upper sleeve seam on one side for the fasteners. This is especially effective as a T-shirt made with lightweight jersey. (E)

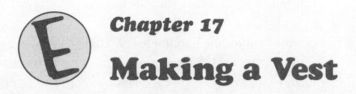

Chapter 17
Making a Vest

Vests of different styles seem to come in and out of fashion, but they never completely go away. Perhaps that is because there are so many different things you can do with vests. They can be dressy or casual, appliquéd, embroidered or painted, with or without pockets, ties, and lapels. And all can be made from one simple, easily modified pattern.

Making a Pattern

The vest pattern diagram shown in **FIGURE 17-1** is similar to the infant's gown in Chapter 16 except that the dimensions are not labeled. You will need to take your own measurements to determine those. Make a quick sketch of the vest pattern in **FIGURE 17-1**. Add the measurements to your sketch as you determine them. Use this sketch to help you draw your final pattern from your sketch.

Begin with the double-pointed horizontal arrow that is shown on the pattern near the bottom of the vest. This length should be approximately ¼ of your chest measurement plus ⅝". The distance from the back shoulder to the bottom of the back vest piece should be the length you want your vest to be plus 1¼" (or two seam allowances). For most vests, measure from the shoulder near the neck where a shoulder seam would be, down the back, and to a couple of inches below the waist.

The armhole and neckline curves and the lower front shoulder will all be proportional to these dimensions. The front curve of the vest and the shape of the bottom front are very flexible. Straighten them, round them off, or do whatever suits your tastes.

This method can be used to make vests for children, whether you're sewing for a little cowboy or cowgirl or a young ring bearer.

FIGURE 17-1

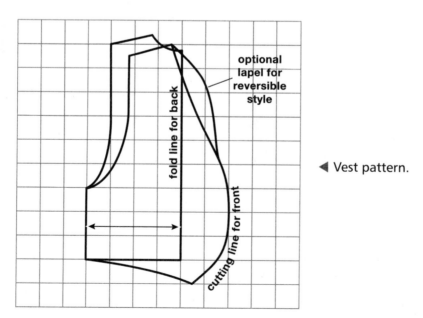

◀ Vest pattern.

You can make a trial vest out of interfacing. Sew the side and shoulder seams together and try it on. Use it to help you get the pattern just right. Since most things call for only small pieces of interfacing, you can cut pieces from the trial vest pieces later for some other project and won't have wasted much. Or you can keep the interfacing vest as a pattern to make the vest again.

Shopping and Cutting

When you have your pattern just the way you want it, you're ready to choose your fabric and start your vest. The front is lined, so you will need a main fabric and a lining. The main fabric can be anything from denim to brocade. Or it can be a background for some decoration that you're planning to design.

The lining should complement the main fabric. A satin fabric will make the vest dressier. Chambray or muslin might be a better choice with denim. A solid-color cotton lined with a coordinating print is another suggestion. The back of the vest can be made from either the main fabric or the lining fabric. The back of the vest isn't lined in this version, so you'll only cut one piece with the center back on the fold of the fabric.

If you are planning to decorate your vest with embroidery, either by hand or with your machine, it is better to mark out the cutting line of the pieces and embroidery within these lines before you cut the pieces out. This will prevent the edges from fraying or stretching because of the embroidery hoop.

Decorating with Crayons

If you have decided to decorate the front of your vest, do it before you begin sewing so that you will have a flat piece of fabric to work with. If you are looking for something unusual, try coloring a picture on your vest with crayons. You fabric must be light enough for the crayons to show and must be able to take the high temperature required to set the crayons.

Begin by drawing your picture onto your cloth. You can place your fabric on top of the picture on a light box and trace it with a hard lead pencil or a disappearing fabric marker. (A light box is simply a piece of glass with a light source under it.)

Before you try to color in your picture, iron a piece of butcher paper on the back to stabilize it. You can also place it on a thin piece of batting or interfacing to keep it from shifting. You might try fine sandpaper as well. Any of these things are going to add a different texture to your coloring, but the textures will probably melt out when you set the color. Color your picture, using heavier and lighter pressure to add dimension. You can also combine colors for shading.

Set your picture by placing the fabric face down on a paper towel on your ironing board. With your iron on the cotton setting without steam, apply the iron and hold it down for about twenty seconds. The color will begin to bleed through to the wrong side of the fabric. Your colors will lighten a little when they are set. If they seem too pale, color over your pictures and set them again.

You can accent your picture by stitching around them, adding details. You can do this with zigzag stitches and free-motion embroidery, with simple straight-stitching, or a combination of both. Crayon pictures will fade a little with washing. Cold water will fade them more slowly than hot, so avoid hot water and keep laundering to a minimum to make them last as long as possible.

Adding a Slashed Pocket

A patch pocket can easily be added to your vest. You can make it square or with a pointed bottom. You can turn under the edges and hem the top, or line it and turn it to finish the edges. If you want to get a bit clever, you can hide a pocket behind a welt. The welt stands up and hides the hole where the pocket lining is attached, and the pocket itself is hidden between the vest front and the lining. This is called a slashed pocket because it is made through a slash in the garment.

Cutting the Pieces

You will need a 3½" by 2" piece cut from leftover vest-front fabric. This will be the welt. If your vest is made from a print fabric, you might want the welt to contrast with it instead, since you will not be able to match the print exactly to hide it. If your lining is of the same or nearly the same weight, you might consider using it.

QUESTION?

What is a welt?
A welt is simply an insert, often for decoration, but in this case it serves a purpose. The basic idea is to stitch two pocket lining pieces and the base of a welt to a hole on your vest, then push these through to the other side.

You will need two pieces for the pocket lining. You can use the lining fabric, muslin, or any other leftover fabric. Just be sure the fabric you choose won't show through either the vest or lining fabrics and will be strong enough to take the usual wear of a pocket. These pieces should be 3½" by the depth of your pocket plus ½" for seam allowances. The back lining piece, which will be sewn above the slash, should be about ½" longer than the other.

Be sure to take the location of the pocket into account when you decide on the depth. If your pocket is in the lower left front where an old-fashioned watch pocket might be, the distance to the bottom of the vest will limit the pocket's depth. The welt will essentially add ¾" to the depth of the pocket.

Making the Welt

Begin by folding the welt piece in half the long way with the right sides together. Sew ¼" from the ends. Clip the corners, grade the allowance, turn, and press. This creates a piece 3" by 1".

Decide exactly where you want to put your pocket. Mark a 3" line on the *right* side of your vest approximately where the center of the welt should be. The slash will actually be ¼" below this, and the welt will extend ½" above it. The pocket will hang below it.

Line your welt up on the right side of the vest, with the folded side pointing downward and the raw edge along the line.

Adding the Pocket Lining

Place the front pocket lining, the slightly shorter one, on top of the welt, lining up one edge with the raw edge of the welt. The pocket lining should extend ¼" beyond each side of the welt.

Machine-stitch ¼" below the marked line and raw edges, stopping and starting your stitches at the edge of the welt. This will leave ¼" of the pocket lining on each edge unstitched.

Carefully cut the vest fabric just above the stitching. This will be somewhat below the marked line. Stop and start the cut a stitch inside the line. If you cut clear to the end of the stitching, the welt will not be able to hide the ends of the slash.

Next, on the right side of the vest, put the other pocket lining piece *above* (not on top of) the first. Line one raw edge up with the upper side of the slash. The sides of the pocket lining should extend evenly beyond both ends of the slash. This half of the pocket lining will finish the upper edge of the slash and be sewn to the front pocket lining after they've both been turned through the slash.

Sew as close to the raw edge as practical. You should be quite close to stitching on the marked line although, since it is covered with the pocket lining, you won't be able to see it. Be sure the stitches do not extend clear to the edge of the pocket lining, but only to the edge of the slash or approximately ¼" from the side edges of the lining.

Finishing the Pocket

Poke the two lining pieces and the seam allowance of the welt through the slash. With the right side of the vest facing you so you don't iron creases around the slash, press the pocket down and the welt up.

Keeping the pocket flat, flip up the vest fabric, and pin the pocket sides and bottom together. You may need to trim one lining piece to fit the other. Sew around the sides and bottom of the pocket, getting as close to the edge of the slash as possible without catching the vest front under the needle. Blind-stitch the sides of the welt to the vest front.

FACT

You can decorate the vest by making a patchwork of several fabrics, perhaps using 3" squares. Cut the vest front from this pieced fabric. Or you might sew scraps of cloth on your vest front in a crazy-quilt style. Zigzag-stitch the raw edges, or turn them under.

Adding Back Ties

If you want to add ties to the back of your vest, you need to attach them to the back piece before it is sewn to the front. The ties should be made out of something lightweight, such as the lining fabric, preferably matching the back fabric.

For ties that will be tied in a double knot at the back, cut them about 4" longer than half the width of the back. Cut the ties about 2¾" wide. This will make the finished ties just over 1" wide. If you are fastening the back with a small buckle, you may want the buckle side to be shorter. The buckle itself will determine the width of your ties.

Fold the ties in half the long way with the right sides together. Sew across the long side and across one end with ¼" seams. Clip the corners, and grade the seam allowances. Turn the ties right side out by pushing against the closed end with something blunt like the handle of a wooden spoon and pulling the fabric over it. Press the ties flat. Sew the unfinished end to the side seam allowance a few inches above the bottom. Be sure to sew both ties at an equal distance from the bottom.

Constructing the Vest

Because the vest is partially lined, it goes together somewhat differently than either the dress or the baby gown of the previous two chapters. The lining finishes the front edge and the front armhole and, if done correctly, can hide the side and shoulder seam allowances as well.

Hemming the Back

Because the back isn't lined on this vest, the lower back, back armholes, and the back of the neck all need to be hemmed. Press these raw edges under $5/8$", and then press the raw edge under within that allowance.

An alternative is to use narrow seam binding. This will allow you to clip and trim the seam allowances at the curves. Your choice will be determined by how casual your vest is—the hem will look more casual than the more polished binding—and whether or not you can match the back fabric with the seam binding. Refer to the different choices for finishing the neck edge of the baby gown in Chapter 16 for details on using the seam binding.

Stitching the Side Seams

When the armholes, neckline, and lower edge of the back are finished, you can sew it to the front pieces. Put the right sides together. The front pieces will still have their $5/8$" seam allowances and will be larger. Be sure you center the back sides between these allowances. Sew $5/8$" seams, and press them toward the front pieces. Grade the seam allowances by trimming the front's allowance to about half of the back's.

ALERT!

Do not stitch the shoulder seams yet. Leaving them open now allows you to turn the lining to the back when you sew it to the front in the next step.

Adding the Front Lining

Before you sew the front lining to the front pieces, turn the side seam allowance and the shoulder seam allowance of these lining pieces toward the back and press them. Pin the lining on top of the front pieces, right sides together. The side seam fold you just pressed on the lining should match the stitched side seams, and the fold at the shoulder should be $5/8$" below the raw edge of the front pieces.

Stitch around the armhole and down the front from the neck and across to the side seam. Clip and grade the seams. Using the open sides, turn the lining to the back. Press the edges. Blind-stitch the lining to the side seam, being careful your stitches don't show on the back fabric.

Reversible Alternative

If you want to make a more casual vest, or you don't like the idea of the back being made from lining fabric, you can make your vest fully lined. This will also make it possible for your vest to be reversible.

To do this, simply cut one back piece from your main fabric and one from your lining fabric, the same as you did the front. The section on the pattern diagram labeled for optional lapel can be used if you want. It will fold down against the front, and the lining will show as a lapel. When you turn the vest the other way, the lining will be outside, and the main fabric will fold over as the lapel.

Sew both the lining and the main vest front and back pieces together at the side seams. Press these seam allowances open. Grade them by trimming all the allowances on the lining. Press under the shoulder seam allowances on the lining front.

Put the lining and main vest together, with right sides facing. Sew all the way around the armholes, all the way around the outside edge, and across the back of the neck. In other words, sew all around the vest except the shoulder seams. Clip the curves, and grade the seam allowances. Turn the vest right side out through one of the shoulder seams. Press.

FACT

In the nineteenth century what we call vests were called waistcoats. They usually had two pockets: one for a watch, and the other for the fob, which was essentially an ornamental counterweight to the watch that allowed the watch chain to drape between the pockets.

Sewing the Shoulder Seams

You now have a nearly finished vest and are finally ready to sew those shoulder seams. Whether you have lined the back or hemmed it, you will finish these seams the same way. If you lined the back, treat both layers as if they were one.

With right sides together, pin the back shoulder edge to the front's main fabric. You will probably want to sew with the front of the vest on top so you don't accidentally catch the lining under the needle. This means pinning the pieces together with the pins tucked under the lining. Sew from neck edge seam to armhole seam. Trim this seam allowance, and tuck it and the lining seam allowance inside the front between the main fabric and the lining. Press. Blind-stitch the lining's shoulder seam to the back the same way you did the side seam.

Adding Buttonholes

Even if you don't plan to button your vest, don't discount the decorative value of buttons and buttonholes. The biggest problem with placing them on the vest is locating the appropriate spot. Depending on how you shaped the front, the buttonhole might belong at the widest point.

Try the vest on, and use straight pins to mark the edge of the overlapping side on the underside. With the vest off, use the pins to help you recreate the overlap.

Try out some buttons to see if you like the effect. Mark the lines for the buttonholes when you decide what you like, and follow your sewing machine's guide for making them. Or, if you are using one large button and want your buttonhole to be decorative, you can refer back to the description of mending a buttonhole in Chapter 4 and make it by hand. Use embroidery thread or two strands of regular thread if you can't find buttonhole twist thread. Add the button or buttons to the other side, and you're done.

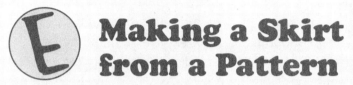

Chapter 18

Making a Skirt from a Pattern

A skirt is a versatile addition to any woman's wardrobe. For casual wear in the summer, skirts are cooler than pants and more appropriate in a lot of settings than shorts. And who can resist the basic black skirt? When you make your own, you have so many more options for fabrics than buying ready-made.

Choosing a Pattern

Skirts get their shape from darts, seams, gathers, pleats, or elastic. They may have front, back, or side zippers, or—in the case of elastic waist skirts—none at all. Some skirts have a waistband, though many of the newer styles do not, instead often riding 1" or more below the natural waist. Narrow skirts often have a slit to make moving easier. Some have patch pockets; some have pockets hidden in the seams.

Before you go shopping for your skirt pattern and fabric, take your waist and hip measurements. Also take inventory of your closet to see what you'll want your skirt to go with. As you study the pattern books to pick out your skirt, don't worry about how each of the features mentioned above is constructed. Choose whatever style of skirt will be most flattering for your figure and will fit with your activities.

FACT

If you want to use a skirt pattern over again but want your skirts to look different, try adding different belt carriers. Consider wide tab carriers that come to a point and are decorated with a button. Or perhaps you'd like a group of three narrow loops side by side. You'll be surprised how much they can change the look of a skirt.

Shopping and Fitting

When fabric shopping, consider what your pattern recommends for fabric and when and where you plan to wear your skirt. Synthetic fabrics or cotton-polyester blends are more wrinkle-resistant and easy to care for than natural fibers. A long skirt will drape better and be more flowing in a silk or silk-type fabrics. Gathered and elastic waist skirts should be of lightweight fabrics to keep them from seeming too bulky around the hips. Remember to check the notion list on the back of the envelope to get your interfacing, zipper, buttons, or elastic.

To fit your pattern with several sizes on the tissues, mark the cutting line for the appropriate size at the waist and the appropriate size at the hips, as described for the dress pattern in Chapter 15. Remember to cut the waistband or waistline facings in the size that corresponds to your choice for the waist.

If your pattern only has one size in the envelope, or you fit a size somewhere in between the pattern's size groupings, you should probably choose the size that most nearly fits your waistline. The hips are easier to alter if the waist has darts or curved seams for shaping.

If you have chosen a silk, suede, or other fabric that will show pinholes, you will not be able to redo seams if you don't get them right the first time. Try out your pattern first on something that will handle some altering so you know the pattern fits just right before you cut out your more expensive fabric.

Cutting and Marking

Unless you've chosen a fabric that must be dry-cleaned, prepare it by washing and straightening. Lay out your fabric as recommended in your pattern guide. If you are working with silk or synthetic suede, be sure to keep your pins within the seam allowances so they won't scar your fabric.

You will need to transfer markings onto your fabric if your pattern has any of the following features:

Zipper
Slit
Darts
Pockets
Waistband

Mark the appropriate dots indicated on the pattern pieces in any of the different ways described in Chapter 15.

Sewing Darts and Seams

As with the dress pattern from Chapter 15, your guide will probably tell you to begin with stay stitching and darts. If your skirt gets its shape from additional front seams, you will probably sew them next.

Remember to be aware of markings for slits or side pockets before you sew any of the seams. Also, if your skirt has a zipper, it is much easier to sew it to two garment pieces before those pieces have been stitched to others and even before the darts have been added. Add the zipper first, then go back and do the seams and darts according to the guide sheet.

ALERT!

If this is your first skirt with this pattern, don't trim and finish the seam allowances yet. Wait until the basic construction is done and try it on, in case you need to let out a seam.

Inserting a Lapped Zipper

If your skirt's zipper is on the side or in front, you will need to insert a lapped zipper rather than a centered one. The idea is that rather than having the two folds of fabric meet on top of the zipper teeth, there is one flap of fabric that laps over the zipper teeth and just a little of the fabric on the other side of the zipper.

Sewing the Zipper to the Seam Allowance

Begin by basting the seam closed like you did for a centered zipper. Press the seam open. Fold the garment pieces away from the seam allowance that will *not* be the side of the exterior overlap. This should be the seam allowance belonging to the back piece if the zipper is on the side. If the zipper is in the back or in the front, you need the seam allowance that belongs to the *right* side piece.

Line the top edge of the zipper tape up with the upper edge of the seam allowance. The zipper should be face down, and the outside edge of the teeth should be right along the seam. In other words, one side of the zipper tape and all of the actual zipper hardware should be lying on the seam allowance. Stitch along the tape close to the teeth, as shown in **FIGURE 18-1**.

FIGURE 18-1

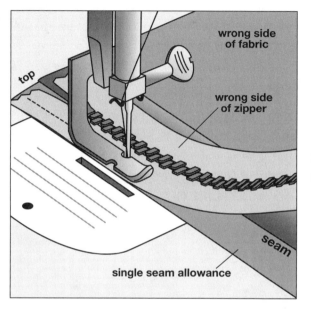

◀ **Lapped zipper, step 1:** Sew the zipper tape to one seam allowance.

FIGURE 18-2

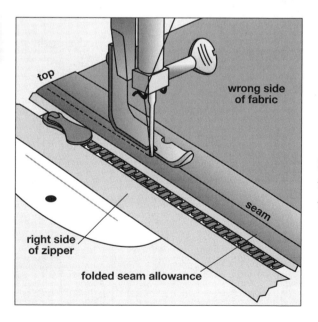

◀ **Lapped zipper, step 2:** Sew along the fold between the seam and the zipper teeth.

Making the Lower Lap

Fold the zipper out and the seam allowance under. Adjust the fold of the seam allowance so it is close to the teeth but not over them. Stitch along the fold of the seam allowance between the seam itself and the zipper teeth, as shown in **FIGURE 18-2**. You are still only sewing through the zipper tape and the one seam allowance.

Making the Upper Lap

Now open out the garment, laying the zipper flat. This is similar to pinning down a centered zipper, except it is already anchored on one side and you can see that it isn't actually centered. Sew across the bottom just below the metal stop and up the previously unstitched side close to the teeth, as shown in **FIGURE 18-3**. Take out the basting stitches.

FIGURE 18-3

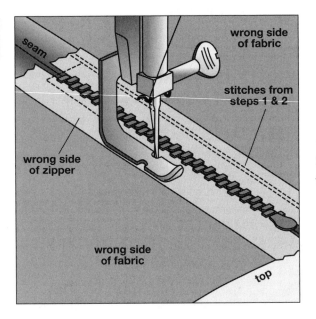

◄ **Lapped zipper, step 3:** Sew the zipper to the skirt, forming the upper lap.

Two-Step Alternative

There is a quicker way to put in a lapped zipper, but it will probably not turn out quite as neat. If you are making something very casual, or you are practicing on cotton before tackling that synthetic suede, you might want to try this shortcut.

Stitch the bottom of the skirt seam, but don't baste the zipper area closed. Turn the left or front seam allowance under ⅝" and the right or back under ½". With the zipper and skirt both right side up, lay the ½" folded allowance along the edge of the teeth. Stitch close to the teeth. Lay the ⅝" fold over the zipper, simulating the closed seam. Sew this side of the fabric to the zipper, down the side, and across the bottom. You may need to sew from the outside instead of the underside in order to be sure the lap stays straight.

If you want to avoid zippers as much as possible, consider making a wrap skirt. Cut a skirt back and two skirt fronts, which you sew to either side of the back. Add ties to either side of a long, narrow waistband, and hem the sides and bottom.

Possible Pockets

If your skirt has pockets, your guide will probably tell you to sew them in place before the side seams. If you want to add pockets that are not part of your pattern, you can do that now as well.

Patch Pockets

Patch pockets are easy to make and have been described already. The only thing tricky about them on a skirt is getting them placed exactly where you want them. Crooked pockets are a sure giveaway that you were improvising.

If you are adding one pocket, pin it in place, then pin the parts of your skirt together and try it on. This will give you a good idea of how the pocket will look and feel where you've pinned it. If you are adding two pockets, pin the first and try on the skirt. Then lay the two front pieces back to back, and pin the second pocket in place exactly over the first. Try the skirt on again to be sure they look balanced.

Half-Hidden Pockets

Another possible pocket on your pattern is a half-hidden pocket. These are styled very much like the standard jeans pocket. The front piece of your garment ends with the pocket top, usually at an angle near the side seam. The pocket consists of two pieces, one of which completes the side front.

Your pattern guide will take you through the steps of construction. Generally, the pocket front is sewn to the garment, turned, and topstitched. The pocket back may or may not have a dart at the waistline. It is sewn to the pocket front and perhaps part of the skirt above the pocket top. Then the pocket and front are treated as one piece and sewn to the back of the skirt.

Hidden Side Pockets

Hidden side pockets are sewn onto side seam allowances before the side seams are sewn. If you want to add this kind of pocket to your skirt, you can create your own pocket insert pattern.

Making a Pattern

The easiest way to make this pattern is to find a similar pocket in one of your own skirts or dresses and use it to make your pattern. If you don't have anything with this type of pocket, draw your own.

The shape is essentially the same as half a heart. The point of the heart, however, is rounded to form the top of the pocket. For an adult, you probably won't want your pocket to be more than 10" or 11" from top to bottom, including seam allowances, or more than 6" across.

Along the straight side (the center of the "heart"), add a $5/8$" seam allowance. Extend this from the upper edge to as far down the pocket as you want to go. Remember, the seam line has to fit the side seam of your skirt. Don't allow this line to curve outward with the pocket. The farther this seam goes, the more the pocket will be anchored to the seam allowance of the skirt.

Attaching the Pockets

Determine the location for your pockets. Generally, if there is only one pocket, it is on the right side. However, if you are left-handed, you might want to put it on the left side of your skirt. Put them at a comfortable distance below the waist.

Sew the pocket pieces along the seam allowances, right sides together. Make sure the pocket pieces are equal distances from the waist on both the front and the back so they will match when you sew the side seam. Press the seams toward the pocket.

With the right sides together and the pocket pieces extending outward, away from the skirt, pin the side seams and pockets together. Sew the side seam from the waist to the pocket seam and around the pocket, then up to the pocket/skirt seam. Pivot the needle, and sew down the rest of the skirt seam. You might want to topstitch along the front edge of the pocket opening to encourage it to lay forward under your skirt.

Finishing the Waistline

Before you finish the waistline of your skirt, be sure it fits properly. If you need to let out or take in a seam, it will be easier to do now. If you alter the skirt at the waistline, be sure you make the same adjustments on the waistband or facing. When the skirt fits, finish the seams with zigzag stitches or pinking shears if you are afraid the fabric will fray.

QUESTION?

What if my pattern calls for lining?
Don't panic. The lining is put together just like the skirt, except you simply press the seam allowance under where the zipper would be. Line it up inside the skirt when you're ready to add the waistband.

Adding a Waistband

Generally, waistbands call for interfacing on half of the band. You can cut it out much the same way you did the interfacing for the neck and sleeve facing on the dress in Chapter 15. One edge of your waistband will probably be straight and the other will be notched. Press the straight side under ⅝".

Lay the center of the fabric waistband piece along a straight edge of the interfacing with the notched side of the facing on the interfacing. Cut the interfacing, and either stitch and trim or trim and fuse it to the waistband. If the waistband is narrow, it may not call for interfacing.

With the right sides together, pin the notched edge of the waistband to the waistline of the skirt, matching the notches. The waistband will extend beyond the skirt on both sides of the zipper. Press the seam allowance toward the waistband. Grade the seam allowance, and clip the curves if necessary.

With the entire waistband piece extending above the skirt, fold it in half with right sides together. The fold of the straight side should line up with the seam. Sew across the ends. The end seam should line up with the lap side of the zipper, but on the other side, it will probably extend at least 1". This will allow for snaps, hooks, or buttons.

Clip the corners and turn the waistband. Press it flat. Topstitch or blind-stitch the folded side to the inside of the waistband seam.

Finishing a Bandless Waist

Skirts without waistbands are very much the fashion. The top edge of the skirt is finished with facing exactly the way the neck edge was on the dress in Chapter 15.

Sew or fuse interfacing to the facing. Sew the pieces together and turn under the outside edge. Sew the facing to the waist, clip and grade the seam, and turn the facing to the inside. Turn the ends under at the zipper, and tack the facing at the seams and darts. You may topstitch it as well.

Binding Alternative

Some women don't like the bulk of the facing on a bandless skirt or pants. You can solve this problem by using narrow, single-fold bias binding around the waist. Stitch around the waist at $5/8$" if it isn't already stay-stitched. Lay the binding flat side up on the right side of the seam allowance. One side of the binding should be right on the stay-stitching. Sew close to that edge of the binding. Extend the binding beyond the zipper on both sides by about $5/8$".

Trim the waistline seam allowance shorter than the binding, and clip the curves. Turn the binding to the back and press it flat. Wrap the ends of the binding under the seam allowance and ends of the zipper tape, and pin them flat out of the way of the zipper. Stitch close to the lower edge of the binding.

Elastic Waist

If your skirt has an elastic waist, make a casing at the top. Your guide sheet and pattern will tell you how much to turn it under and the width of elastic you should use. Leave a gap in the casing for about 2" at the back seam to insert the elastic. Your pattern might call for a round of topstitching at the top edge of the casing.

You can replace spent elastic on a skirt or pants by opening the casing and pulling the old elastic out. If the elastic is sewn on, remove the stitches, then make a casing with extra-wide bias tape or by cutting a waistband facing from similar fabric.

Measure the elastic around your waist without stretching it. Cut it 1" longer than comfortable. Attach a safety pin to one end of the elastic, and thread it through the casing. Be sure you don't accidentally pull the other end of the elastic through the casing as well. Overlap the elastic and pin the ends together with the safety pin. Try on the skirt to make any final adjustments to the elastic. Sew the layers of elastic together by stitching a square on the overlap. This will lie flatter than sewing them together like a normal seam. The square of stitching will ensure that they hold together securely.

Slip the stitched elastic into the casing, and finish sewing down the casing. If you are afraid the elastic will twist inside, stretch the waistline by pulling from several different places so the elastic is distributed evenly. Stitch in the ditch through the casing and elastic at each seam.

Final Details

Your skirt is going to look nearly finished at this point. Try it on again, and pin up the hem as described in Chapter 15 for the dress. Once it is hemmed, there are just a few more details to take care of.

You may need to add snaps, hooks and eyes, or a button at the waistband. This will depend on your pattern and your personal tastes. If your skirt has a slit, you will need to finish it. Generally this is done by pressing under the seam allowance from the end of the stitched seam to the bottom of the skirt. Turn the edge of the seam allowance under, and stitch it down.

Chapter 19

Little Girl's Jumper

Ruffled dresses are still popular for young girls. This one can be worn as a sundress or a jumper or even over another dress like an old-fashioned pinafore. It is cut primarily by measure, with only two shaped pieces that will require making a pattern. You can make the dress as fancy or as simple as you (and the young lady who will wear it) would like.

Taking Measurements

You will need to spend a few minutes with the future recipient of the jumper to get some accurate measurements. The waist measurement shouldn't be at the true waist but rather slightly higher, as this jumper has what would be considered an empire waist. On a toddler, there probably won't be much difference in the measurement itself. However, other measurements are taken up and down from this same "waistline."

The measurements you will need are the following:

A. *Comfortable* distance around empire waist
B. Distance from waist to length of skirt
C. Distance from waist to desired top of bib
D. Distance from waist to shoulder and diagonally across back to waist

FIGURE 19-1

◀ Little girl's jumper.

QUESTION?

How do I measure from an invisible "waist"?
Try tying a long ribbon around her lower chest to mark the right location while you take the other measurements. If she won't leave the ribbon alone, take off her shirt and use a washable marker.

Choosing Material

The dress fabric can be anything from lightweight cotton chintz or seersucker for a sundress to corduroy or velveteen for a winter jumper. You can leave the ruffle off or add lace to get the effect you want. To fasten the back and the suspenders, you will need three buttons.

For a short dress for a toddler with a waist up to about 23", you will probably need only 1 to 1½ yards of fabric. A long dress will take something over 2 yards. The largest piece will be the skirt, which will be about twice your measurement A in width by measurement B in length plus seam allowances and hem. This piece can be cut in three pieces, but those dimensions will help you know how much fabric you will need. Most of the rest of the pieces are long narrow ones, totaling approximately ²/₃ yards of a 42" fabric.

If you want to trim the bottom of the dress with lace, you will need twice measurement A plus 3" or 4" for seam allowances and possible shrinkage. A lace trim over the ruffle will need about 4 times measurement D plus 6" or 8".

The shoulder ruffles can be made from a contrasting fabric with a matching ruffle added to the bottom of the dress. This is particularly effective with a long dress. The lower ruffle will be about four times measurement A by twice the width you desire plus 1". The shoulder ruffles are each about twice measurement D by about 3½" at their widest point. Use these measurements to determine the amount of contrasting fabric to buy.

FACT

With little girl dresses, it's easy to spend more on lace and ribbons than on fabric. If you're watching for sales, don't worry about the fabric prices—you'll only need a yard or two. Instead, watch for sales on trim and stock up when it's cheaper.

Making the Patterns

There are two pieces of the jumper that cannot be cut strictly by measure. These are the suspenders and the shoulder ruffles. The size you will need for these will depend on your measurements, but you'll have to draw patterns.

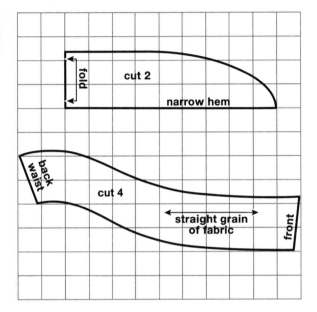

FIGURE 19-2

◀ Ruffle and suspender pattern.

Ruffle

Begin by making the ruffle pattern. As you can see by the pattern diagram in **FIGURE 19-2**, it is cut on the fold. The straight edge will have a narrow hem, and the curved edge will be gathered. For a toddler, the ruffle pattern might be 3½" wide at the center fold. This allows for a ½" hem and a ½" seam allowance, leaving a 2½" finished ruffle at the shoulder. You can make your ruffle wider or narrower, as you choose. The length of the entire ruffle needs to be twice the measurement D. This means your pattern, which is half a ruffle, should be equal in length to measurement D.

Since this is a pattern you are creating for yourself, use ½" seam allowances rather than the standard ⅝". It is much easier to figure and less confusing. For any piece with a seam on both sides, you will add 1".

Suspenders

The suspender pattern has some interesting curves. The idea is for one end to attach to the bib and the other end to attach to the back waist after crossing with the other suspender in the back. The pattern curves so the suspender will lie flat.

The length of the piece should be measurement D *minus* measurement C, which is the bib length. To this remainder, add 3". This will allow for seam allowances and a tab for a button at the back waist. For a toddler, the width should be about 2½". This makes a suspender about 1½" wide.

Draw your pattern on a grid to help you with the curves. Mark off the width and length that your pattern needs to be. Then use the grid marks on the diagram to help you put the curve in your pattern.

Cutting Pieces by Measure

Prepare your fabric if it's washable, which is highly recommended for anything a child is going to wear. Preshrink your trim, if you have any. Begin cutting your largest pieces first.

Skirt

The skirt should be the length of measurement B plus 3" for the seam allowance and hem. The total width needs to be twice measurement A plus 1" for a seam allowance. It may not be practical to cut the entire skirt in one piece, however. If not, avoid a seam in the center front by cutting one piece the width of measurement A plus 1" for the front and two pieces half measurement A plus 1". There needs to be a seam in the back for the opening to allow the dress on and off.

Optional Tie

The next largest pieces will be the ties, if you want to add them. Make them long enough to attach at the side waist and tie with a big bow in the back. Something like 24" will be sufficient for a toddler. If you cut them 3½" wide you can put a narrow hem on each side and still have a nice, wide bow. Cut two of these straight with the grain of the fabric.

Pattern Pieces

Fold your fabric double, straight with the grain. The ruffle is cut on the fold, and you need to cut two of them. You will need to cut four suspender pieces, two from the front of the fabric and two from the back. Lay out both of the patterns on the folded fabric, cut them out, and lay them out again for the other pieces.

Waistband

You will need to cut two of the waistband pieces, too, one for the outside and one to serve as the facing inside. They should each be the length of measurement A plus 3" and 2" wide. For a larger child, you might want the waistband to be a little wider.

If you are running out of fabric long enough to cut the waistband, you can piece it the way you can the skirt. Cut the front half measurement A plus 1". The back pieces can both be cut to half of measurement A plus 3" and trimmed to fit when you sew them on.

Bib

The only pieces left to cut out are the bib and its facing. These pieces are exactly the same size. To make the jumper fit a little better, the bib needs to taper inward slightly from the top to the waistline. Rather than try to cut it exactly, it's easier to cut a rectangle and trim it to fit.

The bib should be measurement C plus 1" by one fourth of measurement A plus 2". Cut two of these rectangles. Take one rectangle, and fold it in half along the line that will be the center front. Mark the bottom edge ½" from the lower, outside corner. Draw a straight line from this point to the upper outside corner. Cut along this line through both layers of the folded bib. An acrylic ruler and a rotary cutter make this very easy. Simply find the mark ½" from the lower edge, and line it up with the upper corner and slice off the excess. Repeat the process with the other bib piece so they are again the same size and shape.

Summary of Pieces to Cut

If all this sounds like a lot of math and story problems at that, here is a list in mathematical shorthand of all the pieces you need to cut:

- Skirt = B + 3" by 2 A + 1"
- *OR* Pieced skirt = 1 (B + 3" by A + 1") and 2 (B + 3" by ½ A + 1")
- Ties = 2 (3½" by approx. 24")
- Ruffle pattern = 2 (D [on fold] by 3½")
- *Curved* suspender pattern = 4 ([D – C] + 3" by 2½")
- Waistband = 2 (A + 3" by 2")
- Bib = 2 (C + 1" by ¼ A + 2")

Constructing the Top

The bib and suspenders go together a little differently than you might think at first glance. The purpose of this particular order is to get all the raw edges tucked neatly under the facing.

Suspenders and Bib

Pick one pair of suspenders and one bib piece to serve as the facing. The other will be the outside front and suspenders. If you are adding an appliqué or other decoration to the front of the bib, do it before attaching the suspenders.

Sew the suspenders to the top of the bib. Refer to the suspender pattern illustration to be sure you're sewing the correct end to the bib. The two suspender pieces should curve toward each other. Match the side of the suspender to the side of the bib at the ½" seam line, and sew the suspenders on. Press the seams toward the suspenders.

Repeat the process with the lining for the bib and suspenders.

Ruffle

Sew a narrow hem to the straight side of both the ruffle pieces. Sew a row or two of gathering stitches along the curved side. Gather the ruffles evenly along the outside edges of the bib and suspenders. The ruffle should end ½" from the waistline and 1" or 2" before the end of the suspender.

Press the seam allowances away from the ruffle. Grade the seam allowance.

Facing

On the bib and suspender facing piece, fold and press the outside edges under ½". These are the edges that correspond to the edges on the outside piece that have the ruffles.

With the right sides together, pin the lining to the bib and suspenders. Sew along the top of the bib, the inside of the suspenders, and across the bottom of the suspenders. You can open the seam allowances out and sew up the end of the suspenders as far as the ruffle.

Clip the corners and grade the seam. Turn the lining to the inside and press. Hand-stitch the lining to the ruffle seam allowance, or topstitch all the way around the suspenders and bib.

Stitch along the bottom of the bib to keep the two layers together.

FACT

It would be possible to sew along both sides of the suspenders and turn the ruffle to the right side, with only the waistline of the bib unstitched. The difficulty is folding the ruffle so it isn't caught in the stitching on either side of the suspenders and still keeping your seams straight. If you have omitted the ruffle, this would be the way to save some time.

Constructing the Skirt

Because of the need to attach the bib, the way we add the waistband to the jumper is different than the way we worked with the skirt in Chapter 18.

Gathering the Skirt

If your skirt is in three pieces, begin by sewing the side seams and pressing them open. Sew the center back seam, leaving 3" or 4" open at the top.

Stitch the edges of the back opening under ¼". Press the seam allowance and the back opening edges toward the right side. This will make it easier to finish the seam allowance for a small overlap. Stitch the right side's seam allowance to the skirt along this fold.

If you know the length you want to make the skirt, a hem would be easier to put in now, while the skirt is still flat. If you added 3" to the measured length, you have 2½" to use as a hem.

Run a row or two of gathering stitches around the top of the skirt. Gather it onto one of the waistband pieces. The waistband should extend ½" beyond the back right edge (the side that is folded and stitched at the seam line). It should extend 1½" beyond the back left edge to provide room for a button. Sew the skirt to the waistband. Grade the seam allowance, and press it toward the waistband.

Attaching Skirt to Front

You will add the bib to the skirt before you finish the waistband. Begin by finding the center of the bib at the waistline and the center front of the waistband. Be sure you measure the center across from the back seam line, not from the edges of the waistband (one extends under the other) or the edges of the opening (one was turned under more than the other).

With right sides together, pin the lower edge of the bib to the upper edge of the waistband, matching the centers. Sew across the bib edge. Your stitches should not quite catch the end of the ruffle. Trim the bib's seam allowance slightly.

Press one long edge of the waistband facing under ½". Line the other edge up with the upper edge of the waistband, covering the bib.

Sew along the upper edge of the waistband, across the end at the right back, across the end, and up to the skirt on the left back. Clip the corners, grade the seams, turn, and press. Hand-stitch or topstitch the lower edge of the waistband.

While topstitching is an option across the suspenders and around the waist, it won't be as neat as blind stitching. For your topstitching to be straight, you will need to be sewing with the right side facing you. What you are trying to stitch into place is on the underside and impossible to watch.

Buttons, Buttonholes, and Ties

Your little jumper is nearly done. The last few details are all that remain.

Buttonholes

Your dress will need three buttonholes in the back waistband. One will hold the skirt closed, and the other two will attach the suspenders. Begin with the one at the center back. This buttonhole should run horizontally so any strain on it tightens it rather than pulling it open. For the same reason, the two buttonholes for the suspenders should run vertically, if possible. This may not be possible with such a narrow waistband and will depend on the size of your buttons.

Before you can make the buttonholes for the suspenders, you'll need to determine where they fall. This can be done by laying the jumper face down on a table and folding the suspenders over imaginary shoulders or a hanger, but it's going to be more accurate to try the dress on the little girl. Use safety pins to mark the spots so you don't scratch her with straight pins.

Adjust the pins so the two buttonholes are an equal distance from the sides of the bib. Follow your sewing machine manual to make the buttonholes, or make them as described in Chapter 4.

Sew the buttons on so that the jumper fits. The buttons on the suspenders and even on the waistband can be moved a little as the child grows.

Ties

If you cut pieces for the optional ties, begin by putting a narrow hem along both long sides of both ties.

To give the ends of the ties a nice point, fold one end of each tie in half, right sides together, and stitch across it. Clip the corner. Turn the tie right side out, and open it out. Press the end so the little end seam lies flat against the underside of the tie. You can topstitch around the point or across the other end of the triangle to keep the point's little "pocket" from opening out.

Fold a pleat in the other end of the ties to make it fit the waistband. Sew across the pleat.

With the right side of the tie against the waistband front, line ½" from the edge of the tie with the center side. If your skirt was made from three pieces, you can use the side seams as guides. Otherwise, a guess is close enough as long as the two ties are the same distance from the sides of the bib.

Sew the ties to the waistband. The ties will fold over these raw edges as it is pulled to the back to tie it in a bow.

Other Possible Trim

If you haven't already hemmed the dress, try it on the little girl and pin it up. You can add lace to the bottom edge along with or as a substitute for a hem. Lace can be added to the edge of the ruffle or across the top of the bib between the suspenders. Simply put the straight edge of the lace against the back of the ruffle or bib and topstitch from the front side. Ⓔ

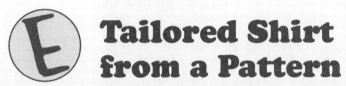

Chapter 20

Tailored Shirt from a Pattern

There are a lot more little pieces required to make a shirt than to make a skirt or basic dress, but you'll still construct it step by step. Don't let pieces labeled neckband, front band, yoke, placket, or epaulette scare you away from a shirt pattern you like. Pick out something and give it a try.

Beginning as Usual

Begin the same as you did the dress and skirt. Use the chart on the back of the pattern envelope to determine your size and the amount of fabric you need. Don't forget to check for interfacing. Also, check the notions list for the number of buttons and what other binding or fasteners you might need.

Preshrink and straighten your fabric. Cut your pattern pieces apart and collect together the pieces you need for your chosen style.

Alter the pattern if necessary using the same steps described in Chapter 15. Lay out your pattern, noting which pattern pieces must be cut on the fold and which need to be cut more than once. Remember to measure from the ends of the straight-with-the-grain arrows to the fold or selvage. Mark things like darts, pocket hems and locations, cuff openings and so on. Collect the pieces that will need interfacing and either cut them out all at once as directed in your guide or cut them from the fabric pieces as described in Chapter 15.

You will probably begin with stay-stitching. The rest of the order will depend on the particular style of the shirt you are making. Finishing the front edge is often the next step. Pockets may come either before or after that. If your pattern has front yokes, they will be sewn onto the front pieces before the front edge is finished and either before or after the pockets. Follow the order of steps as they are presented in the guide.

Finishing the Front Edges

Front edges of shirts are finished a number of different ways. Because there will be buttons and buttonholes added to the front, or in some cases snaps, interfacing is almost always included. You may add a front band to the buttonhole side. Often, the front is hemmed over a strip of interfacing, then folded over and topstitched to simulate a front band.

Other shirts are designed with an extension to the front pieces that serve as facings. You will turn the far outside edge under and stitch it, but you won't fold over the facing until after you've attached the collar.

Making Tailored Pockets

Tailored pockets are done a bit differently than the simple square patch pockets described so far. The primary difference is the shape. The lower corners are usually angled. Occasionally, the pocket comes to a point at the bottom.

Finishing the Edges

Because you won't want the bulk of two layers of fabric in your shirt pocket, these can't be lined and turned. The edges need to be turned under neatly and accurately. Misshapen pockets will detract from the appearance of the entire garment.

Begin by pressing the top edge under ¼". If your fabric takes a crease well, you may not need to stitch this fold down. Fold the top of the pocket again, this time toward the front at the hemline. This will either be marked on the pattern piece or the distance will be noted in the guide. Stitch the ends of the hem at the ⅝" seam line. Clip the corners diagonally and trim the seam allowance of the folded portion to ¼".

Turn the hem to the back and press, making sure the top corners are good, sharp points. Press the rest of the edges of the pocket under ⅝". If your pocket has angled corners, press the sides and bottom first. Press the corners over them, being careful that the overlaps in the seam allowance are smooth and flat.

If your pocket has a pointed bottom, fold the bottom and side corners up to the ⅝" line, and then fold the sides over them. Make sure you are as accurate as possible. If you fold the corners up too far, the corners will have a rounded appearance; not far enough, and the side folds will overlap one another making the corner too thick.

If your pockets are rounded at the bottom, stitch around the bottom and sides at the seam allowance. Clip Vs around the curve. Press the seam allowance under along the stitching. Topstitch ¼" from the edge.

Stitching the Pocket

Sometimes the guide will ask you to topstitch the pocket before it is sewn to the shirt. This may include a line of stitching at the bottom of the hem and ¼" from the outside edge of the rest of the pocket. It may ask for these outlining stitches after the pocket is sewn on the shirt as a way of reinforcing the application stitches. If your fabric doesn't hold a crease well, consider doing it before in order to hold the edges under while you place your pocket.

Locate the marked dots on the shirt front piece or pieces. These dots will be on the underside of your fabric, and you will need to attach your pocket to the outside, of course. From the back, run a pin in and out of the fabric just at the dot. Use the pins to help you place the pocket. Remember to remove these pins before you begin stitching.

If you've altered your shirt pattern, it might be wise to check the placement of the pocket. In front of a mirror, hold the shirt with the front up, using the side seam and neck edge to place it as close as possible to how it will wear. Move the pocket if it looks like it is out of place.

Stitch close to the sides and lower edges of your pocket(s).

FACT

Pocket flaps are easy to add. Stitch the two pieces together at all but the top end. Clip, turn, and press. Topstitch the flap, and add a buttonhole. Place it above the pocket with the raw edge ½" above the top of the pocket. Stitch ¼" from this edge. Press the flap down and stitch ½" from the fold. The raw edge is between these two rows of stitching.

Sewing One- or Two-Piece Collars

After the pockets, the next step is usually the shoulder seams. If there are back darts or a yoke, these will be done first. The yoke facing, if your pattern calls for one, will be added at the base of the yoke, pressed upward and blind-stitched to the shoulder seams. Then you're ready to add the collar.

Types of Collars

The collars on most tailored shirts are rolled collars, meaning the collar itself rolls or folds over. The base of the collar stands up at the neck edge. This base might be made from a separate piece called a stand—making it a two-piece collar—or it might be all one piece. The way to tell if your pattern has a rolled collar is to look at the shape of the seam line that will be attached to the shirt. This will be the notched edge of the collar piece. If it is straight or nearly so, you have a rolled collar.

Another possible shirt collar is a flat collar, which will be shaped more like the neck facing for the dress in Chapter 15. It will lie flat against the neck edge.

A stand collar and a mandarin collar stand up after they are sewn on. They are made from a straight or only slightly curved narrow strip. Think of it as the collar stand of a rolled collar without the collar itself. The difference between the two is the stand collar opens in back, while the mandarin opens in front.

Basic Construction

Any of these collars is going to be constructed essentially the same way. Cut the interfacing, and stitch or fuse it to one of the collar pieces. Trim the interfacing close to the stitching. This piece will probably be the bottom piece of the collar. Sew the two collar pieces together, leaving the notched edge open. Clip the corners and curves, grade the seam allowances, turn it right side out, and press it.

If you have a two-piece collar, the stand pieces will probably be sewn on either side of the collar at this point. One of these pieces will need interfacing as well.

To add collar stays, measure your stay at an angle from the corner seam allowance and place a tiny buttonhole ¼" from the tip. Slide the collar stays through the buttonholes after the collar is together but before you topstitch. The topstitching will hold the stays in place.

Self-Facing Collars

Some shirt collars are self-facing. This actually makes a cleaner inside neck edge because there is no facing to tack to the seam allowances. To make a self-facing collar, fold the notched edge of upper collar or stand under ⅝" *before* you stitch it to the bottom collar or stand.

Line the notched edge of the bottom collar up with the neckline. The neckline's seam allowance will need to be clipped to make it open enough to let the collar lie flat. Pull the folded edge of the upper collar out of the way, and stitch the collar to the neckline.

Some pattern guides will tell you to sew your collar onto the right side of the shirt, while others tell you to sew it onto the wrong side. This depends on how the individual collars are intended to roll. A collar sewn onto the right side will fold midway or so on the collar. The inside is not expected to show; therefore, it is the side with the blind stitching. A collar that's sewn to the wrong side will fold along the faced front, creating a sort of lapel effect. The inside of the collar seam will show more than the outside, which will always be covered by the collar itself. The inside, then, should have the neater, machine stitches.

Faced Collars

Faced collars are made in a very similar fashion, except neither edge of the collar is turned under. The collar is treated as one piece as it is sewn to the neck edge, and then the facing is sewn on to finish the edge.

The facing pieces may be separate and look much like those for the dress in Chapter 15. They may be part of the facing that finishes the front edge. The facing pieces might also be a fold-over facing that is part of the shirt front itself.

The collar might even be finished with a combination of the two techniques. The collar is attached to the neck edge through one layer of the collar only, as if it were self-facing. The front facing is folded over, and the part of the collar in front of the shoulder seam is treated like the usual faced collar. The seam allowance will need to be clipped to allow part of the allowance to fold down under the facing and the rest to fold up inside the collar.

ALERT!

If your pattern calls for epaulettes, put them together just like the pocket flaps. Sew the raw edge at the armhole edge centered over the shoulder seam. Tack down the end, and add a button just inside the point.

Making Cuff Openings

Sleeves with cuffs require an opening in the sleeve itself big enough to allow a hand to fit through. This slit is finished with either a hem, a binding strip, facing, or a placket. Your guide will direct you to finish this opening before you sew the sleeve seam because it is easier to do while the sleeve is still flat.

Hemmed Cuff Opening

For a hemmed cuff opening, the opening is generally a straight slit. Its exact position will be marked on the pattern. Make narrow hems on both sides. Fold the sleeve, right sides together, with these two narrow hems aligned. Sew a sort of tiny dart at the point of the slit to bring the bit of raw edge to the inside and to reinforce the end so the slit doesn't tear farther.

Binding Strip Finish

The pattern piece designed to finish a cuff opening with this type of finish is often called a continuous lap. Press the edges of the long sides under as you would to make a single-fold binding strip.

The sleeve pattern will indicate where the slit should be. Often a stay-stitching line is indicated. Make the slit after the stay-stitching is completed. Open out the slit so it is as straight a line as possible. Sew the continuous lap over the slit much like other applications of seam binding.

If you have lots of patterns, or if you have trouble getting the tissues back in the envelopes, organize them in 9" by 12" envelopes. Label the outside with the pattern number and file numerically. Put the envelopes in plastic sleeves in a notebook, arranged by garment type. Look through your notebook to pick a pattern. Use the number on your choice to find the actual pattern.

Finishing with Facing

A facing piece might be used for the usual long narrow openings in place of either the hem or binding. It would certainly be the choice for a low, wide opening at the cuff that would be difficult to finish with binding or a hem. Follow the markings on the pattern for the exact location for placement and stitching.

Generally, three edges of the facing are turned under ¼" and stitched. The facing is pinned to the sleeve, right sides together, with the unturned side of the facing along the raw edge of the sleeve. Stitch along a marked stitching line close to the location for the slit, much like you would if you were stay-stitching for binding. Cut the slit through the shirt and the facing.

Turn the facing to the back and press. Stitch the facing near the outside edge.

Making a Cuff Placket

A more tailored look to a cuff opening can be achieved with a placket. Often this requires two placket pieces, one to make the underlap and the other to make the overlap. The underlap is made much like the binding, but it is done only on one side of the slit and is wider. The overlap is put on in a similar manner, except it has an extension at the top. After its edges are turned under, this is used to cover the top of the underlap piece and the top of the slit.

Occasionally, the placket is made from one piece. It is put on much like the facing, only with its right side to the back of the sleeve. It is turned through to the right side and used there to create the two laps and finish the edges of the slit.

Adding the Cuffs

Cuffs are always self-facing. There is not a lot of difference between attaching them and attaching a self-facing collar. The difference is mainly with the sleeve itself, rather than the cuff.

QUESTION?

What is a gusset?
A gusset is a fabric insert at the underarms of sleeves that are cut kimono-style, that is, cut all of a piece with the body of the shirt or dress. Gussets make the shirt more comfortable by allowing more arm movement.

Preparing the Cuffs

Prepare the cuff in much the same way as you did the collar. The outer cuff piece will be lined with interfacing. Press under the seam allowance on the notched side of the inner piece. Sew the pieces together along the three unnotched sides, clip the corners, grade the allowances, turn, and press.

If your cuff is one that folds in half, rather than being cut in two pieces, the notched half should be lined with interfacing and the opposite end turned under. This cuff might be sewn onto the sleeve before it is folded.

Before you can attach a cuff, you need to sew any tucks or pleats that your pattern calls for onto the lower edge of the sleeve. If there are no pleats or tucks, the sleeve will likely be gathered.

Sew the sleeve seam, and press it open.

Attaching the Cuffs

If your sleeve is gathered onto the cuff, stitch the gathering stitches from one side of the cuff opening to the other. Gather the sleeve onto the cuff the way you would a ruffle. If the sleeve has pleats or tucks, the cuff should go on flat against the sleeve.

If your sleeves have plackets, the cuffs should fit exactly on each edge of the finished opening. Another type of opening might require the cuff to extend beyond the edge of one side of the opening to create an overlap. Follow your guide to place the cuff correctly.

Generally, the cuff is sewn to the shirt with the right sides together. Then the seam allowance is tucked into the cuff. The underside of the cuff is blind-stitched to the seam. Often cuffs are topstitched to finish them.

Easing in the Sleeves

Occasionally dresses and frilly blouses will have gathered sleeves. These are gathered onto the armhole the way ruffles are. However, a tailored shirt is going to need to be eased on instead. What this means is the sleeve is almost gathered but not enough to make any actual puckers.

Begin by running a row of stitching between the notches on the sleeve. Your guide may have told you to do this before you sewed the arm seam. You will also need to sew the side seams on the shirt itself and press these allowances open.

Turn the shirt inside out. Put a sleeve, right side out, into the proper position at the armhole. Right and left sleeves are not interchangeable. Be sure that the notch groupings on the sleeves correspond to the same groupings on the shirt. Match and pin the pieces together at the notches, the underarm seams, and the center dot on the sleeve and the shoulder seam. Add pins every couple of inches. Use a pin to pull slightly on the easing stitches until the sleeve fits.

Stitch a $5/8$" seam around the armhole. Be careful not to let the needle go through more than one layer of the sleeve at once. The tiny "gathers" in the sleeve that ease it to fit need to be under the loops of thread that make the stitches—not at the point where the needle enters—so they do not show as puckers.

Clip the seam allowance at the underarm curve and press the allowance toward the sleeve.

FACT

Shoulder pads are generally covered with the shirt fabric and tacked to the shoulder seam allowance at both ends. Position them centered on the shoulder seam with the straight end extending about ½" beyond the armhole seam line. They are more often found in dresses and jackets than in tailored shirts.

Finishing with Buttons and Hem

The next thing your guide will call for is probably the hem. This might be straight or curved. The front facing may fold over it before it is top-stitched down.

Buttonholes need to be marked and stitched. Your pattern will show their placement or the guide will recommend a certain distance between them. Don't forget the buttonholes on the cuffs as well. Make buttonholes on both sides of the cuffs if you would rather use cuff links.

Sew the buttons across from the holes. A trick to make sure they align perfectly is to lay the buttonhole side over the button side, making sure they are even at the top. Pin the layers together at the top and bottom. Through the buttonholes, run a pin in and out of the button side. Unpin the layers, and carefully slip the buttonholes over the pins. Sew the buttons where the pins are.

Chapter 21

Advanced Mending and Altering

Now that you've had more experience sewing, you're ready to tackle some of the more complicated mending and altering projects. Remember that invisibility is still the goal. Sometimes you will need to take the garment apart (at least partially), correct the problem, and put it back together again, so that's where your sewing skills will come into play.

Appraising the Problem

You can't expect to be able to make your favorite old garment look like new. Plan, instead, to solve problems that keep you from using certain garments, or to extend the life of favorites. In a sense, every major mending or altering project is an experiment. You don't always know what you're going to turn a garment into when you start ripping out seams. There's always a chance it won't go back together the way you hope. However, if the piece of clothing is not wearable as it is, there's little to be lost in giving it a try.

Little except your time, that is. You need to consider the value of your time as well as the value of the garment. Take into account, also, what you might learn in the process.

If a garment has a whole list of problems, chances are you won't be able to correct them all. Your time will be wasted if there is still something wrong after hours of work. Ask yourself the following questions:

- Is the garment wearable as it is?
- If I can't fix it, can I at least return it to its current condition?
- What is the *best* I can hope for after mending or altering?
- How long is it likely to take?
- What is my time worth relative to the cost of replacing the garment?

Some of these questions will be easier to answer after you've had more experience altering and mending. Sometimes a project is worth tackling for the experience alone. You never know what new construction technique you might discover while you're taking something apart.

Darts and Shaping

Clothing manufacturers tailor their garments to fit some mysterious standard. A lucky few actually fit this standard. Everyone else buys the nearest fit. Sometimes that doesn't seem to be near enough.

Now that you know how garments are constructed, you don't need to be afraid to change a near fit to a perfect fit. This is going to work better with new garments, because stitching lines and fold lines may show in even slightly worn garments. Be sure you aren't working with a fabric that shows pinholes, like silk. Test the hem allowance with a pin before you begin. If your new garment is cotton, there's a chance it'll shrink a little so wash it before you alter it. Otherwise, alter first. Washing will only set the creases in the seams, darts, and hems.

Since it's much easier to make something smaller than it is to make it larger, buy the garment that fits part of you and is too large, rather than too small, elsewhere. This is true even if the next size smaller comes closer to fitting you except for one tight area. Unless the garment has unusually deep seam allowances, you're better off with the larger size. However, if the larger choice is too wide across the shoulders or too long at the waist, you will have to practically take the garment apart and start over to make it fit. It would probably be better to choose another style.

Put the garment on inside out. Pin the seams and darts until the garment fits. If you are altering the back seam, or if you are dealing with a close fitting garment, you might enlist a friend's help. Be careful not to make it *too* small. Sit down and move around in this smaller garment. Take it off carefully so the pins don't either scratch you or fall out.

Shift the pins a little to make sure you are altering each side evenly. Mark along the pins with chalk and stitch the seams and darts. Try the garment on again, right side out this time, then finish the seam allowances.

Shortening Sleeves

Sleeves with hems or simple sleeve bands are easily shortened. Sleeves with cuffs are another matter. The difficulty comes not so much with the cuff as with the sleeve opening. Begin by determining how much you want to shorten the sleeves. If the sleeve openings are deep enough, you may not need to change them.

Taking the Cuff Apart

Carefully remove the cuff by taking out the stitches that hold it to the sleeve. There may be topstitching that needs to be removed as well. Remove the binding or placket if necessary. If the opening is hemmed, you may not need to remove anything but the end dart and the top inch or so of the hem.

Cut off a little less of the bottom of the sleeve than your measurement suggests you should shorten it. Your seam will probably be deeper than what is left of the trimmed allowance. Plus you may have to take a deeper seam in the cuff itself, shortening the sleeves even further.

Fixing the Sleeve

Enlarge the opening in the sleeve if necessary. Finish the edges with the continuous lap or placket or by hemming. If you have trouble replacing the placket, see if you can't substitute a hem in its place.

Because sleeves are tapered, when you cut off the end, it will no longer fit the cuff. You will need to add a pleat or enlarge the existing pleats. Try to put them as close to their original position as possible.

Replace the Cuffs

Pin the cuff to the right side of the sleeve. You may need to take some stitches out of the ends of the cuff to be able to sew it on. Trim the shirt's allowance, finish the ends, and blind-stitch the underside of the cuff. Topstitch to match what was there originally.

Adding Panels

Enlarging garments takes some creative thinking. If the seam allowances don't give you enough fabric, you'll have to find it somewhere else. Rather than making your alterations disappear, try to make them look like original trim and hide them in plain sight. This works best with casual wear, but some dressier clothes might lend themselves to this type of altering, too.

Pants and Skirts

Take out the stitching in the side seams. It may be necessary to cut through the waistband. Take out a little of the hemstitches on each side of the side seams. Press the old allowance flat, and trim the edges so they are even. Cut two strips of fabric as near the same weight as the garment. Cut them as wide as the amount you want to add plus seam allowances. Be sure the strips are long enough to hem at the bottom, and turn under for the width of the waistband at the top.

Sew these strips into place at the sides of your garment. Redo the hem and turn under, and topstitch at the waist.

Cover the side panels with colorful braid or woven ribbon. You may be surprised at what you can find that will go with the color and style of your pants or skirt. Adding a little of the same trim to the edge of the pockets will further encourage the idea that the trim is original. For skirts, you might want to add three off-center stripes to the front rather than at the side seams.

While these panels work well with jeans, they are really best for shorts, skirts, and children's clothing. Unless you are fixing expensive jeans, the ribbon might turn out to be more expensive than replacing the pants.

Shirts and Blouses

To use panels to widen shirts and blouses, choose a contrasting fabric to create vertical stripes down the front. Open up the shoulder seams. Cut vertical lines straight with the grain from hem to shoulder front and back and on both sides. You can sew your panels in with two seams or by folding under the edges and topstitching as you overlap it with the cut edge of the shirt. This latter alternative is more likely to give the appearance of a stripe of trim.

If there are darts in line with where you want to cut, take out the stitches up to a couple of inches from the side seams. Press the darts flat. Make the cuts, and sew in the panels with two seams. Trim the top of the panels to align them with the shoulder seams, and repair these seams. Repair the hem.

If you had to take out a dart, try the shirt on inside out and find the lines for the new darts. Be sure both sides look the same, especially where they cross the panels. Consider replacing sleeve bands with your panel fabric or adding a breast pocket.

If you only need to add a little to a shirt, add a new button panel. Whether this works or not will depend on what the present button side looks like, since it will now show. Keep your addition narrow enough to remain behind the buttonhole overlap.

Sleeves

If a sleeve is too tight, you can put a similar panel along the top of the sleeve. Add a matching panel across the shoulder seams or along the bottom of the shirt.

If the armhole is tight too, open the shoulder seam and widen it with a panel. You can turn it under at the neckline or redo the facing. If there is a collar, you'll need to completely redo the neckline.

Dresses

Dresses without waistlines might be altered with panels the same way as shirts or blouses. If there is a waistline, you might open up the waist seam and sew in separate panels for the bodice and the skirt, but be sure to have them meet.

If the dress is gathered, you might take the skirt off entirely, or at least up to the zipper. Add the panels to the bodice, and regather the skirt onto the larger waistline. If you want the skirt to be fuller, don't remove the skirt except right at the point where you add the panels. Add slightly wider panels to the skirt so it gathers appropriately.

Frayed Cuffs and Collars

You can extend the lives of favorite shirts or dresses if the only problem is fraying on the cuffs or collar. Before you try this with a pair of cuffs, make sure the sleeves are long enough that they will still fit when they are ¼" to ½" shorter. Do both cuffs even if only one is frayed, so they'll be even. Collars must be of a style that will allow them to be reduced in size as well.

Remove the topstitching from the collar or cuffs. Cuff buttons and buttonhole stitches will have to be removed as well. Remove the inside stitching where they attach to the shirt so you can open out the collar or cuff. You may not need to remove them entirely, depending on how they were constructed. Turn the collar or cuff so the right sides are together.

Stitch around the outside edge of a collar, tapering out from the edge that attaches to the neck. You don't want to change the size of that side of the collar. Sew only across the outer side of cuffs. Trim this new seam allowance. Turn, press, and reconstruct the cuffs or collar. Replace the button, and restitch around the buttonholes.

Suit-jacket cuffs can be repaired in a similar manner. Remove the stitches at the lining and at the seam so the jacket fabric can be unfolded. Press it flat. Fold along the original crease with right sides together. Stitch close to the edge, putting the frayed area inside the row of stitches. Turn. Press the sleeve hem so the stitching is just turned to the inside. Refold the lining and blind-stitch it back in place.

FACT

Before the days of effective detergents, shirts became stained where they rubbed against the back of the neck. Homemakers used to turn these collars. That is, the collar was removed and sewn on again upside down, hiding the stain under the fold in the collar. This method will still work if that's where the collar's frayed.

Replacing Worn-Out Lining

The lining in coats often wears out before the rest of it. Leather jackets especially will last much longer than their linings. Replace the lining before it has deteriorated to shreds.

Removing the Lining

Remove the old lining by carefully taking out the stitches. The right or left half will serve as your pattern for the new lining. Choose the side that is in the best shape, and take out the stitches on every dart and turned-under edge. If your lining is quilted or stuffed, this could get messy—all the more reason to replace the lining before it's gone completely to pieces.

Use your pieces to help you determine the amount of fabric you'll need. Buy good-quality suit or coat lining. This is a big enough job that you won't want to have to do it again too soon. If you choose rayon, iron it with a dry iron to avoid water spots.

Iron the pieces that will serve as your pattern. Make note of the amount of seam allowance remaining on the lining pieces. Lay out the pieces on your folded lining fabric. Cut carefully, adding where necessary if the edges are frayed. Mark any darts on the new pieces.

If your old lining had a pocket you don't want to give up, reconstruct it as close as you can to the way the old one was, using the pieces as your pattern. The construction of the welt pocket in Chapter 17 might help you with the details or as a substitute for the original pocket. You might want to use lighter-weight lining inside the pocket.

Reconstruct the lining by sewing the darts, seams, and sleeves. Turn under the outside edges. Slip the lining sleeves into the jacket sleeves, and blind-stitch around the lining's outside edge. Rehem the lower edge and the sleeves.

If you have a favorite garment that fit perfectly but has worn out, take it apart and use it as a pattern for a new one. Take into account the effect fabric has on the appearance and fit of a garment, and try to find fabric close to what your original garment was made of.

Replacing a Broken Zipper

Sometimes a zipper breaks on a garment while everything else is in good condition. Now that you've put zippers in new garments, you shouldn't be afraid to replace them.

Centered Zippers

Centered zippers are, of course, the easiest to work with. Take out the stitches on the zipper and enough of the facing or waistband to baste the seam closed. Sew in the new zipper, remove the basting stitches and repair the facing or waistband.

Lapped Zippers

Lapped zippers are a bit more difficult. Instead of going through the usual steps of sewing one side to a seam allowance, turning, and sewing again, you might want to use the shortcut described in Chapter 18.

Once the old zipper is removed, lay the seam flat, right side down, and lap the allowances the way they were for the old zipper. Lay the new zipper on top, and baste it in place by hand. Turn the garment over, and stitch along the old stitching line. Replace any other stitching you removed.

Flies

Front flies, especially in heavier fabrics such as denim jeans, often have an additional layer of fabric under the zipper that forms an underlap. In this case, remove just enough stitches to get the old zipper out. Put the new zipper in its place. Baste the zipper by hand, with all the layers in as close to the same configuration as they were with the old zipper. Machine-stitch.

You may not be able to do this all in one step. One side of the zipper may need to be sewn to a facing piece or fold before you can sew it to the garment. You may have to get creative if there are riveted buttons. Fold or trim the top of the zipper to avoid them, if necessary.

What if I can't find a zipper the right size?
Buy a larger zipper, and shorten it as described in Chapter 11. For separating zippers, either buy shorter and start or stop a little ways from the ends, or shorten a longer zipper at the *top*. Take looping stitches over the zipper at both sides of the top so the slide doesn't come off.

Camouflaging Mended Areas or Stains

There are any number of ways to disguise a mend or cover a stain. You will have to consider each case individually, using your own imagination and sense of style.

Cover-Ups

Depending on the location of the stain or mend, you might be able to cover it with a pocket, trim, or an appliqué.

The location has to be just right for a pocket to work. Even if it does work, there's the problem of fabric. Generally it is better to use contrasting fabric than it is to try to make the pocket from a near-match fabric. Use the fabric again around the collar, or match it to a new set of buttons. If it's a short-sleeved dress or shirt, you might stitch a narrow fold of your pocket fabric behind the sleeve band and extend it just ¼" beyond.

Whether a row of ruffle or other trim is going to work will also depend on the location. Perhaps a second row in a more logical place will keep the first from looking odd. Maybe three rows of narrow ribbon sewn on the diagonal across one side of a casual shirt and repeated along the bottom of the other side will work, if the ribbons pick up colors in the shirt.

Children's clothes lend themselves to the use of appliqué for cover-ups. If the exact location seems wrong for a single appliqué, consider how it might look if it is part of a scattering of related appliqués.

Cut It Away

Consider how you might modify a garment to get rid of a stain or serious tear. If it's on a sleeve, can the sleeves be cut off above the problem and either banded or hemmed? If it's near the bottom, can the garment be shortened?

If the problem is in the center front of a sweatshirt or sweater, consider slitting the garment down the center, adding ribbing to cover the cut ends, and turning it into a cardigan.

Retro is in. Shop at secondhand stores or garage sales. Redo your finds, dye them, and combine them with what's already in your closet. Some of your "new" creations may surprise you. Have fun.

Sometimes a neckline can be changed to remove the problem. You can use a near-match fabric to face your new neckline. Press it so the stitching is just under, rather than right on, the edge. This is a trick you might use to make something you're tired of look like something new.

Complete Makeover Ideas

If none of the solutions suggested so far is going to help you salvage a garment, it's probably best to replace the item. However, if you really love the fabric or enjoy the idea of turning something useless into something useable again, consider completely making it over.

Using the Fabric

If you love the fabric in a garment, but you have a problem with the style or size, you might take it apart completely and reuse the fabric. This works best with a full skirt or dress with no waistline because the individual pieces will be larger. Also, the fabric must be in excellent condition or it won't be worth your time.

Remove all the stitches in the garment. Press each piece flat. If you are going to buy a new pattern to use with this fabric, make a sketch of all your pieces and label them with the measurements. Take this sketch with you so you'll have a better idea of what you have to work with as you shop for patterns.

Remaking a Dress

A dress can sometimes be remade either into a skirt or a jumper. Consider the style to see if it is appropriate for either. If you turn it into a skirt, you may need to replace the zipper with a shorter one. See if you can piece a waistband from the bodice of the dress. If not, cover it with a belt or a long blouse.

If you decide to make a jumper, cut off the sleeves and recut the armholes. You might want to recut the neckline as well. It's better to make patterns for these changes so your armholes match and the neckline is symmetrical. Use the pattern to cut facings. If there is enough fabric in the discarded sleeves, use it. Otherwise near-match fabric will work. Remember to use interfacing so your armholes and neckline have a crisp, clean look.

Combining Garments

Sometimes you can combine two or three garments to make a new one. Be sure the fabrics go together both in color and texture. For some ideas, look at illustrations in pattern books and clothing catalogs of garments that are made from two or more fabrics. Consider what parts of your current garments fit and what about each keeps you from using it.

As an example, say you have a dress that fits but is too short. Another dress is fine except the bodice is too tight. If the fabrics coordinate, cut off the short dress to bodice length and use it to replace the bodice that's too tight. Perhaps you can add a skirt pocket to match the new bodice or a breast pocket to match the new skirt.

Go through your closet, and pull out all the clothes you never wear. Assess the problems with each one, whether it's style, size, or fabric. See what you can alter and what you can redo. These clothes don't need to simply take up space. You have the skills to change them. Ⓔ

Appendix A

Glossary

appliqué
(V)The act of sewing pieces of cloth onto other pieces for decorative purposes. (N)The piece of cloth which is appliquéd on.

backing
The bottom layer of a quilt, also called lining.

balance wheel
Hand wheel on the right side of a sewing machine used to raise or lower the needle.

baste
To sew pieces in place with temporary stitches.

batik
Method of dyeing in which the area not to be dyed is painted with wax.

batting
The insulating layer of a quilt, usually cotton or polyester, sometimes called filling or padding.

between needle
The short, fine needles used for quilting or topstitching.

bias
The diagonal direction on a piece of cloth.

bias tape
Commercial binding cut on the bias sold in different widths and folds.

binding
Narrow strips of cloth used to cover raw edges.

blend fabric
A fabric that has a blend of more than one fiber, such as cotton and polyester.

blind stitch
The tiny hidden stitches done on the outside of a seam when it is impossible to get inside to machine-stitch.

block
An individual section of a quilt cover.

bobbin
The small spool that holds the lower thread on a sewing machine.

bobbin case
The case that holds the bobbin in the lower area of a sewing machine and rotates when you sew.

bolt
Unit of cloth bought by the retailer, which the shopper's yardage is cut from.

button loop
A loop extended from the buttonhole side of a garment used in place of a buttonhole.

buttonhole attachment
Attachment for a sewing machine that makes buttonholes almost automatically.

buttonhole foot
Clear presser-foot attachment for a sewing machine with marks to help you make a buttonhole.

cap sleeves
Very short sleeves that are cut as part of the body of a shirt or dress.

chain-stitch plate and bobbin insert
Sewing machine attachments that allow you to machine sew the one thread.

chambray
A lightweight cotton woven of dyed warp threads and white weft threads, often used for shirts.

chenille needles
Long, fat needles with sharp or blunt points used for sewing with yarn.

chintz appliqué
An appliqué made by cutting a motif out of a print fabric and sewing it to another.

collar stand
The part of the collar that stands up at the neckline.

comforter
A quilt in which the layers are tied together instead of quilted, sometimes called tied quilt.

continuous lap
Straight binding piece, usually on a cuff opening, that binds both sides of a slit as if it were straight.

corduroy
A cotton fabric with nap in rows, which are called wales.

cotton
One of the most popular fabrics, made from the cotton plant and available in a variety of weights and textures.

cover
The top layer of a quilt, often decorated, sometimes called the quilt top or face.

cover plate
A needle plate for a sewing machine that covers the fabric feeds and used for free-motion sewing such as embroidery.

crinoline
A stiffened fabric used to define pleats in draperies.

daisy stitch
A decorative embroidery stitch that looks like the petal of a flower.

darning needles
Needles that are several inches long to allow you to weave thread over a hole.

darts
Stitched folds in a garment to give it shape.

denim
A heavy cotton twill-weave fabric made from dyed warp threads and white weft threads, generally used for jeans and jackets.

dressmaker's carbon
Carbon paper with a washable transfer used to mark things like darts on fabric.

dressmaker's pins
Standard straight pins used for most sewing.

ease
Make something fit without gathers.

embroidery needles
Needles with elongated eyes to accommodate embroidery thread.

embroidery scissors
Small, short-bladed scissors used for clipping threads.

fabric feeds
Part of a sewing machine that feeds the fabric along under the needle.

facing
Fabric piece used to finish and support an edge such as a neckline.

fat quarter
One half-yard of fabric, cut in half lengthwise.

flannel
A napped cotton fabric with one fuzzy side.

flex-lace
Seam binding made of slightly stretchy lace.

French knot
An embroidery stitch that creates a small dot.

French seam
A finished seam made by sewing the edges together with wrong sides together before stitching the seam.

gingham
A cotton fabric made from dyed yarns woven in a checkered pattern.

glass-headed pins
Thin pins with glass heads, often called silk pins.

grade seams
To trim one seam allowance shorter than the other, with the goal of decreasing the thickness of the seam allowance on a turned item.

gusset
Fabric insert on the underarm to aid movement in kimono sleeves.

half back stitch
Variation on the blind stitch that is stronger and has more give.

heading
An extension above a shirred curtain that forms a small ruffle.

inseam
Seam at the inside of the leg on a pair of pants.

interfacing
Specially designed fabric used to give shaping to areas such as necklines and armholes.

interlining
Lining attached to individual pieces. The lining and outside fabric are treated as if they are one piece.

jersey
A lightweight cotton knit.

kimono sleeves
Long sleeves that are cut as part of the body of a shirt or dress.

linen
Fabric made from the fibers in the stems of the flax plant, used much like cotton.

lining
Fabric layer sewn inside a garment to add drape, comfort, and/or warmth and to conceal the seam allowances.

mitered corners
Corners finished with a diagonal fold from corner to hem or binding edge, making a clean, square corner.

muslin
An inexpensive cotton fabric, which is often undyed.

nap
Texture on the surface of a fabric.

needle board
Small flat board with needle-like side used to press velvet so the nap isn't crushed.

needle plate
Face plate that surrounds the fabric feeds on a sewing machine.

notch
A triangular-shaped marking on a pattern used to match up adjacent pieces.

notion
Any article, other than fabric, used in construction sewing.

nylon
A synthetic fabric.

one-way fabric
Fabric that appears different when turned 180 degrees, due to its print, nap, or shine.

outline stitch
A decorative embroidery stitch that makes a straight or curved line, sometimes called a stem stitch.

panel
A piece of cloth separating the blocks on a quilt cover, sometimes called sashing.

patches
Fabric used to mend a hole; also the name for individual quilt pieces.

patchwork
Anything made with pieces of different fabrics.

pinking shears
Scissors with serrated blades that cut in a zigzag pattern to slow fraying.

piping
Fabric-covered cord used as trim.

placket
Insert that finishes an opening by creating an overlap.

point presser
Small wooden stand used to press sharp points into collars and other turned points.

polyester
A synthetic fabric, often combined with natural fibers to make them easier to care for.

preshrink
Washing a piece of fabric so it will shrink before you cut out your garment or craft.

presser foot
Part of a sewing machine that holds the fabric against the fabric feeds.

pressing cloth
Cloth used to protect a sensitive fabric from the iron.

quilt
(V)To stitch layers of cloth together. (N)Generally, a bed-covering or wall-hanging made from layers of cloth. Other objects are referred to as quilted.

quilting stitch
Tiny in-and-out stitches through the layers of a quilt, done in a rocking motion.

raw edge
Unfinished cut edge of cloth.

rayon
Fabric made from regenerated plant material with many of the same characteristics as synthetic fabrics.

reverse appliqué
Appliquéing a fabric through a hole in the fabric on top of it.

ribbing
A stretchy knit fabric used for cuffs, collars, and waistbands of sweatshirts and similar garments.

rickrack
Decorative trim woven in a zigzag shape.

rolled collar
A collar that folds over so the base stands up at the neck.

rotary cutter
A cutting tool with a circular blade used on a special mat to cut straight lines.

running stitch
A stitch in which the needle weaves in and out of the fabric several times before being pulled all the way through.

satin
Cloth with a shiny finish.

satin stitch
A decorative embroidery stitch made with parallel stitches very close together.

satin-stitch foot
Presser-foot attachment for a sewing machine, with a groove along the center bottom for thick zigzag stitches.

seam binding
Tightly woven narrow ribbon used to support seams and finish hems.

seam guide
Sewing machine attachment used to help you sew seams at the proper distance from the fabric's edge.

seam ripper
Sharp hook-ended tool used for taking out stitches.

seersucker
A lightweight cotton fabric that alternates tightly woven stripes with loosely woven ones.

selvage
The tightly woven edges of a length of fabric.

serger
A type of sewing machine that finishes seams and trims them as it sews.

set
Sew the blocks of a quilt cover together or make a dye or coloring permanent.

shank button
Button with a small loop on the underside instead of holes, used with heavy fabrics.

sharp needle
Long needles used for most hand sewing.

shears
Long-bladed scissors.

shirred
Gathered onto a rod.

silk
Fabric woven from the threads spun by silkworms.

slashed pocket
Pocket made through a cut in a garment.

sleeve board
Miniature ironing board used to press sleeves and other narrow items.

spool pin
Pin on a sewing machine that holds the spool of thread.

stitch in the ditch
Topstitching done exactly on a seam.

straight-stitch foot
Presser-foot attachment for a sewing machine used on delicate fabrics.

straight-stitch plate
Needle plate for a sewing machine with a hole instead of a slot and used with delicate fabrics.

synthetics
Fabrics produced chemically.

T-pins
Heavy pins with long T-shaped heads used for heavy or loose-weave fabrics.

tack
To take a few small stitches on top of each other to hold two pieces of cloth together.

tailor's chalk
A special fabric chalk that brushes off; used to mark seam lines.

tailor's ham
Hard cushion used to press curves.

tapestry needles
Longer version of embroidery needles.

template
A shape cut the size and outline of a desired pattern piece used to mark stitching or cutting lines on a piece of fabric.

tension discs
Part of a sewing machine that keeps the thread taut.

thread take-up lever
Part of a sewing machine that controls the thread as it is fed to the needle.

topstitch
Stitches taken on the outside of a garment for decoration or to hold a turned edge flat.

tracing wheel
Tool with a spurlike wheel used with dressmaker's carbon for marking from a pattern to fabric.

twill tape
Sturdy cotton tape used to strengthen vulnerable cloth behind snaps or buttons.

valance
Short curtain at the top of a window.

velvet
A cotton fabric with a one-way nap.

wales
The rows of nap on corduroy.

walking foot
Presser-foot attachment for a sewing machine that feeds the cloth from the top while the fabric feeds feed from the bottom, sometimes called an even-feed foot.

warp threads
The threads in a woven fabric that run the entire length of the bolt.

weft threads
The threads of a woven fabric that run crosswise or from selvage to selvage.

welt
Insert in a garment, sometimes only for decoration, often to cover a slash pocket.

woolen
Wool fabric made from the shorter fibers, having a rough, hairy texture.

worsted
Wool fabric made from the longer fibers, having a smooth finish.

yard goods
Fabric sold by the yard or fraction of a yard.

zigzag stitch
A machine stitch of variable length and width used to finish raw edges or, when made close together, machine embroidery.

zipper foot
Narrow presser-foot attachment for a sewing machine with needle grooves on both sides; used to sew close to thick areas such as zippers.

Appendix B

Resources

Books

Ahles, Carol Laflin. *Fine Machine Sewing; Easy Ways to Get the Look of Hand Finishing and Embellishing* (Newtown, CT: Taunton Press, 2001).

This is a detailed guide to machine appliqué, twin-needle stitching, and other fancy topstitching techniques.

Atwood, Jennie Archer. *Sew Vintage: New Creations from Found Fabrics* (Newtown, CT: Taunton Press, 2002).

This is full of color photos of not-so-practical but lovely things to do with antique lace, old needlepoint, and vintage fabrics.

Brann, Donald R. *How to Make Valances, Cornice Boards, Draperies and Install Traverse Track* (Briarcliff Manor, NY: Directions Simplified, Inc., 1964).

This book has more information on installing hardware and constructing wooden valances than sewing the actual curtains, but it does have some helpful advice.

Cream, Penelope, ed. *The Complete Book of Sewing: A Practical Step-by-Step Guide to Sewing Techniques* (New York: D K Publishing, 1996).

A detailed guide to most sewing techniques with lots of pictures.

Davidson, Myra. *Pillows, Curtains and More: Coordinated Projects to Sew* (Radnor, PA: Chilton Book Co., 1993).

This is a colorful book with lots of ideas and instructions for home decorating.

Eames, Alexandra. *Windows and Walls, Designs Patterns Projects* (Birmingham: Oxmoor House, Inc., 1980).

This book has lots of ideas for curtains, shades, and wall coverings with basic directions.

Eaton, Jan. *The Encyclopedia of Sewing Techniques* (New York: Barron's Education Series, 1987).
A good quick-reference book for most kinds of home sewing.

Eisinger, Larry, ed. *The Complete Book of Sewing* (New York: Crown Publishers, Inc., 1972).
A good guide to sewing techniques with good illustrations, though the photographs are dated.

Geiger, Jennifer. *Small Quiltcrafts* (New York: Meredith Press, 1989).
This book presents lots of home-decorating and personal items that involve piecing or appliqué. The emphasis is on the quilting rather than the construction, but that is covered as well.

Goldworthy, Maureen. *Mend It!* (New York: Stein and Day, 1979).
A detailed book of directions for mending garments, in some cases beyond what most people would try.

Oppenbeimer, Betty. *Sewing Packs, Pouches, Seats and Sacks* (North Adams, MA: Storey Books, 1998).
This book has lots of practical projects, with detailed instructions and illustrations.

Magazines

Creative Needle
1 Apollo Road
Lookout Mountain, GA 30750
✆ (706)820-2600 or ✆ (800)443-3127
✍ *www.creativeneedlemag.com*

Threads
The Taunton Press, Inc.
63 South Main St., P.O. Box 5506
Newtown, CT 06470-5506
✆ (203)426-8171
✍ *www.threadsmagazine.com*

Sew Beautiful
149 Old Big Cove Rd.
Brownsboro, AL 35741-9985
✆ (800)547-4176
✍ *www.sewbeautifulmag.com*

Web Sites

✍ *www.americansewingexpo.com*
American Sewing Expo's Web site

✍ *www.asg.org*
American Sewing Guild's Web site

✍ *www.csnf.com*
Annual Creative Sewing & Needlework Festival

✍ *www.marthapullen.com*
Annual Martha's Machine Embroidery, Quilting, & Sewing Market

✍ *www.mnag.org*
Marin Needle Arts Guild, San Rafael, CA

✍ *www.vreseis.com*
Naturally colored cotton resource

✍ *www.moonbathshop.com*
Organic cotton and hemp fabrics

✍ *www.cottonplus.com*
Organic cotton from a farmer-owned cooperative

Free Offers

Beacon Fabric and Notions
Free catalog of outdoor fabric and supplies
6801 Gulfport Blvd. So. #10
South Pasadena, FL 33707
✆ (800) 713-8157

Fitting Tips!
Free newsletter for users of pattern-making software
P.O. Box 290651
Nashville, TN 37291
✆ (800) 213-0673

Folkwear
Free catalog of vintage and ethnic sewing patterns
✍ *www.folkwear.com*

Keepsake Quilting
Free catalog
Dept. TM, Route 25B
P.O. Box 1618
Centre Harbor, NH 03226-1618
✍ *www.keepsakequilting.com*

Smoke & Fire Co.
Free catalog of historic clothing patterns and books
P.O. Box 166
Grand Rapids, OH 43522
✆ (800) 766-5334

Wild Ginger Softwear, Inc.
Free demos for computer-generated patterns
✍ *www.wildginger.com*

Index

THE EVERYTHING SERIES!

BUSINESS

Everything® **Business Planning Book**
Everything® **Coaching and Mentoring Book**
Everything® **Fundraising Book**
Everything® **Home-Based Business Book**
Everything® **Leadership Book**
Everything® **Managing People Book**
Everything® **Network Marketing Book**
Everything® **Online Business Book**
Everything® **Project Management Book**
Everything® **Selling Book**
Everything® **Start Your Own Business Book**
Everything® **Time Management Book**

COMPUTERS

Everything® **Build Your Own Home Page Book**
Everything® **Computer Book**
Everything® **Internet Book**
Everything® **Microsoft® Word 2000 Book**

COOKBOOKS

Everything® **Barbecue Cookbook**
Everything® **Bartender's Book, $9.95**
Everything® **Chinese Cookbook**
Everything® **Chocolate Cookbook**
Everything® **Cookbook**
Everything® **Dessert Cookbook**
Everything® **Diabetes Cookbook**
Everything® **Indian Cookbook**
Everything® **Low-Carb Cookbook**
Everything® **Low-Fat High-Flavor Cookbook**

Everything® **Low-Salt Cookbook**
Everything® **Mediterranean Cookbook**
Everything® **Mexican Cookbook**
Everything® **One-Pot Cookbook**
Everything® **Pasta Book**
Everything® **Quick Meals Cookbook**
Everything® **Slow Cooker Cookbook**
Everything® **Soup Cookbook**
Everything® **Thai Cookbook**
Everything® **Vegetarian Cookbook**
Everything® **Wine Book**

HEALTH

Everything® **Alzheimer's Book**
Everything® **Anti-Aging Book**
Everything® **Diabetes Book**
Everything® **Dieting Book**
Everything® **Herbal Remedies Book**
Everything® **Hypnosis Book**
Everything® **Massage Book**
Everything® **Menopause Book**
Everything® **Nutrition Book**
Everything® **Reflexology Book**
Everything® **Reiki Book**
Everything® **Stress Management Book**
Everything® **Vitamins, Minerals, and Nutritional Supplements Book**

HISTORY

Everything® **American Government Book**
Everything® **American History Book**
Everything® **Civil War Book**
Everything® **Irish History & Heritage Book**

Everything® **Mafia Book**
Everything® **Middle East Book**
Everything® **World War II Book**

HOBBIES & GAMES

Everything® **Bridge Book**
Everything® **Candlemaking Book**
Everything® **Casino Gambling Book**
Everything® **Chess Basics Book**
Everything® **Collectibles Book**
Everything® **Crossword and Puzzle Book**
Everything® **Digital Photography Book**
Everything® **Easy Crosswords Book**
Everything® **Family Tree Book**
Everything® **Games Book**
Everything® **Knitting Book**
Everything® **Magic Book**
Everything® **Motorcycle Book**
Everything® **Online Genealogy Book**
Everything® **Photography Book**
Everything® **Pool & Billiards Book**
Everything® **Quilting Book**
Everything® **Scrapbooking Book**
Everything® **Sewing Book**
Everything® **Soapmaking Book**

HOME IMPROVEMENT

Everything® **Feng Shui Book**
Everything® **Feng Shui Decluttering Book, $9.95 ($15.95 CAN)**
Everything® **Fix-It Book**
Everything® **Gardening Book**
Everything® **Homebuilding Book**

All Everything® books are priced at $12.95 or $14.95, unless otherwise stated. Prices subject to change without notice.
Canadian prices range from $11.95–$31.95, and are subject to change without notice.

Everything® **Home Decorating Book**
Everything® **Landscaping Book**
Everything® **Lawn Care Book**
Everything® **Organize Your Home Book**

EVERYTHING® KIDS' BOOKS

All titles are $6.95

Everything® **Kids' Baseball Book, 3rd Ed.** ($10.95 CAN)
Everything® **Kids' Bible Trivia Book** ($10.95 CAN)
Everything® **Kids' Bugs Book** ($10.95 CAN)
Everything® **Kids' Christmas Puzzle & Activity Book** ($10.95 CAN)
Everything® **Kids' Cookbook** ($10.95 CAN)
Everything® **Kids' Halloween Puzzle & Activity Book** ($10.95 CAN)
Everything® **Kids' Joke Book** ($10.95 CAN)
Everything® **Kids' Math Puzzles Book** ($10.95 CAN)
Everything® **Kids' Mazes Book** ($10.95 CAN)
Everything® **Kids' Money Book** ($11.95 CAN)
Everything® **Kids' Monsters Book** ($10.95 CAN)
Everything® **Kids' Nature Book** ($11.95 CAN)
Everything® **Kids' Puzzle Book** ($10.95 CAN)
Everything® **Kids' Riddles & Brain Teasers Book** ($10.95 CAN)
Everything® **Kids' Science Experiments Book** ($10.95 CAN)
Everything® **Kids' Soccer Book** ($10.95 CAN)
Everything® **Kids' Travel Activity Book** ($10.95 CAN)

KIDS' STORY BOOKS

Everything® **Bedtime Story Book**
Everything® **Bible Stories Book**
Everything® **Fairy Tales Book**
Everything® **Mother Goose Book**

LANGUAGE

Everything® **Inglés Book**
Everything® **Learning French Book**
Everything® **Learning German Book**
Everything® **Learning Italian Book**
Everything® **Learning Latin Book**
Everything® **Learning Spanish Book**
Everything® **Sign Language Book**
Everything® **Spanish Phrase Book,** $9.95 ($15.95 CAN)

MUSIC

Everything® **Drums Book (with CD),** $19.95 ($31.95 CAN)
Everything® **Guitar Book**
Everything® **Playing Piano and Keyboards Book**
Everything® **Rock & Blues Guitar Book (with CD),** $19.95 ($31.95 CAN)
Everything® **Songwriting Book**

NEW AGE

Everything® **Astrology Book**
Everything® **Divining the Future Book**
Everything® **Dreams Book**
Everything® **Ghost Book**
Everything® **Love Signs Book,** $9.95 ($15.95 CAN)
Everything® **Meditation Book**
Everything® **Numerology Book**
Everything® **Palmistry Book**
Everything® **Psychic Book**
Everything® **Spells & Charms Book**
Everything® **Tarot Book**
Everything® **Wicca and Witchcraft Book**

PARENTING

Everything® **Baby Names Book**
Everything® **Baby Shower Book**
Everything® **Baby's First Food Book**
Everything® **Baby's First Year Book**
Everything® **Breastfeeding Book**

Everything® **Father-to-Be Book**
Everything® **Get Ready for Baby Book**
Everything® **Getting Pregnant Book**
Everything® **Homeschooling Book**
Everything® **Parent's Guide to Children with Autism**
Everything® **Parent's Guide to Positive Discipline**
Everything® **Parent's Guide to Raising a Successful Child**
Everything® **Parenting a Teenager Book**
Everything® **Potty Training Book,** $9.95 ($15.95 CAN)
Everything® **Pregnancy Book, 2nd Ed.**
Everything® **Pregnancy Fitness Book**
Everything® **Pregnancy Organizer,** $15.00 ($22.95 CAN)
Everything® **Toddler Book**
Everything® **Tween Book**

PERSONAL FINANCE

Everything® **Budgeting Book**
Everything® **Get Out of Debt Book**
Everything® **Get Rich Book**
Everything® **Homebuying Book, 2nd Ed.**
Everything® **Homeselling Book**
Everything® **Investing Book**
Everything® **Money Book**
Everything® **Mutual Funds Book**
Everything® **Online Investing Book**
Everything® **Personal Finance Book**
Everything® **Personal Finance in Your 20s & 30s Book**
Everything® **Wills & Estate Planning Book**

PETS

Everything® **Cat Book**
Everything® **Dog Book**
Everything® **Dog Training and Tricks Book**
Everything® **Golden Retriever Book**
Everything® **Horse Book**
Everything® **Labrador Retriever Book**
Everything® **Puppy Book**
Everything® **Tropical Fish Book**

All Everything® books are priced at $12.95 or $14.95, unless otherwise stated. Prices subject to change without notice.
Canadian prices range from $11.95–$31.95, and are subject to change without notice.

REFERENCE

Everything® **Astronomy Book**
Everything® **Car Care Book**
Everything® **Christmas Book, $15.00**
($21.95 CAN)
Everything® **Classical Mythology Book**
Everything® **Einstein Book**
Everything® **Etiquette Book**
Everything® **Great Thinkers Book**
Everything® **Philosophy Book**
Everything® **Psychology Book**
Everything® **Shakespeare Book**
Everything® **Tall Tales, Legends, &**
Other Outrageous
Lies Book
Everything® **Toasts Book**
Everything® **Trivia Book**
Everything® **Weather Book**

RELIGION

Everything® **Angels Book**
Everything® **Bible Book**
Everything® **Buddhism Book**
Everything® **Catholicism Book**
Everything® **Christianity Book**
Everything® **Jewish History &**
Heritage Book
Everything® **Judaism Book**
Everything® **Prayer Book**
Everything® **Saints Book**
Everything® **Understanding Islam**
Book
Everything® **World's Religions Book**
Everything® **Zen Book**

SCHOOL & CAREERS

Everything® **After College Book**
Everything® **Alternative Careers Book**
Everything® **College Survival Book**
Everything® **Cover Letter Book**
Everything® **Get-a-Job Book**
Everything® **Hot Careers Book**

Everything® **Job Interview Book**
Everything® **New Teacher Book**
Everything® **Online Job Search Book**
Everything® **Resume Book, 2nd Ed.**
Everything® **Study Book**

SELF-HELP/ RELATIONSHIPS

Everything® **Dating Book**
Everything® **Divorce Book**
Everything® **Great Marriage Book**
Everything® **Great Sex Book**
Everything® **Kama Sutra Book**
Everything® **Romance Book**
Everything® **Self-Esteem Book**
Everything® **Success Book**

SPORTS & FITNESS

Everything® **Body Shaping Book**
Everything® **Fishing Book**
Everything® **Fly-Fishing Book**
Everything® **Golf Book**
Everything® **Golf Instruction Book**
Everything® **Knots Book**
Everything® **Pilates Book**
Everything® **Running Book**
Everything® **Sailing Book, 2nd Ed.**
Everything® **T'ai Chi and QiGong Book**
Everything® **Total Fitness Book**
Everything® **Weight Training Book**
Everything® **Yoga Book**

TRAVEL

Everything® **Family Guide to Hawaii**
Everything® **Guide to Las Vegas**
Everything® **Guide to New England**
Everything® **Guide to New York City**
Everything® **Guide to Washington D.C.**
Everything® **Travel Guide to The Dis-**
neyland Resort®, Cali-
fornia Adventure®,

Universal Studios®, and
the Anaheim Area
Everything® **Travel Guide to the Walt**
Disney World Resort®, Uni-
versal Studios®, and
Greater Orlando, 3rd Ed.

WEDDINGS

Everything® **Bachelorette Party Book,**
$9.95 ($15.95 CAN)
Everything® **Bridesmaid Book, $9.95**
($15.95 CAN)
Everything® **Creative Wedding Ideas**
Book
Everything® **Elopement Book, $9.95**
($15.95 CAN)
Everything® **Groom Book**
Everything® **Jewish Wedding Book**
Everything® **Wedding Book, 2nd Ed.**
Everything® **Wedding Checklist,**
$7.95 ($11.95 CAN)
Everything® **Wedding Etiquette Book,**
$7.95 ($11.95 CAN)
Everything® **Wedding Organizer,**
$15.00 ($22.95 CAN)
Everything® **Wedding Shower Book,**
$7.95 ($12.95 CAN)
Everything® **Wedding Vows Book,**
$7.95 ($11.95 CAN)
Everything® **Weddings on a Budget**
Book, $9.95 ($15.95 CAN)

WRITING

Everything® **Creative Writing Book**
Everything® **Get Published Book**
Everything® **Grammar and Style Book**
Everything® **Grant Writing Book**
Everything® **Guide to Writing Chil-**
dren's Books
Everything® **Screenwriting Book**
Everything® **Writing Well Book**

Available wherever books are sold!
To order, call 800-872-5627, or visit us at everything.com

Everything® and everything.com® are registered trademarks of F+W Publications, Inc.